Harry Caplan

Of Eloquence

Studies in Ancient and Mediaeval Rhetoric

BY

Harry Caplan

Edited and with an Introduction by
ANNE KING *and* HELEN NORTH

Cornell University Press

ITHACA AND LONDON

CORNELL UNIVERSITY PRESS

First published 1970

THIS BOOK HAS BEEN PUBLISHED WITH THE AID OF A GRANT FROM THE HULL MEMORIAL PUBLICATION FUND OF CORNELL UNIVERSITY.

International Standard Book Number: 0-8014-0486-X
Library of Congress Catalog Card Number: 66-24262

PRINTED IN THE UNITED STATES OF AMERICA
BY THE MAPLE PRESS COMPANY

Harry Caplan:
An Introduction and Dedication

WE are pleased, for many reasons, to present this collection of some of Professor Harry Caplan's important studies in rhetoric and public speaking. The volume was originally planned as one way of honoring Professor Caplan on the occasion of his official retirement from Cornell University in June, 1967. Since then, however, he has continued to teach and lecture throughout the country, and it is no small part of our pleasure that the volume can appear at a time when he is still active in the classroom as well as the study.

I

It is to Professor Caplan himself that we offer this volume, with the hope that it will express some part of the affection and esteem felt for him by a multitude of his students, colleagues, and friends. We should add, however, that there is considerable doubt whether he would wish us to demonstrate our regard in this way. Indeed, we have had to override his original objections to the appearance of this book. Our real strength to withstand, if not to convince, him came from the comforting knowledge that we were here meeting a genuine need. Numerous teachers and students of rhetoric, already familiar with many of the essays in the volume, have indicated their desire to have these materials more readily available. And it is part of our pleasure too that in presenting this book, we can fulfill another of our intentions: we can make it possible for an even wider audience to know and use Professor Caplan's work.

II

If Professor Caplan will not easily accept the tribute implicit in this volume, he will certainly reject out-of-hand any explicit statement of appreciation. At our back we always hear his critical comments thundering near: he will rebuff praise as hyperbole, fullness of detail as wordiness; he will unerringly note any unconsidered cacophonies and solecisms, and will scrutinize the very semicolons, used and unused. Daunted by that prospect, and even more by the impossibility of doing justice in brief space to his full and varied career, we have placed a *vita*—along with a bibliography of his writings—at the end of this volume. We refer the reader to both items for fuller lists of dates and for details which reflect in themselves, far better than we in our comments here can hope to do, much of the range, the interests, the achievements and honors which have marked his career thus far.

Close ties have been forged between Harry Caplan and Cornell for over fifty years. At Cornell, since 1912, he has been an undergraduate and graduate student, a teacher of public speaking and of Latin and Greek, for seventeen years chairman of the Department of Classics, full professor since 1930, and, since 1941, Goldwin Smith Professor of the Classical Languages and Literature. And though he has, during the years, taught and lectured at other leading institutions throughout the country, he has usually accepted such invitations only for summer sessions, faithfully returning to Cornell in September for the new academic—and football—season.

The breadth of his scholarly interests is suggested by the many and varied groups to which he belongs—groups representing classical, mediaeval, Renaissance, and modern literatures, as well as specialized speech and linguistic associations. Of the numerous ways in which his scholarly achievements have been recognized, we can here call attention to only a few. He has twice been a Guggenheim Fellow, in 1928–1929, when he was one of the first Cornellians so honored, and again in 1956. He served as President of the American Philological Association in 1955, and was elected a Fellow of the Mediaeval Academy of America in 1957.

But for generations of Cornell students all such distinctions may well seem subordinate to a single achievement: Professor Caplan's impact as a teacher. In courses ranging from "Baby Greek" to Literary Criticism, from Classical Rhetoric to Horace, from Demosthenes to Mediaeval Latin, graduates and undergraduates have felt that impact far beyond the doors of the classroom, and long after the books have been shut.

Some part of his success as a teacher no doubt comes from his own rhetorical skills, from his ability to combine good-humored raillery with pointed criticism, to look pained, pleased, or skeptical at need. Yet such classroom methods, however effective and memorable—and inimitable, as so many of his graduate students have discovered—are far less significant than the attitudes fundamental to all aspects of his career.

For Professor Caplan, there is no separation of teaching from scholarship, of the university from its departments or its students. It is not simply that all are vital, but, more important, that all achieve their greatest vitality only in their interaction. If he played an important role in keeping the classics an essential part of the University during the seventeen years of his chairmanship, it is surely because he communicated to others this relationship of the part to the whole. In the same way, much of his success as a teacher has stemmed from the fact that he has never found it necessary to decide whether one should teach a subject or a student. Because he has always been equally concerned for, equally enthusiastic about, both student and subject, he has made each more truly vital.

And it is this same concern, surely, that has given his office its distinctive character, and indeed makes it necessary to include some reference to 121 Goldwin Smith in any picture of Professor Caplan. Less an office, in fact, than a way of life, there he resided and presided, from 11 A.M. to 11 P.M. every day for forty-five years. Seated behind the large double desk, surrounded by books bursting from the crowded shelves on all sides of the room, hidden, often, by other books piled high before him, he might seem at first to epitomize the scholar retired from the hurly-burly of activity to the seclusion of the study. But the opposite was more nearly true. Often the room seemed almost as full of people as of books—of students discussing their work, students bringing parents or fiancés, alumni with their offspring, and friends and colleagues from far and near. And the scholar behind the desk was also, according to the occasion, teacher or host or adviser or friend, sharing with and communicating to his visitors his own interest in the people and the books around him.

III

If the publication of this volume serves to honor Professor Caplan's general contributions as a scholar and teacher, its contents reflect and pay tribute to his special achievements in the field of rhetoric; that his devotion to Rhetoric has been faithful, long-standing, and productive, the volume itself bears witness.

The selections of previously published work include early as well as recent pieces, arranged, with one exception, in the chronological order in which they first appeared, and with here and there some changes from their original form. The two papers that complete the volume were delivered as addresses, and now appear in print for the first time. The one piece taken out of its chronological position, the comprehensive Introduction to the Loeb edition of the *Ad Herennium*, which appeared in 1954, is here placed first to serve as a kind of general introduction to the often more specialized essays that follow. It is also the one selection which has been slightly cut, so as to omit those few sections which could be understood only with the actual text or translation of the *Ad Herennium* at hand. Footnotes marked by asterisks are those of the editors.

In all fairness to Professor Caplan, we should also add that our decision to include essays of the 1920's, allowing only limited changes by the author, ignored his own wishes to revise them completely. We felt justified in this decision not only by the knowledge that readers were continuing to find these early essays—when they could find them at all—useful in their original form, but also by the promise of their increased usefulness when brought together in a single volume. Here, the wide range of Professor Caplan's concern with rhetoric is seen. In time, the essays range from articles published in the 1920's to a speech delivered in 1964. In form, they include translations, hermeneutics and criticism, and history and theory of rhetoric. In tone, they range from the scholarly to the more popular, as Professor Caplan practices the fundamental rhetorical principle of adapting his style to the audience and the moment. Finally, the essays, important in themselves and in relation to one another, also show Professor Caplan, early and late, as a leader in the study of ancient rhetorical theory and its rich influence on classical and mediaeval civilization and on modern criticism and taste.

February 1970

ANNE KING
Adelphi University
HELEN NORTH
Swarthmore College

[ix]

Acknowledgments

THE editors wish to thank the following publishers and journals for permission to reprint the material indicated: "Introduction to the *Rhetorica ad Herennium*," by permission of Harvard University Press and the Loeb Classical Library, from [*Cicero*] *Ad C. Herennium de Ratione Dicendi* (1954); "The Latin Panegyrics of the Empire," by permission of the Speech Association of America, from *Quarterly Journal of Speech Education*, X (1924); "A Late Mediaeval Tractate on Preaching," from *Studies in Rhetoric and Public Speaking in Honor of James Albert Winans* (1925), courtesy of Appleton-Century-Crofts, Division of Meredith Publishing Company; "Rhetorical Invention in Some Mediaeval Tractates on Preaching" and "The Four Senses of Scriptural Interpretation and the Mediaeval Theory of Preaching," by permission of the Mediaeval Academy of America, from *Speculum*, II (1927) and IV (1929); "Classical Rhetoric and the Mediaeval Theory of Preaching," by permission of The University of Chicago Press, from *Classical Philology*, XXVIII (1933), as revised for *Historical Studies of Rhetoric and Rhetoricians* (Cornell University Press, 1961); "'Henry of Hesse' on the Art of Preaching," by permission of the Modern Language Association of America, from *PMLA*, XLVIII (1933); and "The Decay of Eloquence at Rome in the First Century," by permission of Cornell University Press, from *Studies in Speech and Drama in Honor of Alexander M. Drummond* (1944). The editors are indebted to a number of persons, above all to Professor W. Samuel Howell of Princeton University, for

[xi]

Acknowledgments

his initial encouragement and his continuing interest and assistance, and to Professor Everett L. Hunt of Swarthmore College, for his wise counsel and invaluable support at every stage of the project. For helpful advice we are beholden to Professors Donald C. Bryant of the State University of Iowa and Raymond F. Howes of the Claremont Graduate School and University Center, and we are grateful to Miss Dorothy Grosser of the Cornell University Library, who compiled the bibliography of Professor Caplan's writings. The late Mrs. Catherine North of Swarthmore, Pennsylvania, and Mrs. Jeanne Naef, secretary to the President of Adelphi University, typed and set up for the printer much of the manuscript; we deeply appreciate their assistance. We also thank Miss Rachel Kitzinger, of Swarthmore College, who helped compile the Index Locorum. We are under special obligation to the editorial department of Cornell University Press, whose aid went well beyond the call of duty.

The author gratefully acknowledges assistance from The Charles Edwin Bennett Fund for Research in the Classical Languages.

Contents

Of Eloquence

Studies in Ancient and Mediaeval Rhetoric

I
Introduction to the
*Rhetorica ad Herennium**

THE Greek art of rhetoric was first naturalized at Rome in the time of the younger Scipio, and Latin treatises on the subject were in circulation from the time of the Gracchi. But the books by Cato, Antonius, and the other Roman writers have not come down to us, and it is from the second decade of the first century B.C. that we have, in the treatise addressed to Gaius Herennius, the oldest Latin Art preserved entire. Like Cicero's incomplete *De Inventione*, which belongs close to it in time, this work reflects Hellenistic rhetorical teaching. Our author, however, gives us a Greek art in Latin dress, combining a Roman spirit with Greek doctrine. It is a technical manual, systematic and formal in arrangement; its exposition is bald, but in greatest part clear and precise. Indeed the writer's specific aims are to achieve clarity and conciseness, and to complete the exposition of his subject with reasonable speed. He seeks clarity through the use of Roman terms, and of specially selected examples; he seeks conciseness by keeping practical needs always in view, by scrupulously avoiding irrelevant

* Reprinted from [*Cicero*] *Ad C. Herennium de Ratione Dicendi* (*Rhetorica ad Herennium*), edited and translated by Harry Caplan (Loeb Classical Library, Cambridge, Mass. and London, 1954), vii–xxxiv. The final sections, on the translations, editions, and text, have been omitted, and a few references which are relevant only to the text and translation have been deleted.

matter, and by presenting methods and principles, not a host of particular illustrations of a given point.[1]

The fact that the treatise appeared, from Jerome's time on, as a work by Cicero[2] gave it a prestige which it enjoyed for over a thousand years. Because of its position in the manuscripts following *De Inventione*, it was in the twelfth century called *Rhetorica Secunda;* perhaps because of a belief that Cicero wrote the treatise to replace his juvenile *De Inventione*, it was later called *Rhetorica Nova*.[3] But Cicero never refers to any work of his which might be identified with our treatise; the disparaging reference in *De Oratore* I. 2. 5 to those "crude and incomplete" essays of his youth is obviously to the two books *De Inventione*. The picture we draw of our author does not fit the early Cicero, and his doctrines in many crucial instances, as will be seen later, are in sharp contrast with those of *De Inventione*. Furthermore, the thought and style of the work are unworthy of the mature Cicero. Finally, Quintilian[4] (who often cites *De Inventione*),[5] and similarly Gellius,[6] Marius Victorinus,

---

[1] See Martin Schanz, *Geschichte der römischen Literatur* (Munich, 1909), I, 466–473.

[2] The uncritical editor who, before Jerome's time, made this ascription may also have been responsible for the division of the work into six books. He may have thought the untitled work Cicero's because of its resemblance to *De Inventione*, and may have interpreted the *inchoata ac rudia* of *De Oratore* I. 2. 5 as referring to two distinct works. An interesting interpolation, based on the belief in Ciceronian authorship, appears in the MSS at I. xii. 20: [*Tullius*] *heres meus* [*Terentiae*] *uxori meae.*

[3] For like parallel designations of literary works in the Middle Ages, see E. R. Curtius, *Europäische Literatur und lateinisches Mittelalter* (Bern, 1948), p. 161.

[4] It is argued, for example, that if Quintilian at 4. 5. 3, where he considers the view that the propositions in a Partition should not exceed three (cf. the like principle for the Enumeration in our treatise, I. x. 17), or at 3. 6. 45, where he deals with the three Types of Issue (cf. our treatise, I. x. 18), had known that these were identical with, or akin to, Ciceronian notions, he would not have kept silent on the point.

[5] Usually under the title *Libri Rhetorici.*

[6] Gellius, *Noctes Atticae* 13. 6. 4, says that he has been unable to discover

Servius, and Cassiodorus show no acquaintance with any Ciceronian work of this nature. Although the belief in Ciceronian authorship has still not entirely disappeared, all the recent editors agree that the attribution is erroneous.

The first to doubt that the treatise was worthy of Ciceronian authorship was Lorenzo Valla (middle fifteenth century). Then Raphael Regius in 1491 positively divorced the work from Cicero's name. The question of authorship has occupied the attention of scholars at intervals ever since, but has never been settled to the satisfaction of all. It is wisest, I believe, to ascribe the work to an unknown author, although a good many reputable scholars have made out a case, at first glance attractive, for assigning it to a rhetorician named Cornificius.[7] These rely on citations in Quintilian which correspond with passages in Book 4 of our treatise. Cornificius is mentioned, and always with disapproval, in the following places:

In 5. 10. 2 Quintilian, discussing *arguments*, criticizes Cornificius for calling a Conclusion from Incompatibles *contrarium; contrarium* appears in our treatise as a *figure* (of diction).

In 9. 2. 27 Quintilian tells us that *oratio libera*—which he would allow to be called a figure only if it is simulated and artfully designed—is by Cornificius called *licentia; licentia* is the term used by our author (4. xxxvi. 48) for a figure which, in one form, fulfils Quintilian's requirements.

In 9. 3. 69–71 Quintilian, dealing with *adnominatio*, gives three examples of flat punning to be avoided, not imitated; Cornificius, he says, calls this word-play *traductio*. Two of these

---

whether the term *barbarismus* was used before the Augustan age; cf. our treatise, 4. xii. 17.

[7] The first to ascribe the work with assurance to Cornificius was Petrus Victorius in 1582; Regius had vacillated, assigning it variously to Cornificius, Verginius Flavus, and Timolaüs. Recent scholars who have upheld the theory of Cornifician authorship are Johannes Tolkiehn, *Jahresb. des philol. Vereins zu Berlin*, XLV (1919), 73, and Wilhelm Kroll, *Glotta*, XXII (1934), 24, and *Philologus*, LXXXIX (1934), 63.

[3]

examples are used by our author, one to illustrate *traductio* (4. xiv. 21), but the other to illustrate *adnominatio* (4. xxi. 29). To meet this real difficulty, the advocates of Cornifician authorship maintain that *adnominatio* and *traductio* are brought together by Quintilian because they are indeed kindred figures, but these scholars are forced also to blame Quintilian for casual excerpting at this point, or for drawing upon his memory—a charge hard¦to prove against so careful a workman.

In 9. 3. 91 Quintilian criticizes Cornificius and Rutilius for regarding *finitio*, which is no figure at all, as a figure of diction; *definitio*, somewhat differently characterized, appears as a figure of diction in our treatise (4. xxv. 35).

In 9. 3. 98 Quintilian tells us that Cornificius lists ten figures of diction of which the first five must be regarded as figures of thought: *interrogatio* (cf. 4. xv. 22), *ratiocinatio* (4. xvi. 23), *subiectio* (4. xxiii. 33), *transitio* (4. xxvi. 35), *occultatio* (4. xxvii. 37), and the other five as not figures at all: *sententia* (4. xvii. 24), *membrum* (4. xix. 26), *articuli* (*articulus* = 4. xix. 26), *interpretatio* (4. xxviii. 38), *conclusio* (4. xxx. 41).[8] These all appear in our treatise, in the places indicated in parentheses.

Quintilian mentions Cornificius in two other places. In 3. 1. 21, sketching the history of writers on rhetoric, he says: "Cornificius wrote a great deal (*non pauca*) on the same subject (rhetoric), Stertinius something, and the elder Gallio[9] a little. But the predecessors of Gallio, Celsus and Laenas,[10] and in our own day Verginius,[11] Pliny,[12] and Tutilius wrote with greater care. And even today there are distinguished authors. . . ."

---

[8] Georg Thiele, *Göttingische gelehrte Anzeigen*, II (1895), 725 ff., compares the order of the figures in this passage with that which they follow in our treatise, and sees in the comparison an argument for Cornifician authorship; Curtius Koehler, *De Rhetoricis ad Herennium* (Berlin, 1909), pp. 8 ff., presents the refutation.

[9] Long survived the elder Seneca, who died *c.* A.D. 39.

[10] Both A. Cornelius Celsus and Popillius Laenas fl. under Tiberius.

[11] Verginius Flavus fl. under Nero.

[12] The Elder (A.D. 23/4–79).

To this passage may be joined 9. 3. 89, where Cornificius appears in a list of authors who devoted whole books (*non partem operis . . . sed proprie libros*) to the discussion of figures: "Caecilius, Dionysius,[13] Rutilius,[14] Cornificius, Visellius, and a number of others, although there are living authors whose glory will match theirs."[15]

An examination of these passages, especially in their context, leads us to several conclusions. First, Cornificius lived after the time of Cicero and near (but before) Quintilian's own day. In 3. 1. 8 ff. Quintilian is obviously preserving a chronological order: Cornificius appears after Cicero (rather than immediately after Antonius) and before the writers *aetatis nostrae.* Again, in 9. 3. 91 and 9. 3. 98–99 Cornificius, Caecilius, and Rutilius are mentioned following discussions of Cicero. Finally, in 9. 3. 89 Cornificius is listed with writers of the Augustan age, and we assume that he was contemporary with them or flourished soon after them.[16] It would seem preposterous to place a writer of Marian times in this group.

[13] Both Caecilius and Dionysius fl. under Augustus.

[14] P. Rutilius Lupus fl. in the late Augustan period.

[15] In five other places Quintilian gives examples which, with greater or less completeness, appear also in our treatise: 9. 3. 31 (*complexio,* 4. xiv. 20); 9. 3. 56 (*gradatio,* 4. xxv. 34); two examples in 9. 3. 72 (*adnominatio,* 4. xxii. 30 and 4. xxi. 29), the wording of one differing slightly, that of the other a great deal, from that in our treatise; 9. 3. 85 (ἀντιμεταβολή = *commutatio,* 4. xxviii. 39); 9. 3. 88 (*dubitatio,* 4. xxix. 40). None of these examples is assigned by Quintilian to Cornificius or to any other author; whether they appeared in Cornificius' book and were from there borrowed by Quintilian we cannot know. Some or all of these examples may have been common to a number of manuals. The well-known remark attributed to Socrates ("I do not live to eat, but eat to live"), which Quintilian uses as an example in 9. 3. 85, he may have found in a Greek source.

[16] The efforts that have been made to identify Cornificius with anyone of that name who lived at this time have come to nought. Nor have the many scholars who have ascribed our treatise to a Cornificius, and so sought to identify him with an earlier bearer of that name, agreed in their identification. C. L. Kayser's choice, *Cornifici Rhetoricorum ad C. Herennium Libri IIII* (Leipzig, 1854), the Q. Cornificius who with Cicero was candidate for the consulship in 64 B.C., was favored for a time.

Of Eloquence

We further conclude that Cornificius was the author of a special book on figures,[17] and that this is the source from which Quintilian makes his citations in Book 9. That Cornificius produced additional work in the field of rhetoric is possible;[18] the phrase *non pauca* in 3. 1. 21, however, does not permit us to be certain whether this was in the form of a complete Art of Rhetoric,[19] or of several works on single parts of the subject.

[17] It is likely that this work did not contain a section on tropes. Quintilian, 8. 6. 1 ff., never cites Cornificius on this subject, nor refers to any of the several resemblances, in rules and examples, that exist between his treatment and our author's. In large part, however, his treatment differs from our author's. If Cornificius had discussed tropes, it is perhaps safe to assume that passages from his book would have been excerpted by Quintilian. Again, in 9. 1. 2 Quintilian mentions Proculus as among the writers who call tropes "figures"; our author, too, attaches the tropes to the figures in this way (4. xxxi. 42), but Quintilian does not name Cornificius along with Proculus.

The separation of tropes from figures was first made, we think, in the Augustan age. If Cornificius dealt only with figures, that fact, too, might be evidence for placing him at a time not earlier than that period.

[18] Marx, however, believes that Cornificius wrote only the special work on figures. See Friedrich Marx, *Prolegomena* in his *editio maior* of the *Rhetorica ad Herennium* (Leipzig, 1894), pp. 69 ff.

[19] Thiele (*Gött. gel. Anz.*) and G. Ammon believe that it was such a complete Art of Rhetoric. Thiele identifies it with our treatise; the special book on figures was a portion (=Bk. 4) of this Art. In his review of Marx, *ed. maior*, *Blätter für das Bayer. Gymn.-Schulwesen*, XXXIII (1897), 409 ff., Ammon argues as follows: The division, in the MSS, of Book 4 (which is especially large) into three books indicates that we have in our treatise a contamination of Cornificius' complete Art and his special work on figures. The "Art" extends to 4. xiii. 18, at the end of which there is a lacuna; 4. i. 1 to 4. xiii. 18 corresponds to "Book iv" of the MSS. The special book on figures also perhaps included two books; "Book v," dealing with figures of diction, extends from 4. xiii. 19 to 4. xxxiv. 46, and "Book vi," treating figures of thought, extends from 4. xxxv. 47 to the end. In the union a portion of the complete Art of Rhetoric was lost—a short exposition of the two types of figures, and the beginning of their treatment. That Cornificius' attitude towards the use of one's own examples differed in the two works Ammon thinks is not significant. But Ammon's hypothesis is not acceptable, since the division into four books follows from the author's own words; the lacuna at 4. xiii. 18 is brief (only a transition is indicated); neither are the first three books of uniform length; and the author's special interest in *ornatus* justifies the length of Book 4, which in any event may as it stands lay claim to unity.

Introduction to Ad Herennium

Cornificius, then, lived in a later period than our author, and so cannot have written the *Rhetorica ad Herennium*. The book by Cornificius which Quintilian cites is not the *Rhetorica ad Herennium*, and there is no evidence that Quintilian knew or made use of our treatise.[20] The agreements between Cornificius' work and our author's we explain by assuming a common source,[21] and we should remember, too, that some of the matter, especially some of the examples, shared by both can be classed among the commonplaces of the subject.

Who, finally, was the real author? We have no evidence to determine that question, and so must assign the work to an *auctor incertus*.[22]

The original title is as unknown to us as the name of the

---

[20] Further arguments (see Koehler) rest frankly on the *argumentum e silentio.* For example, Quintilian often refers to Cicero's *De Inventione* but never mentions the agreements between that work and "Cornificius." Again, in 9. 2. 54 he lists four terms used for the figure Aposiopesis, but not the term used by our author (*praecisio*, 4. xxx. 41); this silence leads some to question whether, had he known our treatise, he would not in such cases as this have referred to the terms our author employs. Or again, in 9. 3. 99 ἠθοποιία and χαρακτηρισμός are cited from Rutilius among figures supplementary to those found in other authors. Since Cornificius has just been mentioned, it is inferred that his book lacked these figures; but they appear in our treatise as *notatio* (4. i. 63) and *effictio* (4. xlix. 62). Or again, in 3. 6. 45, where Verginius Flavus is referred to as favoring the Antonian classification of the Types of Issue (cf. our treatise 1. x. 18), Cornificius is not mentioned—but as I should remind the reader, the advocates of Cornifician authorship believe that Quintilian was not interested in the first three books of our work, or in 4. i. 1–4. xii. 18, because on the subjects there treated he had recourse to better material elsewhere.

[21] Teuffel-Kroll and others, however, believe that Cornificius probably used our treatise directly. See W. S. Teuffel, *Geschichte der römischen Literatur*, revised by W. Kroll (6th ed.; Berlin, 1916), I, 305–309.

[22] Other attributions, none of them seriously pressed to-day, have in the course of time since the fifteenth century been made to: Verginius Flavus (time of Nero), Timolaüs (time of Aurelian), M. Tullius Tiro and M. Tullius Laurea (freedmen of Cicero), the rhetor Junius Gallio (friend of the elder Seneca), M. Antonius Gnipho and L. Aelius Stilo (teachers of Cicero), M. T. Cicero (son of the great orator), L. Ateius Praetextatus (died after 29 B.C.), and Papirius Fabianus (time of Tiberius).

author. Marx, on the basis of the introductory remarks in Book I, suggests, with plausibility, that this might have been *De Ratione Dicendi*, which was also the title of Antonius' treatise on rhetoric.

Our author dedicates his work to Gaius Herennius; we know several Herennii[23] of this period, but no one definitely identifiable with the addressee. Marx, influenced by the apparent fact that the work remained unnoticed for five hundred years, believed that it was intended only for private use, and not for publication, but this hypothesis does not receive universal acceptance.

As we have said, the treatise is altogether Greek in doctrine. The Rhodian[24] rhetor who represents its original source sought to bind rhetoric to philosophy, and the book as it stands is a synthesis of various teachings: pre-Aristotelian (Isocratean and "Anaximenean"), Aristotelian and Peripatetic, Stoic, Hermagorean, and possibly Epicurean. Hellenistic theorists selected from all schools what they needed, and indeed some of the precepts were by then a common possession.[25] We must remark, too, in our author's case the thoroughly practical motives to which he constantly gives expression. The notes in the Loeb edition attempt in many instances to indicate the ties by which he is bound to the traditions of different schools. To illustrate briefly, and almost at random: the threefold purpose of the Direct Opening is pre-Aristotelian doctrine; the concept of the *officia oratoris* is Aristotelian; the "virtues" of Style go back to Theophrastus; the detailed treatment of

[23] They were of plebeian stock, and were allied to the family of Marius.

[24] Many Romans came to Rhodes, a great centre of rhetorical studies, and in 87 B.C. Apollonius Molo visited Rome. The notes in the Loeb edition indicate a number of echoes of Rhodian life and thought.

[25] Cf. Cicero, *De Inv.* 2. 3. 8: "[Isocratean theory and Aristotelian theory] were fused into one by their successors." Interdependence is often hard to trace definitely even in the earlier periods.

Delivery belongs probably to post-Theophrastan theory; the discussion of Solecism and Barbarism shows a debt to Stoicism; the definition of rhetoric is Hermagorean, and so too, though in modified form, is our author's *status* system—indeed every art which had a *status* system was beholden to Hermagoras; the opposition to amphibolies may be Epicurean; and in the case of some principles the Sophists and Plato play an originating or participating rôle.

The precepts are often illustrated by excellent examples, many of them allusions to the recent and the contemporary political scene, especially the Marsic and Marian Wars, and many bringing back to life the older Roman eloquence. Of the older Latin orators, our author shows special admiration for Gaius Gracchus and Crassus (4. i. 2; 4. ii. 2), but he tells us that Cato, Tiberius Gracchus, Laelius, Scipio, Porcina, and Antonius also commonly serve as models in the field of style. Poets and historians, too, may be models (4. v. 7); he has praise for Ennius and Pacuvius (4. iv. 7), but he does not hesitate to use these poets and Plautus[26] and the historian Coelius Antipater in illustration of faults of argumentation or of style. Examples of figures of speech (whose sources he does not name) are drawn from Greek authors as well; the speeches of Demosthenes (especially *De Corona*) and Aeschines are special favorites, but sayings originated by Homer, Simonides, Pythagoras, Isocrates, Socrates, Theophrastus, Aristarchus, Apollonius ὁ μαλακός, and others also appear, as do references to Greek mythology. The author's experience and mastery of Greek literature, however, do not seem to have been great; this Greek lore was transmitted to him from the schools.

The schools emphasized declamation and the study of models, and the treatise is in this respect an image of school practice. Declamatory exercises—the author again and again

[26] And probably also Accius; see 2. xxvi. 42.

stresses the importance of exercise[27]—are represented in the form of *progymnasmata* of various types (including training in epideictic), of deliberative questions (*deliberationes, suasoriae*), and of judicial cases (*causae, controversiae*). The deliberative questions are all taken from events of Roman history, none of them antedating the war with Hannibal.[28] Of the judicial cases drawn from Roman history, almost all date from the end of the Jugurthine War to the end of the Marian War; a number are also Greek in origin, and occasionally are altered to fit Roman conditions. Our author doubtless used collections of declamations current in his day.

The organization of the treatise is rather complicated.[29] The author is heir to two structural schemes—the pre-Aristotelian, based on the *partes* of the discourse (μόρια λόγου), and the Peripatetic, based on the five *officia* (ἔργα) of rhetoric. In his discussion of judicial oratory—which held the foreground in Hellenistic rhetoric, and claims most of his attention —both schemes are fused, "in order to make the subject easier to understand" (1. iii. 4), and with interesting results. The *partes* are treated under Invention, and not, as in the Peripatetic system, under Disposition. Disposition, which is therefore narrow in scope and rather sterile, becomes an adjunct of Invention[30] (3. ix. 16), and is treated directly after it, where in

[27] But never a word about declaiming in Greek; cf. on the other hand the custom followed by Cicero (*Brutus* 90. 310).

[28] For events connected with the Hannibalic War Coelius Antipater may have served as a source, for the subsequent period the orators, and perhaps also Cato's *Origines;* see H. E. Bochmann, *De Cornifici Auctoris ad Herennium Qui Vocatur Rerum Romanarum Scientia* (Zwickau, 1875).

[29] See Karl Barwick, *Hermes*, LVII (1922), 1 ff.; Georg Thiele, *Quaestiones de Cornifici et Ciceronis Artibus Rhetoricis* (Greifswald, 1889), pp. 96 ff.; Ioannes Radtke, *Observationes Crit. in Cornifici Libros de Arte Rhetorica* (Koenigsberg, 1892), pp. 22 ff.; Friedrich Solmsen, *Amer. Journ. Philol.*, LXII (1941), 35–50, 169–190.

[30] The conflation results in certain inconsistencies; see, e.g., the reference to Invention at 1. x. 16, and the note on 3. x. 17. Certain other inconsistencies in the order are, however, not the result of conflation; the author at times in his

the Peripatetic structure we should expect a discussion of Style. The Types of Issue are subjoined to Proof, which is one of the *partes*, and not as in Aristotle a primary and central function of the whole art. The discussion of the deliberative and epideictic kinds, on the other hand, is more in line with the Peripatetic method: in both cases Invention receives first consideration, and then comes the Development of the cause based on the parts of the discourse.

Each book has a Preface and a Conclusion, which, by brief summaries and transitions characteristic of lecture or text-book style, serve to tie the parts together, and to keep the plan of the work clear in the reader's mind.

The first two books deal with Invention in judicial causes; Invention in deliberative and epideictic speaking is discussed much more briefly in a part of Book 3. Disposition is also accorded little space for the reasons set forth above. But the treatment of Delivery, Memory, and Style is of special interest and importance.

The doctrine of Delivery had been developed in post-Aristotelian times, and our author is familiar with books on the subject. He is dissatisfied with these and wishes to treat the subject with greater care and completeness than had characterized the work of his predecessors (3. xi. 19). In the section which he devotes to Delivery two observations will present themselves to the modern student of public speaking. The rules are for the most part prescriptive; the speaker is told precisely what use of voice, pause, and gesture he ought consciously to make in a variety of situations. And secondly, the doctrine represents a salutary reaction against Asianism; piercing exclamations and the continual use of the full voice are more than once reprehended (3. xii. 21 ff.), and the speaker

---

treatment transposes his original order of topics (e.g., in 1. xiv. 24 and 2. xvi. 23; and cf. 1. xiv. 24 ff. with 2. xiv. 21 ff.).

is more than once warned against imitating the delivery of the stage-actor (3. xiv. 24; 3. xv. 26).

The section on Memory is our oldest surviving treatment of the subject. Based on visual images and "backgrounds," the mnemotechnical system which it presents exerted an influence traceable to modern times. Here too the author refers to previous writers on the subject in order to combat their theory; he specifies that these are Greek, but he does not mention any of them by name.

In Book 4 we have the oldest systematic treatment of Style in Latin, indeed the oldest extant inquiry into the subject after Aristotle. It offers, furthermore, the oldest extant division of the kinds of Style into three, and the oldest extant formal study of figures. Our author gives more space to Style than to any other of the departments of rhetoric, and much more to *ornatus*—which is limited to the figures—than to the other aspects of Style. The exceptionally large enumeration of figures is of course more in accord with Isocratean than with Aristotelian doctrine; our author, together with the younger Gorgias (through the translation by Rutilius), provides us with an important source for our knowledge of Hellenistic theory in this field. The treatment of the figures is not always bald and jejune, despite their formal array. Occasionally our author writes good literary criticism; read for example the advice, anti-Asian in character, which he gives on the use of the Gorgianic figures (4. xxi. 32). He is often sensitive to the effect which a figure of speech, well-used, can work upon the hearer. He never advocates the tricky cunning which would have justified the scorn that Longinus (*De Sublim.*, chap. 17) expressed for the "petty figures (σχημάτια) of the rhetorical craftsman." His counsel is for moderation and the consideration of propriety—in the use of Apostrophe (4. xv. 22), Maxims (4. xvii. 25), Disjunction (4. xxvii. 38), Onomatopoeia

(4. xxxi. 42), Metaphor (4. xxxiv. 45), and Comparison (4. xlviii. 61). The author is not always at ease among technical terms (see 4. vii. 10, and also 4. x. 15 and 4. xi. 16), since not all of these had yet become stable in Latin.

A number of questions concerning the treatise are vigorously debated. How old was the author when the work was composed? Is the treatise nothing but the notes of lectures delivered by his Latin teacher? Does our author favor the *populares?* What is his philosophical bias, if any? And most baffling, what relation does the treatise bear to Cicero's *De Inventione?*

Whereas in the nineteenth century it was customary to praise our author for "manly independence of thought," it is now, especially since Marx's work[31] appeared, common to make him out an uncritical and very young man, or a boy, who copied down, virtually word for word, the lectures of his Latin teacher, and worked these up with only slight additions, mostly represented by the Introductions and Conclusions to the several Books. The style does show puerilities, and signs of immaturity are sought and found here and there in the thought. But not everything labelled as puerile by some critics justifies the label, and in some degree the charge would have to be shared by the teacher. The confusion between student and teacher arises necessarily from the theory that we have here only a student's notebook.[32] Actually our author seems old enough to have spent (*consuevimus*, 1. i. 1) time in philosophical studies,[33] older enough than his kinsman Herennius to have composed the book for his use, and to encourage him in industry (1. i. 1; 2. xxxi. 50; 3. xxxiv. 40; 4. lvi. 69), young

---

[31] See n. 18 above.

[32] Cf. Quintilian, 3. 6. 59, on Cicero, *De Inv.*: "Such faults as [this collection of school-notes] has are assignable to his teacher."

[33] Which he thinks conduce more to the good life than does the study of rhetoric; he is not a professional rhetorician.

enough still to practise with him (3. i. 1; 4. lvi. 69), and to make plans for the future—he expects to write on Grammar (4. xii. 17), on Military Science and State Administration (3. ii. 3), on Memory (3. xvi. 28), and (if encouraged) against the dialecticians (2. xi. 16). We have no reason to believe that when he speaks of the pressure of private affairs (1. i. 1) and the demands of his occupations (1. xvii. 27) he is merely following a literary convention or indulging in rhetorical fiction. He charges Greek writers with childish argumentation in respect to the use of examples (4. iii. 4), warns against puerilities in the use of Isocolon and Paronomasia (4. xx. 27; 4. xxiii. 32), and finds recourse to amphibolies silly (2. xi. 16). His apologies for slow progress and references to the magnitude of his task and the care he has devoted to it (e.g., 1. xvii. 27; 2. xxxi. 50) are inconsistent with the picture of one who is merely working over dictated material. He professes to have taken pains in assembling his material (*conquisite conscripsimus*, 1. xxxi. 50, and *studiose collegimus*, 4. lvi. 69), and this seems to imply the use of sources, although we cannot know how wide this use or how comprehensive his study of them may have been.

Lecture notes doubtless form the core of the treatise, but the author probably made use of other sources as well, and worked the matter over with some degree of independence. Some of the very incongruities that we find in the treatise may derive precisely from this weaving together of material drawn from a number of places. Dependence on his teacher is explicit only in connection with a disputed point, on the number of Types of Issue[34] (1. x. 18). We go too far if we assume that the precepts all belong to the teacher and very little more than the Introductions and Conclusions to the author. And one won-

---

[34] Who the teacher (*noster doctor*) here referred to was we do not know.

ders how the teacher would have regarded the release of his own work, even if only for private use, as the work of his pupil.[35]

Does our author favor the Popular party? It is believed that his teacher may have belonged to the school of L. Plotius Gallus and the *rhetores Latini*. These teachers of public speaking, whose identity and innovations remain obscure to us, apparently as a matter of principle taught their subject in Latin, rigidly suppressing the Greek language; they probably were Marian in sympathy and had as students only the sons of the *populares*.[36] Our author can indeed in his examples praise or sympathize with the Gracchi, Saturninus, Drusus, and Sulpicius (2. xxviii. 45; 4. xxii. 31; 4. lv. 68; 4. xv. 22), and advise us to bring our adversaries into contempt by revealing their high birth (1. v. 8), but he can likewise accuse Gaius Gracchus of promoting panics (4. xxviii. 38), praise Caepio's attack on Saturninus as patriotic conduct (1. xii. 21; 2. xii. 17), warn Saturninus against the excesses of the popular mob (4. liv. 67), attribute the future revival of prosperity to the Conservatives (4. xxxiv. 45), and regard their slaughter as a disaster (4. viii. 12). The themes of the *causae* are variously Popular and Conservative in spirit, and we must infer that our author took his material where he found it and used it to suit his primary purpose—technical instruction in the art of rhetoric. If he really belonged to the Popular party, then he still must have believed in giving the Conservative cause a hearing.

Nor again should our author's attitude to the Greeks be represented as an antagonism approaching hatred. True, he

[35] See Schanz, p. 470. Quintilian, 1. Praef. 7, regrets that two books of lecture notes, taken down by pupils, and by them published under his name, but without his consent, are in circulation. Marx, of course, maintains that our treatise was never intended for circulation.

[36] See Marx, pp. 141 ff., and Aubrey Gwynn, *Roman Education from Cicero to Quintilian* (Oxford, 1926), pp. 58–69.

deliberately takes most of his historical *exempla* from Roman history, repeatedly finds fault with the methods of Greek rhetoricians (1. i. 1; 3. xxiii. 38; 4. i. 1), and suppresses the names of Greek writers whose examples he uses in Book 4. But he also omits the names of Roman authors whose examples he uses in that Book. Furthermore, he professes to know Greek books, occasionally uses Greek technical terms and other Greek words, and praises the Greeks for their invention of the art of rhetoric (4. vii. 10).

A few traces of Epicureanism in the work have given rise to the notion that our author was an adherent of that school of philosophy. A maxim of Epicurus, in altered form, is quoted without attribution (4. xvii. 24); in another example, religion and the fear of death are listed among the motives that impel men to crime (2. xxi. 34); and the dialecticians are censured for their love of ambiguities (2. xi. 16). But, as the notes in the Loeb volume illustrate, the examples are drawn from the literature of various philosophical schools—a condition one would expect, inasmuch as manuals of rhetoric reflecting diverse schools were then extant, and these manuals may well have had much material in common.

But the most vexing problem—and, as Norden[37] says, one of the most interesting in the history of Roman literature—concerns the relations between our treatise and *De Inventione*. We are not even sure of the respective dates of composition. The reference in *De Oratore* 1. 2. 5 to the "essays . . . which slipped out of the notebooks of my boyhood, or rather of my youth"[38] does not enable us to fix upon a particular year for the composition of *De Inventione*, but internal evidence points to *c*. 91 B.C. By this we mean only that the work contains no reference to any event that took place during or after the

---

[37] A. Gercke and E. Norden, *Einleitung in die Altertumswissenschaft* (Leipzig–Berlin, 1910), I, 471.
[38] Cf. Quintilian, 3. 6. 59 and 3. 1. 20.

Marsic War.[39] Cicero may, of course, have worked the material into its final form later. When he published the book remains uncertain; allowing even for the possibility that in the passage above Cicero understated his years with ironic intent, we may not suppose a date much after 86 B.C. Likewise on internal evidence we assign our treatise to *c.* 86–82 B.C. The reference in 1. xv. 25 to the death of Sulpicius, which took place in the year 88, supplies us with a *terminus post quem* for the composition of Book 1.[40] 4. liv. 68 contains a reference to Marius' seventh consulship, which he held in the year 86. And since nothing in the work mirrors the conditions which obtained in the State under Sulla—for instance, the first illustration in 4. xxxv. 47 reflects a jury system still comprising both senators and *equites*—we may set the year 82 as the *terminus ante quem*. But again these dates regard only the contents; our author could have collected his examples by the year 82 and have composed the treatise later—not much later, probably, for he is eager to complete the work and send it to Herennius. It seems then likely, though not certain, that *De Inventione* was composed before our treatise.

Agreements are so frequent that obviously there is a close tie between the two works. Some precepts are set forth in virtually the same language, and some of the illustrations are identical. This is not the place to enumerate these likenesses, nor the differences,[41] which are even more striking; the

---

[39] See Marx, pp. 76 ff.

[40] In 3. i. 1 it is implied that separate books were sent to Herennius.

[41] See Marx, pp. 129 ff. Our author differs from Cicero in the method of presenting his material, in organization, and in spirit; for example, in many technical terms; in the doctrine of Proof, of the Types of Issue, of the sources of Law; in the number of *genera causarum;* in his emphasis upon the judicial kind of discourse as against Cicero's full treatment of all three kinds; in his much briefer discussion of many topics; in his less accurate quotations; in the more limited scope of his historical references (Cicero uses events in Roman history that antedate Hannibal); in his thoroughly Latin spirit. Marx's analogy is telling: our author is to the *togata* as Cicero, who is much more learned in Greek literature, is to the *palliata.*

treatises have been compared in several studies, but the last word on the subject has not yet been said. I may here only review recent opinion.[42] No one now believes that our author used *De Inventione*. On the other hand, the belief that Cicero used the *Rhetorica ad Herennium* still finds adherents; but since it is probable that Cicero's work antedates our treatise, we hesitate to accept this notion. Other critics postulate a common source. That both authors had a single Greek original in common is not acceptable, for it would be unbelievable that two independent translators should have rendered their text in precisely the same words; furthermore, the illustrations from Roman writers shared by both make such a solution impossible.[43]

Or did both make direct use of the same Latin source? This view is popular, and takes two forms: (1) that both had the same Latin teacher, the differences being explained by the assumption that they heard this teacher at different times—our author later, and when the teacher had changed his mind on a number of points; and that Cicero used other sources in addition;[44] (2) that both used the same Latin manual,[45] our author only this manual, and without many changes—except for certain transpositions and abridgements, some omission of examples, and slight additions (e.g., the Introductions and Conclusions)—and Cicero with greater alterations; and that Cicero further used Hermagoras.[46] Marx, on the other hand,

[42] I have not seen M. Medved, "Das Verhältnis von Ciceros libri rhetorici zum Auctor ad Herennium" (unpub. diss., Vienna, 1940).

[43] See William Ramsay in Smith's *Dict. of Greek and Roman Biography and Mythology* (London, 1880), I, 727.

[44] In *De Inv.* 2. 2. 4 he professes an eclectic method of excerpting from his sources.

[45] This second view is that of Georg Herbolzheimer, "Ciceros rhetorici libri und die Lehrschrift des Auctor ad Herennium," *Philologus*, LXXXI (1926), 391–426.

[46] Whether directly or through an intermediate source; the point is debated.

finds that the contrast between the two works is too sharp to permit a theory either of direct dependence or of a single immediate common source, whether teacher or manual; he posits two Latin teachers, and behind these, two Rhodian masters who advocated opposing doctrines, our author inheriting the older theory and Ciccro a fuller and more recent system.

Without accepting Marx's thesis that the treatise is entirely a set of lecture notes—for I would assign more of the work to the author than Marx allows—I believe that something like his hypothesis is required. The differences between the two works seem to rule out a single immediate common source; the likenesses we may best refer to the use by both authors (or by their teachers) of Latin treatises like the *De Ratione Dicendi* of Antonius.[47] We cannot appraise the influence of these older Latin arts of rhetoric which are lost to us, but it may well have been considerable.

Our main difficulty when we compare the two works is in explaining the following coincidence. In 1. vi. 9 our author distinguishes three occasions (*tempora*) for the use of the Subtle Approach, and in 1. ix. 16 maintains that this is his own innovation; in *De Inventione* 1. 17. 23, however, a like threefold classification occurs, but instead of occasions we have "motives" (*causae*). Again diverse explanations are offered, but in the end we are, I believe, forced either to accept Marx's view that the classification is of Greek origin or to take the author's words at their face value. Marx finds the context here thoroughly

---

[47] Most now believe that the influence of Antonius' book (cf. Cicero, *Brutus* 44. 163, *De Oratore* 1. 21. 94; Quintilian, 3. 1. 19) is apparent in our treatise; see Rudolfus Kroehnert, "De Rhetoricis ad Herennium" (diss., Koenigsberg, 1873), pp. 23 ff. (who thinks, however, that Antonius was our author's Latin teacher), Marx, p. 131, and Koehler, pp. 35–38, but also Heinrich Weber, *Über die Quellen der Rhetorica ad Herennium des Cornificius* (Zürich, 1886), pp. 22 ff., and Thiele, *Quaestiones*, p. 94. Antonius' book appeared sometime before 91 B.C.

Greek, even though we do not know any specific Greek source for the threefold classification, and hurls the charge of fraud and impudence at our author; the principle, he is sure, originated with the Rhodian rhetor whose doctrines our author followed, and Cicero in his turn received it from his own teacher in a modified form. Some of those who, like Marx, consider our treatise merely lecture notes, and yet wish to absolve the writer of the charge of fraud, make the point that he may not have known that his teacher had borrowed the precept from a Greek source; but the notion that the author did not know Greek well enough for his purposes would require proof. Schanz and others believe that Cicero borrowed the principle from our treatise, but that hypothesis would be more acceptable if we could be certain that the *Rhetorica ad Herennium* was actually published and available to Cicero before his publication of *De Inventione*. As a matter of fact, the precept appears in a somewhat different setting in *De Inventione*, where its use is confined to the *admirabile* kind of cause. Our author doubtless depends on a Greek source for his general treatment of the doctrine of the Subtle Approach. Yet he always writes with practical motives, and on this particular point specifically says that his purpose is to provide a sure and lucid theory. When, therefore, he claims as an innovation the slight distinction between *tempora* and *causae*, we find him guilty, not of fraud, but of the exaggerated self-esteem which is also elsewhere characteristic of him.[48]

The chief basis of Marx's charge of deceit is provided by the Introduction to Book 4, considered in relation to the examples used in that Book. This Proem, organized and developed

[48] He has not been moved to write by hope of gain or glory, "as others have been" (1. i. 1); "no one else" has written with sufficient care on Delivery (3. xi. 19); he "alone, in contrast with all other writers," has distinguished three occasions for the use of the Subtle Approach (1. ix. 16); cf. also 1. vi. 10; 3. vii. 14; 3. xxiv. 40; and 4. lvi. 69.

like a *chria*[49] according to the rules of the class-room, is rather graceful and learned; in language, too, it is smoother than the purely technical parts of the treatise; and its contents are Greek in character. Marx and others contend that it did not belong in this place originally, but was in its main outlines taken from a Greek source, inserted here, and made over to seem a Latin product. In this Preface our author presents a long argument against a theory, which he labels as Greek, of using borrowed examples, and promises to give only those of his own creation (except in the case of faulty ones). But the execution does not fulfil the promise, for he then proceeds actually to use borrowed examples, and without naming his sources, many of which are Greek. The author (or rather his teacher) thus got into trouble when, having used a Greek art which employed borrowed examples, he tried to adjust to it the contrary precepts of another Greek author who created his own examples. This is the person, say his critics, who in 1. i. 1 accuses Greek writers of futile self-assertion.

According to another interpretation, which is intended to save the honor of both student and teacher, the young student here put down the notes of a lecture once delivered by his teacher, thinking this to be an appropriate place, but being no master of Greek, he was unaware that his teacher had in the rest of what comprises his Book 4 taken so many examples from Greek sources.

It seems best, however, to grant the author some degree of literary individuality, and to regard his claim to the use of his "own" examples as at least an honest one. The notion that he did not know Greek well enough for his purpose is gratuitous. To be sure, one cannot deny the contradiction between promise and fulfilment, nor assign to the author more than a relatively small share in the fashioning of the Proem, the

[49] See the figure, Refining, 4. xlii. 54 ff.

Greek origin of which is obvious. But he made good use of this Proem, which as it stands coheres well enough with the text that follows it; he would naturally use material that he had heard or read, perhaps not always knowing where he had picked it up;[50] and what is most likely, he may have considered his free translation of the Greek examples and alteration of the Latin a large enough task to justify his feeling that they were now his own. He is sometimes adroit in transposing the original examples and adjusting them to Roman conditions.[51] The claim to originality becomes then a pardonable, or at least an understandable, exaggeration, rather than evidence of misrepresentation.

Since the treatise stands near the beginnings of Latin prose,[52] its style has been the subject of close study. The faults have received special attention, especially those resulting from the author's quest for variety and for refinements in forms and constructions—for example, *abundantia*, artificially balanced clauses, the love of synonyms, of word-play, hyperbata, and asyndeta, the inflated language of the Conclusions to each Book, and other extravagances of rhetorical style; also the awkward transitions and the author's tendency merely to reiterate, under the guise of remarks concluding the treatment of a precept, what he has already said. Further peculiarities are the arbitrary use of pronouns, the omission of subjects of verbs in the infinitive, the mixture of present and future in the sequence of tenses, the frequent employment of the first person future active indicative, of substantives in -*io*, of the *ut* . . .

[50] In Cicero, *De Oratore* I. 34. 154, Crassus tells how in his practice declamations, trying to choose diction different from that of the poetic passage by Ennius or speech by Gracchus on which he was practising, he would discover that the best words had already been used by his model.

[51] See, e.g., in 4. xxix. 40, how the example of the figure Indecision from Demosthenes, *De Corona* 20, receives a Roman character.

[52] Of extant complete prose works only Cato's *De Agri Cultura* is older.

ne . . . construction, and of the indicative in indirect questions. The dry style of the precepts usually contrasts with the lively and smooth style of the examples. Although the style is in general not highly developed nor fluent, and there are several passages of which the meaning is obscure, our author in greatest part achieves, as I have said, his aim of clarity. It would not be fair to class his treatise with the crude text-books (*libri agrestes*) disparaged in *De Oratore* 2. 3. 10. The language is up to a point "plebeian" and there are puerilities, but some of the qualities thus designated are rather to be assigned to what we may call the schoolmaster's manner and to the nature of technical, text-book style. Some of the irregularities perhaps also derive from the author's desire to make haste and to be brief, and from the process of translation; here and there the language betrays a Greek origin.

Our author is fond of periods formed with rhythmic clausulae. It is another echo of the school practice of his time that the dichoree, favorite of Asianic style, plays the chief rôle, but other cadences are also frequent. In the examples illustrating the three types of style in Book 4, rhythms are chosen with a fair degree of taste so as to correspond to the character of the different types.

We may say that the style is within limits archaic, and sometimes reminiscent of Roman comedy; yet today it is no longer set in such sharp contrast as formerly to Ciceronian style. Kroll[53] looks upon it as having been formed on the same principles as those of the Roman orators whom Cicero regarded as his own forerunners.

In the present century it has been customary to undervalue the treatise because of its shortcomings—which in large part are those inherent in the nature of a text-book—even as its virtues were often exaggerated in the nineteenth century, when

[53] *Glotta*, pp. 24 ff.

more than one critic (e.g., Chaignet)[54] held the work up as superior to Quintilian's *Training of an Orator*. Regarded from a historical point of view, the treatise presents no strikingly novel system; for us, however, it has literary importance because it is our only complete representative of the system it teaches. We may further readily admit that the work lacks the larger philosophical insight of Aristotle's *Rhetoric*, but that is not to deny its excellence as a practical treatise of the kind doubtless used by Roman orators. It is, moreover, itself not without usefulness for the modern student of the art. We ought now to redress the balance, to recognize that, though Greek in origin and inspiration, it marks a significant stage in Roman rhetorical theory, to assign due value especially to Book 4, and to bear in mind that the work exerted a beneficent influence for hundreds of years. One of the distinguished modern students of rhetoric, Spengel,[55] called it "a book more precious than gold."

LATER HISTORY

Interpreting a *subscriptio* in manuscript H, Marx assumed that the book first came to light in Africa in the middle of the fourth century and was soon thereafter brought to Lombardy.[56] Therefore the first references to it appear late—in Jerome (in works written in the years A.D. 395 and 402), the grammarian Rufinus (fifth century), Grillius[57] (late fifth century), and Priscian (early sixth century). Manuscripts of the M class were

[54] A-Ed. Chaignet, *La rhétorique et son histoire* (Paris, 1888), p. 63, n. 8.

[55] Leonhard Spengel, "Die Interpolation in der Rhetorik ad Herennium," *Rheinisches Museum* (*Neue Folge*), XVI (1861), 391.

[56] See Marx, pp. 1 ff. Not all believe that the work could have lain so long in oblivion; some think that it was used by Cornificius [see p. 7, n. 21, and p. 8 above].

[57] See Josef Martin, *Grillius: Ein Beitrag zur Geschichte der Rhetorik* (Paderborn, 1927), p. 156 (48. 15).

known to Servatus Lupus, as we learn from a letter he wrote in 829 or 830, and indeed our oldest extant manuscripts, which belong to that class, date from the ninth and tenth centuries. Later the treatise was much used, abstracted, annotated, and interpolated; it shared favor with Cicero's *De Inventione*, which, as against modern taste, seems to have been preferred to his *De Oratore*. The great number of manuscripts of the *Ad Herennium*—we have more than a hundred—is in itself an index of its popularity. Complete commentaries began to appear as early, perhaps, as the twelfth century, translations as early as the thirteenth. The full story, however, of the influence which the treatise enjoyed in education and in the poetry and prose of the Middle Ages and Renaissance has yet to be worked out.

II

The Latin Panegyrics
of the Empire*

I AM aware that any paper treating of ancient oratory or rhetoric is likely to irritate the sensitive feelings of valiant modernists, such as have in our *Quarterly* recently raised the war-cry: "Dam this deluge"—of scribblings by pusillanimous hero-worshippers of the ancient dead.[1] Those of us who are convinced that we have much, very much, to learn from the rhetoric of the high periods of Greece and Rome are smitten hip and thigh, as proper punishment for neglect of the present time, for a deification of men who were but mortal, and whom adulation anyway would do no good. With extreme trepidation, then, do I discuss a product of the civilization of ancient Rome which some critics have considered the most worthless bequest of antiquity.

But while a study, even a brief one, of the Panegyrics of Imperial Rome will demonstrate the excessive severity of this condemnation, I am mindful that the Romans at this time of their decadence will be revealed to be but human indeed in their artistic depravity. I likewise believe that if we will, we may learn from this depravity a profitable lesson for the present time.

I justify the present undertaking on several grounds. First,

---

* Reprinted from *Quarterly Journal of Speech Education*, X (1924), 41–52.
[1] This paper was read at the meeting of the Speech Association of America in Cincinnati on December 27, 1923.

our generally inadequate histories of oratory do not deal suffi-
ciently with the time of the Empire even as history. Secondly,
we may profit something from the example even of the vicious
and the depraved. Thirdly, these speeches, as typical products
of the activity of the schools, should be of especial interest to
teachers of public speaking. Fourthly, the period is made particularly significant to us by the fact that the orators were professors of rhetoric. Fifthly, as an age when Gaul was "nurse of
orators" and held undisputed precedence over the rest of the
world, it marks the beginning of French eloquence, later so
richly colored by a high development of the eulogy. Sixthly,
the panegyric as a speech form and these examples in particular are interesting in themselves.

Histories repeat the observation of Tacitus that Augustus
pacified the world, and eloquence also. Free speech died with
the death of the Republic. Of so early as A.D. 25 Tacitus tells
us (*Annals* 4. 34. 1): "In the reign of Tiberius, Cremutius
Cordus was impeached upon a novel charge, now heard for
the first time—that in his History he commended Marcus
Brutus and called Gaius Gracchus 'the last of the Romans.'"
Although, to be sure, the orator of the law-courts continued to
serve or subvert the ends of justice, the political oratory of
Cicero and Hortensius belonged to a past golden age. Every
form of high activity was at low ebb. After the age of Silver
Latin, good poetry was silent; history flourished in abridged
text-books only; law and medicine alone throve. Great oratory
could hardly prosper in the world of the first several centuries
of our era, a world such as a cursory survey of Gibbon reveals:
a world of emperors and princelings following one another in
tragic succession, of might, murder, intrigue, violent change,
of wars against Gaul, Goth, and German barbarian.

Though it no longer exerted great political influence,
oratory never lost its glamour. An affected eloquence still

remained, in the pay of rulers who inspired only such speaking as contributed to the gratification of their pride of power. Senators still harangued and maintained the fiction of a Republic and the image of the old Constitution, but they did not address their fellow citizens as of old. The public lecture-halls still were crowded to the doors to hear distinguished professors lecture, but the speakers delivered no message. To hear the invectives hurled against tyrants in the schools would give one the impression that here were progress and truth, but the spirit was not alive. They were not a Hyde Park.

The new type of oratory was the declamation, a direct product of the schools of the rhetoricians. Now declamation was meant to be a practical training in persuasion and argument through the treatment of subjects resembling actual cases pleaded before the courts. But the teachers supplanted the discussion of general and lively questions with the deliberative *suasoriae* and the judicial *controversiae*. The former employed fictitious subjects taken from history. A typical *suasoria*, for example, would be a speech persuading Caesar to cross the Rubicon. The latter employed civil causes drawn from private life, subtle, complicated, unlikely situations. I can here find time to present only one *controversia*—a less objectionable one: a father, thinking his son plans to kill him, orders his second son to slay his brother. The second son refuses. He is brought up on the charge of disobedience. The defendant in extenuation pleads that he heard his mother's voice forbid him do the deed. Is he guilty? More ingenious combinations of such circumstances were later tried, to an extreme of incredulity. An artificial and absurd staple pabulum of poisonings, murders, and other social crimes was fed the young student without range or variety for several centuries. It absorbed much of his time at school. Quite natural that early the premium was placed on ingenious turn of phrase, on bizarre treatment, on sparkling form. In particular would the rhetor shine in these qualities when he amended the student's version for the class; and royalty and society, seeking diversion, would attend the public recitals and applaud. Clearly great speaking can not be expected of this instruction. It seems that the education was not even effective for simple appearance in court. It is told of the great rhetorician Latro, that when suddenly called from his class-room to appear in behalf of a relative, he retired in a funk. He could not endure the open sky.

What by proper attention to content might have been valuable training, by absurd themes was rendered a training in mental gymnastics. Declamation became not an exercise, a means for education in public speaking, but an end in itself.

It is not my purpose to analyze the decay in oratory. The ancients themselves were well aware of it. Seneca the Elder treats the subject in the Preface to Book I of his *Controversiae*. Quintilian wrote a work, unfortunately not preserved, entitled *On the Causes of the Decay of Eloquence*. Tacitus wrote a dialogue on the decadence of oratory. Nor can the human tendency to belittle one's own time, paralleled in every field of history, be accounted the motive for this universal realization of artistic poverty. What I do regard as highly significant is the frequent inclusion, among the causes assigned for the decline, of this faulty instruction of the schools. Quintilian, who sees in declamation a potentially useful medium of instruction, says (2. 10. 3): "The practice however has so degenerated through the fault of the teachers that the ignorance of declaimers has been one of the chief causes that have corrupted eloquence."[2] . . . Tacitus writes: "The men of

---

[2] *Institutio Oratoria*, ed. and tr. H. E. Butler (London–New York, 1920–1922). Lucian's keen satire, entitled "The Rhetorician's Vade Mecum" by H. W. and F. G. Fowler in their translation, III (Oxford, 1905), 218–230, shows how the rhetors were likewise damaging the education of the East.

former days were well aware that in order to attain the end in view, the practice of declamation in the schools of rhetoric was not the essential matter—the training merely of tongue and voice in imaginary debates which had no point of contact with real life" (31). "The exercises in which the schools engage largely defeat their own objects.—Good heavens! what poor quality is shown in their themes, and how unnaturally they are made up. In addition to the subject matter that is so remote from real life, there is the bombastic style in which it is presented. And so it comes that themes like these: 'the reward of the king-killer,' or 'the outraged maid's alternatives,' or 'a remedy for the plague,' or the 'incestuous mother,' and all the other topics that are treated every day in the school but seldom or never in actual practice, are set forth in magniloquent phraseology" (35).[3] It is no surprise to hear Petronius (*Satyricon*, chap. 1), through the mouth of Encolpius, inveighing against the teachers of rhetoric: "I believe college makes complete fools of our young men, because they see and hear nothing of ordinary life there. It is pirates standing in chains on the beach, tyrants pen in hand, ordering sons to cut off their father's heads, oracles in time of pestilence demanding the blood of three virgins or more, honey-balls of phrases, every word and act besprinkled with poppy-seed and sesame. People who are fed on this diet can no more be sensible than people who live in the kitchen can be savory. With your permission I must tell you the truth, that you teachers, more than anyone else, have been the ruin of true eloquence. Your tripping, empty tones stimulate certain absurd effects into being, with the result that the *substance* of your speech languishes and dies. . . . I certainly do not find that Plato or Demosthenes took any course of training of this kind. . . .

---

[3] *P. Cornelii Taciti, Dialogus de Oratoribus*, ed. A. Gudeman (Leipzig-Berlin, 1914), ed. and tr. Sir William Peterson (London–New York, 1920).

Great style, which, if I may say so, is also modest style, rises supreme by virtue of its natural beauty."[4]

Perhaps Nisard[5] is right in concluding from the history of oratory in Greece and Rome that eloquence passes through three stages. First, there is the epoch of simple art, spontaneous public speaking born of simple feeling, not devoid, of course, of the quality of communicativeness, nor of happy organization, nor of natural facility. Secondly, there comes the epoch in which orators employ artistic principles of some elaborateness. From these theories arise. Genius and art combine. Liberty and public expediency guard against over-refinement. But both Demosthenes and Cicero represent the maturity preceding the decay which characterizes the third epoch. This is the oratory of over-elaborateness, of over-embellishment, of over-emphasis on external "form."[6]

The fostering of every tendency to ornament, the proclivity for the half-poetic style, the excessive emphasis on display, the complete neglect of inner form and dignified content, the straining to delight their hearers, this direct fruit of the teachings of the schools found a rich nourishment in that class of demonstrative speaking called the panegyric. It was the crowning achievement of the schools. Although a teacher of vision like Quintilian would not divorce from it a practical value (3. 4. 12–14) derived from the subject matter, epideictic had always been primarily devoted to display. A long distinction of funeral oratory was now supplemented by an avid cultivation of the panegyric. It became a rival to the stage in public interest. Anxiously anticipated far in advance, the

---

[4] *Petronius*, ed. and tr. M. Heseltine (London–New York, 1913). [The passage is presented in fuller form on p. 167, below.]

[5] D. Nisard, "Juvenal, ou la déclamation," in *Etudes sur les poëtes latins* (Paris, 1849), I, 423–431.

[6] Compare, in the theory, the over-subtle rules in the Greek scholastic treatises, of Hermogenes, for example.

speech, once delivered, was a topic of wide public discussion for months. And the public greed for recreation was gratified.

The Roman panegyric must be distinguished from the Greek, which was a speech delivered before a *panegyris*, an assembly of the whole nation on the occasion of the national games and festivals. In such the populace was exhorted to emulation by praise of the mighty deeds of their ancestors. As Lincoln did in his Gettysburg Address, the orator would use the occasion for stimulating his hearers to unanimous coöperation in the plans of the nation. Of course the classic examples of the Greek type are the *Panegyricus* and the *Panathenaicus* of Isocrates, the great professor of rhetoric. In Rome, particularly with the growth of the Empire, the panegyric became a eulogy of a living individual, usually the Emperor. A congratulatory address on any auspicious event, it might be on a national festival, the Emperor's birthday, the receipt of the honor of a consulship, any suitable opportunity for requesting renewal of favors. The most renowned rhetoricians, men of force in their community, would deliver it before the Prince himself. And these schoolmasters were indeed highly esteemed by the public and by royalty, being endowed with high honors and more than a respectable annuity. One of the panegyrists represented in the corpus which we are considering today received a salary of 600,000 sesterces, which he returned for the reorganization of his school at Autun (Eumenius, *Paneg. Lat.* IX(IV), II).

These Latin Panegyrics consist of twelve speeches, all but the first (which was addressed by Pliny to Trajan in A.D. 100) dating from the third and fourth centuries.[7] Four are ascribed severally to Claudius Mamertinus, Eumenius, Nazarius, and Pacatus Drepanius, and the other seven to *auctores incerti*.

---

[7] *XII Panegyrici Latini*, ed. W. Baehrens (Leipzig, 1911).

All of them so far as we know were Gallic rhetoricians. The occasions were variously celebrations of military victories, of a royal marriage, of the bestowal of a consulate, of the rebuilding of a school, of the anniversary of accession to the purple, of the birthday of Rome. Besides Trajan, the emperors addressed were Constantius, Constantine, Maximian, Julian, and Theodosius. If we remember that these speeches are almost all[8] that have come down to us of a type which was extremely popular, one which also in the provinces was enthusiastically cultivated and employed at every opportunity, and if we accept the hypothesis that usually what has been preserved for us is the best that might have been preserved, we may gain a fairly clear idea of what the mass of panegyrics was like.

I have selected for translation[9] the shortest of the collection, yet one which is typical. This panegyric, assigned in some editions to Claudius Mamertinus, was delivered before the Emperor Maximian at Trèves on April 21, A.D. 289. On May 1, A.D. 285, Diocletian had elevated Maximian, his fellow soldier, to the rank of Caesar and the title, Cousin. They divided sway. Diocletian, taking the title of Jovius, directed. Maximian, later (286) accorded the name Herculius and the status of Brother, carried the directions into execution. The coins of the period contain the images of both; the decrees that have come down to us are signed by both.

---

[8] There are extant Latin panegyrics by Symmachus (fourth century), Ausonius (fourth century), and Ennodius (fifth century), and also several poetical ones— which often achieve a high degree of good form—dating from the last century of the Republic and the first six centuries of the Christian era.

[9] I have found it necessary to excerpt only essential parts of this speech, and by a free, although I hope not unfaithful rendering, slightly to reorganize them into some semblance of unity, pruning away only expansive excrescences of the main thought. It was convenient to gain some help from the plan suggested by the condensation made by E. Allain, *Pline le jeune et ses héritiers* (Paris, 1902), III, 416. The panegyric is No. X (II) in W. Baehrens' edition.

Of Eloquence

Most sacred Emperor, all feasts should be celebrated in your honor as in divine honor. But especially on this most festive and most joyful day, under your rule, should the veneration of your divinity be joined with the solemn worship of the Holy City. At this hour when your piety celebrates the birth of the immortal mistress of the nations, it is fitting and proper that we sing, before all, *your* praises and render *you* thanks, Invincible Emperor. Indeed one can rightly speak of you and of your brother as the Founders of Rome, since it is to you that she owes her restoration, so very like to her foundation. And if this her natal day marks the origin of the Roman people, the first days of your reign preëminently mark her deliverance.

Where shall I begin? Shall I recall the obligations of the Republic to your fatherland? For who doubts that if Italy is by antiquity of glory the Sovereign of peoples, it is Pannonia which is Sovereign by valor? Or shall I rehearse the divine origin of your race, to which you bear witness as well by immortal deeds as by your adoption of the name? Shall I recount how you were educated and trained on that great frontier, that home of the bravest legions? Of Jove are such things invented, whereas of you they are true, O Emperor. Or shall I attempt to enumerate your exploits? But he who would wish to include all these themes, must hope to have innumerable years, aye centuries—a life as long as *you* deserve.

When you were summoned to restore the Republic by your kindred divinity, Diocletian, you were more the benefactor than the benefited. When all the barbarian nations of Gaul, united, threatened destruction, and when not alone the Burgundian Goths and the German Alemanni but as well the Chaibones and the Herulians—even these, who are chief of the barbarians in might and remotest in distance—would have invaded these provinces in impetuous attack, what god would have brought us hope in such despair, had you not been at hand? What need of a multitude, since you in person contended, you yourself fought to a decisive issue everywhere, all along the line? So fiercely did you rush upon the enemy, that neither they nor our soldiers deemed you were but one. They could not follow you even with their eyes. Truly you were so carried away all through the battle, as a mighty stream enhanced by winter showers and snows is wont to invade the field on every side. So all the Chaibones and the Herulians, all were cut down and slain in the great destruction; and not a fugitive of the battle but the glory of your victory reported their extinction to wives and mothers left at home.

I pass in silence over your numberless contests and victories in all of Gaul. Indeed what discourse would suffice for the multiplicity and grandeur of such achievements? You were the first Emperor to prove that the Roman Empire had no boundary, except such as was set by your arms. In former times the Rhine was regarded as a natural barrier of protection for the Roman provinces against barbarian inhumanity. Ever were we terrified when a mild season diminished the waters of the Rhine. But you, invincible Emperor, subdued these wild and savage peoples by devastation, combat, slaughter, fire, sword. Thanks to you we are now of free and easy mind. Let the Rhine dry up! There is no fear. What I see beyond the Rhine is Roman.

You both are generous, both most brave. In this resemblance you are more and more in harmony; and, what is surer than all kinship, are become brothers in the virtues. It is a fact that in your sharing this great Empire there is no envy on either side. You have but a single spirit—to guide the Republic. The considerable separation in your residences does not hinder your governing as if with right hands clasped. You place such a premium on concord, Emperor, that those who serve at your side you have bound to you by a personal intimacy and affinity with you. You think it admirable that you have the adherence not of the timidly servile but of the devotedly loyal. It is this especially that we admire in you, O Emperor. Just as all blessings seem to derive to us from the power of diverse divinities, but in reality flow from the highest sources, namely, Jove, Sovereign of Heaven, and Hercules, Peace-Maker of the earth; so of all our most excellent benefits, Diocletian furnishes the stimulus, and you the accomplishment.

It is a mark of your good fortune, I repeat of your felicity, O Emperor, that already have your soldiers victoriously attained the Ocean, that already the ebbing floods draw in the blood of enemies slain on its shore. Fleets, admirable to the extreme, have been built and equipped to assail the sea as well as all the rivers. How prosperous issues will follow you in your naval projects, anyone can easily understand, from the seasonableness of the weather which already attends you.

May it be vouchsafed me to end as I have begun this pious duty. Happy, O Rome, are you in such leaders! Happy, I say, aye much happier now than under your Romulus and your Remus. They were twin brothers, yet they quarreled, vying each to give you his own name; and they chose each separate hills and different auspices. Whereas your preservers of today, when first they return to you in triumph, are eager to be borne together in the same chariot, together to ascend the Capital, together to dwell in the Palace. No doubt soon will that great day dawn when it will not be necessary to set forth the good examples of the Camilli, and the Maximi, and the Curii, and the Catos, for emulation, when rather it will ever and again reveal you two, before our very eyes the most eminent exemplars of governmental wisdom.

And, Emperor, when you have insured the security of the whole world, the City, Mother of your Empire, will receive you. We pray that for this end your loyal hands may from time to time be loosed of their oppressive burdens. And may you in special (for I believe the East makes a similar request of Diocletian) be able frequently to make happier, by the visit of your divinity, these your provinces which enjoy renown, prosperity, and a most firmly established peace. You see, O Emperor, how great is the power of your heavenly benefactions to us. Rejoicing in your presence up to now, we already desire your return.

*   *   *

The models of the panegyrists were Cicero and Pliny, the former not a precedent in the specific speech-form, but exemplary in the manner of excessive laudation, as in his currying of Pompey's favor in the speech on the Manilian Law. Then, of course, there were also many precedents of obsequiousness in poetry. But the lapse from Pliny was very great. Read his panegyric to Trajan, thanking him for the Consulship; read this best Roman panegyric, and though you will find it in part dull and dry, though to Trajan are assigned all the blessings and virtues, you will clearly see the orator's high-minded sincerity and noble purpose, some dignity and force, and at least decency in the relations of orator and patron.

The panegyrists seem to have followed carefully and conscientiously in disposition, topics, attention to figures, the rhetorical works of epideictic; their speeches are in character close to the plan and doctrine of the treatises ascribed to Menander Rhetor (third Christian century), who gives special directions for the composition of various types of demonstrative oratory, including those in praise of a sovereign, of a country, of a city, the farewell speech to one departing, and others, the employment of which you may have observed in "Mamertinus."

Critics disagree concerning the value of these speeches. Everyone who reads them in Latin will agree that, from the literary point of view, the pure classic diction, the clarity, the grammatical correctness and a certain finish must be admired. When the Latin tongue was decaying all about them, the use of Cicero as a standard, even though it resulted in book Latin, lends credit to these schoolmen. To be sure, as is perhaps to be expected of an academic product, the speeches are invariably uniform. But no adverse criticism can be made on grounds of error in external form. They receive the condemnation that they do because of their unhealthy content. The public discourse of perhaps no other period can match that of these professors for fulsome flattery, the bad taste of abject adulation, usurpation of the place of thought by words, passion for strained and turgid thoughts, the use of grand and stately words for little things, the love of epigram, antithesis, and exaggerated hyperbole. The over-use of hyperbole, which must have required audacity, approaches ludicrous parody. The orator can find no comparison in history with the exploits of the subject. One orator compares a decree to Amphion's wonderful music. The present age is proclaimed greater than the golden age of Saturn. Enemies are never spared an avalanche of curses. Divine impetus is discovered to move every royal journey. Crimes and vices are made into virtues. The emperors, superior as they were to many of their predecessors and successors, were never historically the great geniuses here depicted. Maximian, for example, though a brave and active general, was a greedy and bloodthirsty prince.

I can catch the fervor of their modern apologists and accept the contention that these Roman orators were perhaps true patriots. I can, and must of course, view their attitude from the perspective of the dangerous and debased time in which they lived, with its emperor cult and divine right, view it with consideration of the restraints and prohibitions imposed by the imperial system. But an inescapable conclusion is that this eloquence was in too large part empty of ideas; that these orators were mannerists, specialists in externals.

I cannot now trace the history of the panegyric in the Middle Ages, the Renaissance, and the modern world. Such speeches were delivered at the dedication of churches in the days of the Holy Empire. There was a great renewal of panegyrical epideictic in the early Renaissance in Italy, and in England during the fifteenth and sixteenth centuries. Erasmus wrote a great panegyric on Philip II of Spain. The French have a long history of the speech form, which flourished particularly under Louis XIII and Louis XIV, Richelieu and Mazarin, and throughout the eighteenth into the early nineteenth century. And I am not sure that we must study the oratorical history of peoples with a temper different from ours like the French or Italians, or of peoples with institutions different from ours, like the Germans under the Kaiser, in order to find approximate modern analogues to the Roman panegyric. It is necessary only to hear or read speeches delivered in our own country at inauguration ceremonies, the awarding of honorary degrees, and particularly the nomination of presidential candidates.

III

A Late Mediaeval Tractate on Preaching[*]

I

IN *The Decay of Modern Preaching*, Mahaffy bewails the lack of attention in courses of homiletics to the rhetoric of theological learning. He declares that without it the learning is dead and, as it were, sealed in a tomb.[1] Pleading for the establishment of more chairs of rhetoric in modern theological schools, he yet warns against naming them chairs in *sacred* rhetoric, since the appellation would rest on the false assumption that sacred rhetoric differs from any other rhetoric.[2] On the other hand Phillips Brooks, equally concerned for the good training of the preacher, with excellent use of the oratorical device of *praetermissio*, asserts: "Of oratory, and all the marvelous mysterious ways of those who teach it, I dare say nothing. I believe in the true elocution teacher, as I believe in the existence of Halley's comet, which comes into sight of this earth once in about seventy-six years."[3] Involved, of course, in this difference of opinion is the persistent question of a definition of oratory and of rhetoric. Brooks obviously

[*] Reprinted from *Studies in Rhetoric and Public Speaking in Honor of J. A. Winans*, edited by A. M. Drummond (New York, 1925), pp. 61–90.

[1] J. P. Mahaffy (New York, 1882), p. 73.

[2] *Ibid.*, p. 141.

[3] *Lectures on Preaching* (New York, 1888), p. 178. For a similar position, cf. A. S. Hoyt, *The Work of Preaching* (New York, 1909), p. 43.

distrusted not only a type of instruction which, one now readily admits, was not always effective, but also over-embellishment of style, display, and inappropriate pulpit devices of delivery. Indeed, Brooks's *Lectures on Preaching* deal largely with the rhetoric of preaching, with invention and disposition and persuasion, and the preacher's personality. Patently, he was led into an erroneous divorcement of rhetoric from oratory, and into the false identification of oratory with delivery, or rather, with bad delivery.

The suspicion which Brooks avowed, as against the more discerning penetration of Mahaffy, was largely shared by preachers of the Middle Ages. To be sure, the pagan rhetoric of Cicero and Quintilian was well known, and used, by Cyprian, Augustine (who had taught it in the secular schools), Gregory, and many others. Yet Augustine finds it necessary to defend the use of rhetoric by a Christian teacher.[4] No doubt the frequent condemnation of eloquence by the mediaeval teachers, as by Brooks, arose from zeal to avoid ostentation and a style ill fitting the elevated tone of the preacher's calling. St. Thomas Aquinas says: "He who has to preach must make use of both eloquence and secular learning."[5] "The use of secular eloquence in Sacred Scripture is in one way commendable and in another reprehensible. It is the latter when one uses it for display or when one aims mainly at eloquence. He who strives mainly for eloquence does not intend that men should admire what he says, but rather tries to gain admiration for himself. Eloquence is commendable when the speaker has no desire to display himself, but wishes only to use it as a means of benefiting his hearers, and out of reverence for Holy Scripture." "It is laudable in preaching to make use of a har-

---

[4] *On Christian Doctrine* IV. 1 and 2.

[5] For these quotations from St. Thomas, see J. Walsh, "St. Thomas on Preaching," *Dominicana*, V (1921), 6–14.

monious and learned style, if it be not done from motives of display, but for the instruction of hearers and the persuasion of opponents." This is sound rhetoric. Gregory Nazianzen's censure[6] of preachers who used the eloquence of the theatre was a reproof of bad rhetoric. Of course the belief of mediaeval teachers that pagan books generally should be handled with care, against the contingency of exposure to impiety,[7] did have an effect on the use of classical rhetorical works. But though secular learning was subordinated to sacred, it was by no means neglected.[8]

By the thirteenth century, rhetoric throve in the schools of Europe. The sermons and the homiletical text-books of the late mediaeval period show a highly developed rhetoric of invention, particularly in the application of the ancient rhetorical commonplaces, an organic system of disposition, and a shrewd attention to delivery. The uniqueness of the subject-matter of the sermon and the peculiar differentiation of the preacher's function should not misdirect us to the conclusion that there was an absence, in theory and practice, of the same broad rhetorical principles which operate equally in ancient or modern public speaking of any kind.

A late mediaeval treatise on preaching, representing a method of the twelfth, thirteenth, and fourteenth centuries, should give us insight into a very important period in the history of oratory, and particularly in the history of the oratory of the pulpit, since preaching had then, after a long development, risen to a high level of excellence. The rise of new orders, the spread of mysticism, the growth of scholasticism, and the superior general culture of the time affected both

---

[6] See P. A. Beecher, art. "Homiletics," *Cath. Encyc.*

[7] See A. Lecoy de la Marche, *La chaire française au moyen âge* (Paris, 1886), p. 476.

[8] See L. Bourgain, *La chaire française au XIIe siècle* (Paris, 1879), p. 251.

the extent and method of preaching. I may not here attempt the hazardous task of reviewing the vast field of mediaeval preaching and preachers;[9] but suffice it to say that in the development of the sermon form, the time from the Apostolic Age to the twelfth century represents one period—that of the inorganic form. The sermon grew out of the custom of improvising a brief exposition of the Biblical passage for the day, following the order of the verses. It was an exegetical abstract, worked over, or it was a patristic homily. The homily was an informal discourse, a "conversation" (in Latin, *tractatus popularis*), a doctrinal interpretation of Scripture in a familiar way, without formal introduction or divisions. It might be treated sentence by sentence, or by concentrating the entire Gospel on one idea, or by selecting a virtue or vice from the Gospel to discuss, or by paraphrasing and applying the whole Gospel. Bede, Gregory, and Origen used homilies. The sermons of the period of conversion of the barbarians, those of Boniface and Caesarius of Arles, for example, achieved energy and color in notable degree. After the great missionary epoch, during the time when the clergy were recruited from the barbarians, there followed one of comparative decadence in preaching; then, with the age of Charlemagne, a gradual renascence. By the twelfth century in France, and the thirteenth in the rest of Europe, pulpit eloquence was at a peak in its progress. The "mellifluous doctor," St. Bernard of Clairvaux, aroused multitudes to enthusiasm.

As distinguished from the method of the homily, the preachers of this later phase—Albertus Magnus, Bonaventure, Thomas Aquinas—used sermons (*sermones*) in expounding the

[9] See E. C. Dargan, *A History of Preaching* (New York, 1905); R. Cruel, *Geschichte der deutschen Predigt im Mittelalter* (Detmold, 1879); A. Linsenmayer, *Geschichte der Predigt in Deutschland* (Munich, 1886); J. S. Maury, *Essai sur l'éloquence de la chaire* (Paris, 1877); Lecoy de la Marche, *op. cit.*; Bourgain, *op. cit.*; J. M. Neale, *Mediaeval Preachers and Mediaeval Preaching* (London, 1856).

Gospel, following a systematic method. In the tractate to be presented, the strictly systematic scheme will be apparent.

The method of the thirteenth century, it will be seen, was to unfold the sermon from the internal essence of the truth with which it was concerned, by explaining the text and by deducing associated lines of thought, with strong dependence on what Bossuet later called, perhaps properly, the "banal" art of amplification.[10] But the analytical design of organization was at times so good that it could easily sustain attention. The diversification of each member must not have presented difficulties to the attainment of clearness and orderly sequence. The scholastic influence appears in the resemblance which the sermons bear to philosophical discussions—in definitions, distinctions, dialectical inquiries, and argumentation. When allied to talent, the methodical spirit must have been highly efficacious, even though the sermons may in many cases have been too replete with divisions and trivial comparisons. Since the people had complete faith, it was instruction which they sought. Nor were the teachings always devoid of feeling. Sometimes majesty and great religious power were achieved. The principle of amplification it was probably necessary to use against the failure of inspiration. To be sure, they abused the habit of drawing too much out of one word; Eckhart gave a sermon devoted only to the word "and."[11] Always the sermon rested on Scripture, whereof the preachers' knowledge seemed intuitive, on the Fathers, and on the liturgical books, but often the severity was relieved by embellishment, and the discourse made lively by physical action. The mysticism in symbolical interpretation was often simple to comprehend, and at other times obscure. Moral points were not usually

---

[10] See pp. 60 ff. below and the "Henry"-tract, pp. 155 f. below. "St. Bonaventure" discusses the expansion of sermons in *De Arte Concionandi*, Part III.

[11] Linsenmayer, p. 159.

developed to their full extent, but merely proposed and applied by a figurative interpretation.

Response to preaching was on occasions exciting. Often the preachers were heckled.[12] Often they were so popular that they left town secretly in the dead of night lest their departure be prevented by their devotees. Jacques de Vitry tells[13] that Foulques de Neuilly needed a new cassock each day, to replace that usually torn by the crowds, who came from distant countries to hear the holy man and share with him some of his sanctified possessions. In their efforts to amuse, some preachers were condemned for yielding to extravagance. Jacques de Vitry himself would suddenly lift his voice to shout: "That man sleeping there in the corner will never learn my secret."[14] An abbé, in the midst of his talk, awakened his sleeping flock by a swift change of subject: "There was once a king called Arthur." They started from their doze only to be chastised for lack of attention.[15] Every method of preparation for delivery was employed. Some preachers, like Bede, spoke extempore, from prepared outline; some, like Anthony of Padua, read from notes. The author of the tractate before us has interesting observations on delivery.

The preachers studied their audiences. Gregory the Great devotes a whole chapter[16] to the mere enumeration of the different types to be admonished by the preacher. The discourses of Jacques de Vitry are addressed to one hundred and twenty categories of auditors. They preached to all and everywhere; men and women, rich and poor, day and night, in

---

[12] Lecoy de la Marche, p. 216.

[13] S. Baring-Gould, *Post-Mediaeval Preachers* (London, 1865), p. 11.

[14] Lecoy de la Marche, p. 214.

[15] Lecoy de la Marche, *ibid.* Still one does not read of extravagances in this period comparable to those of later practice, e.g. that of Olivier Maillard [see p. 239 below].

[16] *Pastoral Rule*, Part III, i.

public places and streets and fields. Perhaps their greatest skill was shown in adjustment, in matter and diction, to illiterate audiences. Nothing was taken for granted; every thought was put in the most vivid and intelligible language, often with striking stories and homely proverbs. Were space allotted me, I should here clearly illustrate this by introducing an entire sermon. Thereby the characteristic unity of the mediaeval sermon might also be apparent. But something of the spirit of direct communicativeness with a simple audience may be caught from the following translation of an excerpt from a thirteenth century sermon. It is entitled "On the Angels,"[17] and was delivered by the great Franciscan, Berthold von Regensburg, in the German vernacular of his day.[18]

We celebrate to-day the feast of the Great Princes, the Holy Angels, who are to the whole world a great miracle, and through whom Almighty God has created many great miracles. And if a man did not wish for any other reason to go to heaven, he might nevertheless easily go to heaven for this reason: merely to see what wonders and wonders are there. And of the wonders there is no end, the wonders with which God has endowed the Holy Angels. And they are the messengers of our Lord—for angel means, in Greek, a messenger. Our Lord had great joy, for He was without beginning, just as He is also without end. I speak of Divinity, of the Crown. Before He created anything such as we are, He had great delight within Himself and of Himself. Then He planned to create. He wished to create two creatures, two kinds of creatures, so that these might be sharers of His joy—but that He Himself because of them should have not less joy. And however much joy and delight He gave to them, on that account no less joy had He—just like the sunshine. However much of its light the sun gives us day by day, itself has no less light. So God made two creatures; they were man and

17 In F. Pfeiffer and J. Strobl, *Berthold von Regensburg* (Vienna, 1880), 2. 174 ff.

18 It is perhaps safe to say that after the tenth century. Latin was not understood by the common people of Europe.

angel. Then God made a thing. And it was the very best thing of all things that God had ever made. And He never made a thing so well among all the things which God made in order that man and angel should share in His joy; so good and so useful was it. And so God brought it about that men and angels should have therefrom more and more joy. And however useful was the thing, and however much honor and blessedness lie therein, still were there some angels in heaven who wished not to retain the thing. And they were shut out from the eternal joys, and thrown into eternal torture. And all the people who retained the thing remained with Almighty God in eternal joys, because they retained the thing which is so good, among all things the best [virtue]. . . .

And so we celebrate to-day the feast of the Angels who remained with God, and did not fall. And so we celebrate to-day the feast of St. Michael and the Holy Angels; and that we do not celebrate the feast of the Holy Angels often in the year, therein our Lord did wisely and well. However easy it would be that we should celebrate their feast three times yearly, our Lord did well and wisely therein, and it is better that we do not celebrate their feast often. Why? See, for this reason. If we should celebrate their feast with singing and with reading, we should also have to preach about them, and if we had to preach often about the angels, perhaps a blasphemer would come along, and perhaps be so blasphemous that he might preach of the heresy of the Holy Angels. For Our Lord has wrought so many wonders with the angels that we do not know them all for sure. He has wrought some miracles or wonders with the angels of which we do not know fully, but only guess. And whoever guesses a thing does not know it for sure. And so Our Lord has done many a thing with them that we well know. Whoever, therefore, might wish to preach the things which we guess, might possibly preach heresy. And so no one should preach anything except that which we know for sure!

St. Thomas Aquinas' own preaching, and advice collected[19] from his writings, appear consistent with the doctrine of our

---

[19] See Fr. O'Daniel, "Thomas Aquinas as Preacher," *Ecclesiastical Review*, XLII (1910), 26–37; especially Walsh, *art. cit*; and R. B. Vaughan, *Life and Labours of St. Thomas of Aquin* (London, 1871–1872).

treatise, the author of which claims adherence to the Thomistic school. Vaughan's biography discusses the Angelic Doctor's simple style, the strong intellectual element in his sermons, and his great powers of delivery. One of his sermons was greeted with such lamentation that he could not for a time continue. On another occasion he was applauded—an experience which Chrysostom of the fourth century often enjoyed, but which in the thirteenth was rare. His preserved[20] sermons are either bare sketches as reported by pupils and listeners, or perhaps the final recapitulations, such recapitulations as the author of our tractate refers to. Leo XIII thought so highly of Thomas' method as to commend it to all preachers.[21]

Some of his precepts relate to the subject-matter of sermons, the preacher's function, and his ethical qualities as preacher. "The matter of preaching is twofold; what is useful for the present life, as concerns God, or our neighbors, or ourselves; and what we hope to have in the next life." "All preaching should be directed to two purposes: demonstrating God's greatness by preaching the faith; and showing forth His goodness by elucidating the truth." "A preacher must have three qualities: stability, to ward him from error; clearness, to avoid obscurity in his teaching; utility, to seek God's glory rather than his own." "A preacher must have three powers: he must be endowed with a fulness of knowledge of things sacred, to prove to others; he must be able to prove what he says; he must fitly set forth to his audience the things he conceives." "Two things are necessary for preachers, that they may lead to Christ. The first is an orderly discourse; the second is the virtue of good works."

[20] *Divi Thomatis Aquinatis Doctoris Angelici Sermones et Opuscula Concionatoria*, ed. A. J. Raulx (Paris, 1881).

[21] See the Encyclical Letter (1879) on the Restoration of Christian Philosophy, prefixed to the Dominican Fathers' translation of the *Summa Theologica*.

Another injunction of Thomas warns against the telling of stories or fables.[22] This advice, consistent with the omission from our treatise of any discussion of the *exemplum*, is an interesting divergence from a favorite practice of thirteenth century preachers, even among the Dominicans.[23] Some preachers, notably Jacques de Vitry[24] and Caesarius of Heisterbach, realizing that many listeners who were not moved by bare doctrine could be stirred by illustrative stories with pointed morals, used such *exempla* with great effectiveness. Some of these tales were of the saints; many concerned the devil. Almost all were full of superstition, but a great number were characterized by genuine morality, shrewd knowledge of the world, and fancy and humor. Great collections[25] of fables, bestiaries, and *exempla* were available for the preacher and were used throughout Europe.

As is to be expected, the theory of preaching, in point of time, succeeded the practice. In France, Guibert de Nogent's *Liber Quo Ordine Sermo Fieri Debeat* appeared at the beginning, and Alain de Lille's *Summa de Arte Praedicatoria* at the end, of the twelfth century. The *De Eruditione Praedicatorum* of Humbert de Romans—who promises to teach a way of producing a sermon for any set of men and for every diversity of circumstance[26]—belongs to the beginning of the thirteenth. Even before the twelfth century, the preacher could have recourse to collections of homilies (some as early as the eighth century),

[22] For these passages from St. Thomas, see Walsh, *op. cit.* With the last injunction, compare Dante's complaint of the use of fables in the preaching of his day, *Paradiso* XXIX. 103–120. The mediaeval tractate of Humbert de Romans encourages the use of *exempla;* Lecoy de la Marche, p. 301.

[23] E.g., the famous collection of Stephen of Bourbon.

[24] See T. F. Crane, *The Exempla of Jacques de Vitry* (London, 1899).

[25] See T. F. Crane, "Mediaeval Sermon-Books and Stories," *Proceedings of the American Philosophical Society*, XXI (1883), 49–78; and "Mediaeval Sermon-Books and Stories and their Study since 1883," *ibid.*, LVI (1917), 369–402.

[26] Book II.

collections of text-materials for sermons, of sermons for each day, of commentaries, glosses, alphabeted Biblical vocabularies, and homiletical lexicons. Such preachers' anthologies, "The Garden of Delight," "The Flower of the Apostles," "The Book of Sparkling Points," were common in the European libraries. This apparatus, although it made for a general high level of preaching, must have suppressed originality in the less competent preachers.

It would require special linguistic training in the various tongues of mediaeval Europe to make a substantial study of the influence of the sermon on the history of the period, or its influence particularly upon the development of the modern tongues. As the almost exclusive source of knowledge for the common people, the sermon was undoubtedly a great instrument of civilization. But a more practical and more promising inquiry for the student of rhetoric would be a comparison of the mediaeval sermon in content, form, methods, and function with that of later periods. The preaching of the Renaissance, in theory, marked a return to greater dependence on the Greek and Roman rhetoricians, and, in practice, specialized in long exordia and an interest in the civil law. Reuchlin's *Liber Congestorum de Arte Praedicandi* is largely a repetition of Cicero and Quintilian. In his *Ecclesiastes*, Erasmus glances back with ridicule at mediaeval preaching. Yet an examination of the sermons of a John Donne of the seventeenth century would yield surprising discoveries of spiritual similarity with the sermons of the Middle Ages. Surely it was a far cry from the thirteenth-century sermons—tools in an instrumental art, serving the humble and illiterate—to those of the period of Louis XIV, when the eloquent divine preached in the drawing-rooms of fine ladies, and skeptics of the nobility were offered the entertainment of the latest fad in preachers. The eighteenth century had very little esteem for

the thirteenth, condemning it for bad taste, dryness, a barbarous scholasticism, overcredulity, and complete lack of
eloquence—this at a time when, in England, Doctors of
Divinity were delivering before criminals awaiting execution
sermons prepared for university audiences.[27] And perhaps
most useful would be to contrast the mediaeval pulpit orator
with the Brookses and Beechers, or with his present-day
counterpart, who sermonizes on social and political questions,
uses longer texts, and opposes formalism. It is to be hoped that
students of the history of rhetorical theory will be encouraged
to make such necessary and illuminating studies.

II

The treatise which we are considering, and that attributed
to Henry of Hesse, the *Tractatus de Arte Praedicandi*, were the
first homiletical texts to appear in Germany.[28] The copy of the
tractate used by the translator is found in the library of
Cornell University, bound together with other, unrelated,
ecclesiastical works, in a quarto volume of incunabula.[29] The
treatise covers nineteen pages. No date or place of publication
is indicated. Most probably it was printed in the last decade
of the fifteenth century.[30] Misprints, faulty punctuation,
obscure contractions, suspensions, and special symbols make
the reading at times difficult. Nor is the thought always clear.
And the imperfect and anacoluthic Latin in some places
makes translation even more difficult. In translating, I have

[27] Neale, p. xv.

[28] Cruel, p. 596. [For a translation of the Henry-tract, see pp. 143–159 of this
volume.]

[29] Press No. 7546 A15: *Tractatulus Solemnis de Arte et Vero Modo Predicandi.*

[30] See L. Hain, *Repertorium Bibliographicum*, Nos. 1351–1359, 1361–1362; J.
McGovern, "A Mediaeval Manual for Preachers," *Ecclesiastical Review*, LXX
(March, 1924), 299 ff. The earliest copy known is a Nürnberg edition of 1477,
according to Linsenmayer, p. 102.

attempted to give the reader some impression of the style of the original.

We do not know the Dominican author-compiler; neither do we know of any such tractate of Thomas[31] as that referred to by the compiler in the title.

The reader will observe that the author frequently quotes from memory. Steeped though he is in Scriptural lore, he is often guilty of false quotation. His fondness for the rhetorical principle of accumulation is evident. His use of the various senses of explication illustrates the influence of Alexandrian philosophy and theology on the thought of the Middle Ages.[32] Almost every idea in this logical, detailed, precise exposition of the ancient method of invention is shrewdly developed by authoritative passages; the author practises the art of which he is expositor.

III

A Short Formal Treatise on the Art and True Method of Preaching, Compiled from Divers Writings of Holy Men of Learning, and chiefly from a certain short treatise composed by the Most Holy Doctor of the Christian Church, Thomas Aquinas, in which he proceeds in the manner and form of the material here presented.

As I WISH to communicate to my best beloved the following material on the method of popular preaching, after my many labors vouchsafed me by the All-Highest (who gives every good but not the bull by the horns), I am therefore submitting to them an abridged tractate on this art, laboriously compiled from sundry books of holy men of learning.

---

[31] No reference is found either in P. Mandonnet, *Des écrits authentiques de St. Thomas d'Aquin* (Fribourg, 1910), or in M. Grabmann, *Die echten Schriften des Heiligen Thomas von Aquin* (Münster in Westphalia, 1920).

[32] [See pp. 96 ff. below.]

It does not suffice to possess learning or command of the materials of preaching in order to preach correctly and fitly, but art and method also are required. So Gregory at the beginning of his *Pastoral Rule*[33] tells us that the art is based upon the Word of God. The appropriate method of preaching may be a gift of God, who gives to preachers of the Gospel the Word, with abundant virtue, art, and also learning. As St. Augustine says, this gift is to be assisted in many ways, for nothing is more presumptuous than to teach before one has learned the method of teaching.[34] According to Tully, in the second book of his *Rhetoric*,[35] it is not enough to have something one ought to say, but there is required the very business of speaking as the quality of the hearer demands and exacts. For how can anyone speak if he know not the means of knowing how he should speak? Likewise St. Augustine, *On Christian Doctrine*,[36] emphasizes not only what is said, but the way in which it is said. Primarily he who penetrates the hearts of his audience present kindles and inflames his hearers, for, as Gregory says, the way of the Lord is directed toward the heart when the doctrine of Truth is heard. Hence the hearing of God's Word is the way of conversion from sin. A sermon of the Lord is food for the mind. For of such great virtue is preaching that it recalls men from error to truth, from vices to virtues; it changes depravity to rectitude and turns rough to smooth; it inculcates faith, raises hope, enkindles charity; it dislodges the injurious, implants the useful, and fosters the honorable. For

[33] Prologue; and Part I, chap. 1: "The government of souls is the art of arts." The compiler is in the habit of quoting generally rather than literally or accurately. In this and some of the subsequent quotations it has not been possible to discover the exact references.

[34] Possibly a general reference to *On Christian Doctrine* IV. 1–4, and 10.

[35] The statement in this form is not found in either the *De Inventione* or *Rhetorica ad Herennium;* but see Aristotle, *Rhet.* 3. 1. 2.

[36] See, e.g., 4. 16. 33; for the reference to Gregory which follows, cf. *Pastoral Rule*, Part III, Prologue.

it is the way of life, the ladder of the virtues, and the door of Paradise. It is therefore not only an art, but the art of arts,[37] and the science of the sciences. William of Paris in approving and recommending the art of preaching says: "Since so many volumes of rhetoric have been written by the band of rhetoricians, is it not much more just and worthy that their own art and doctrine should enjoy treatment by the band of preachers, so that they will be divine rhetoricians?"[38] Especially so, since, in its profit and utility, the eloquence of oratory cannot compare with this eloquence of preaching.

Preaching, then, is the fitting and suitable communication of the Word of God.

Now, three kinds of preaching have been used concomitantly. One is by word of mouth, as indicated in "Preach the Gospel to every creature."[39] Another kind is by writing. Hence the Apostle is said to have preached to the Corinthians when he wrote them the Epistles containing God's Word. The third kind is by deeds. So Gregory says that every act of Christ is instruction for us. For He, the Supreme Master, our Lord Jesus, in order that nothing should be wanting in His teaching, took most diligent care to instruct in each kind, by works and by sermon, as it is written of Him in the first chapter of the Acts. Jesus undertook to do and to teach, or rather, first to do and then to teach. To denote this, each faithful preacher today is held to preaching first by deed and then by sermon. Would indeed that each preacher today were to become such a diligent imitator of Christ Jesus, that he should preach not with the word alone but also with works! Whence Pope Leo: "Teaching is more complete by deed than by voice, for the

---

[37] See note 33 above.

[38] See William of Auvergne, *Rhetorica Divina*, chap. 1.

[39] Mark 16:15. For the reference to Gregory which follows, cf. *Pastoral Rule*, Part I, chap. 3.

effective method of preaching rests on the agreement of life with doctrine."[40] Gregory: "It follows that his preaching is condemned whose life is contemned." Aristotle, in the *Ethics*,[41] says that they whose works are at variance with their speech will be despised. Bernard, in a sermon: "Then, too, does the seed of God easily germinate, when the preacher's piety strengthens these truths in the heart of the hearer. For this end, unless I err in my judgment, the preacher must live justly and rightly, lest he render his words null by contradicting deeds." Paul: "I dare not speak of any of those things which Christ worketh not by me [for the obedience of the Gentiles, by word and deed],"[42] deeming it shameful to preach or teach what he failed to perform in act.

Here follows a definition of preaching.

Thus preaching by word or voice—our present subject—is open and public instruction in faith and morals, devoted to the informing of men, and proceeding along the path of reasoning and from the source of authorities. It will be open preaching, since, if it were secret, it would be subject to suspicion and would seem to let loose heretical dogmas. It will be public, because it is to be set before the many, not one individual. If it were set before the one, it would properly be not preaching, but exposition of doctrine. That is why preaching is termed instruction in faith and morals.

Two aspects of theology whereof use is to be made in preach-

[40] Most probably Leo I, the Great, but I have not found the passage here ascribed to him. For the reference to Gregory which follows, cf. *Pastoral Rule*, Part I, chaps. 1, 2, 10, 11; Part II, chaps. 1–4; Part III, Prologue, and chap. 40.

[41] Possibly *Eth. Nic.* 4. 13, on boasters and humbugs, or 10. 10, on sophists. I have not found in St. Bernard the passage which here follows, but cf. in "Sermons on the Canticles" 16.2 (Migne, *Pat. Lat.* 183, p. 849) the threefold cable by which the preacher draws souls to the kingdom of heaven: *recte sentire, digne proloqui, vivendo confirmare.*

[42] Rom. 15:18.

ing are involved: the rational, which strives after knowledge in things divine, and the moral, which offers information in ethics. For preaching is instruction now in divine matters, now in moral conduct. This is imaged forth by the angels descending and ascending on the ladder which Jacob saw.[43] Mystically, the angels are those learned men who ascend when they preach heavenly things. They descend when they conform to things mortal.

In fact the efficient cause of a sermon is twofold: principal and instrumental. The principal cause of every sermon is the Lord of Glory. That He may be moved by the preacher's tongue as agent, prayer is made to Him. Thus the preacher acts as an instrumental cause.

Also, the art of preaching is the science which teaches address on some subject. The subject of this art is the Word of God. The subject of the sermon, on the other hand, is the preacher's purpose—and the like that can be added.

The preacher's principles of action can be used as follows. If the sermon delivered is from some authority of the Bible or the Saints, he must preach vigorously, so that his utterance may leave his mouth vigorously and abide in the listener's heart. Hence the preacher must sometimes try to speak with wonder, as in delivering the passage: "Have I not dissembled? Have I not kept silence?"[44] Sometimes he must speak with grief and lamentation, as in: "O my son, Absalom! my son, my son Absalom!"[45] Often with horror and agitation: "Except ye be converted."[46] At times with irony and derision: "Dost thou still continue in thy simplicity? [Bless God and die.]"[47] Sometimes with gracious countenance and drawing together

[43] Gen 28:12.
[44] Job 3:26.
[45] II Sam. 18:33.
[46] Matt. 18:3.
[47] Job 2:9.

of the hands: "Come unto me, all [ye that labor and are heavy laden, and I will give you rest]."[48] With a certain elation: "From a far country have they come to me."[49] At times with impatience and indignation: "Let us appoint a captain," and so forth.[50] At other times with joy and lifting up of the hands: "Come, ye blessed [of my Father, inherit the kingdom prepared for you from the foundation of the world]."[51] Often with hate, and turning away of the face: "Depart from me, ye cursed," and the rest.[52] Thus the preacher's gesture should conform to that which he must believe Christ used when He said: "Destroy this temple,"[53] by placing his hand above his heart and looking at the temple.

From these suggestions and others that will follow, any preacher can easily collect and acquire the principles of action—the true art and method—which are, so to speak, the instruments guiding him in his activity. One is not hindered by learning to know also many other things—for example, that it is possible to be ignorant of method. Very few and limited are the things we know in proportion to those we do not.

The theme is the beginning of the sermon. In regard to it there are many requirements: first, that it be taken from the Bible; that it have a fully perceived meaning; that it be not incongruous; that it be not too long nor too short; that it be expressed in predicable terms—in all its verbs, participles, and the rest.

Again, the theme is the prelocution, made for the proof of the predicable terms contained in the theme, through authori-

[48] Matt. 11:28.
[49] Cf. Josh. 9:6, 9.
[50] Num. 14:4.
[51] Matt. 25:34.
[52] Matt. 25:41.
[53] John 2:19.

tative passages from the Bible and theologians, and by bringing in authorities of philosophy through some simile, moral point, proverb, or natural truth.

Likewise what is said in the theme and its division is called the theme, since the division of the theme is the very theme itself. For from the theme the divisions proceed as from a root (as is clear in our tree below). That is why the division is called the theme.

Note that there are four parts of a sermon: the theme, the protheme or prelocution, the division or distinction, the subdivision or subdistinction. To them two principles apply: the deducing of these parts I have mentioned—through demonstrations of, and exhortations to practice, the virtues—and the avoidance of faults.

Faults in Sermons

The preacher's ignorance
Lack of fluency
Excessive noisiness
Sleepy delivery
Finger pointings
Tossing of the head
Remote digression

The prelocution, too, can be formed by adducing authorities with reference to the theme. For illustration, let this theme be assumed: "O death, how bitter is the remembrance of thee."[54] Now the prelocution of this theme can be taken from definite authorities: the Psalmist, "The death of the wicked is very evil";[55] Kings, "Behold, in peace is my bitterness most bitter";[56] Ecclesiasticus, "Remember thy last end, and thou

[54] Ecclus. 41:1. [Cf. Henry-tract, p. 148 below, as also for n. 55.]
[55] Vulg. Ps. 33:22.
[56] Wrong reference. Is. 38:17.

shalt never sin";[57] Solomon, "Nothing is surer than death, nothing less sure than the hour of death";[58] Augustine, "Of all terrible things death is most terrible";[59] and also the authority of a philosopher. So the wise man says, "O death, how bitter is the remembrance of thee." These were the words of the theme taken up in the first place.

Next let the theme be posited with its divisions and subdivisions. After that comes the invocation of the Holy Spirit through angelic prayer—*Ave Maria* and the rest.

Then [the theme is developed] by arranging the parts one after another, by dividing and subdividing.

First Division

Death is twofold, spiritual and corporeal. Of things spiritual some are virtuous, some vicious. This is the subdivision of the first member. On the first is said: "For ye are dead, and your life is hid with Christ in God."[60] On the second, the verse of the Apostle: "Blessed is he who hath been freed from a second death."[61]

Subdivision of the Second Member

Of deaths corporeal, some are natural, some violent. On the former the passage from Kings is quoted: "We all die, and are as water spilt on the ground."[62] On the latter, the verse from Jeremiah: "Let us condemn him to a most shameful death."[63]

This theme fits our purpose because, the gospel omitted, the prelocution is formed through definite authorities.

After the prelocution comes the division of the theme, and

[57] 7:40.
[58] Actually St. Augustine [see below, Chapter VII, note 31].
[59] Cf. Aristotle, *Eth. Nic.* 3. 9 [see below Chapter VII, note 32].
[60] Col. 3:3.
[61] Cf. Rev. 20:6, 14; 21:8.
[62] Auth. Vers. II Sam. 14:14.
[63] Wisd. of Sol. 2:20; cf. Jer. 11:19.

then the subdivision of the principal parts of the theme, as has been made clear by the examples.

The theme, prelocution, division, and subdivision of the theme now fixed, the sermon is not yet complete unless some principal part is amplified through other materials, to wit through adduced authorities. Otherwise the sermon would become too short and simple. For that reason reliable methods of expanding the whole sermon as agreeably as possible must be provided.

Likewise observe how the main material of all sermons, yes, rather of all of Sacred Scripture is comprised of these ten topics: God, the devil, the heavenly city, hell, the world, the soul, the body, sin, penitence, virtue. Very few indeed and limited are these in proportion to the multitude of sermons. But even these topics, expanded according to the need of the hearers, grow as if into infinity.

The amplification of sermons is to be accomplished in nine ways: first, through agreement of authorities; second, through discussion of words; third, through the properties of things; fourth, through a manifold exposition or a variety of senses; fifth, through similes and natural truths; sixth, through marking of the opposite, to wit, correction; seventh, through comparisons; eighth, through interpretation of a name; ninth, through multiplication of synonyms. These means have been clarified in their order on the tree sketched at the end of the present treatise. After I have successively expounded each single method, together with its materials and examples, there will be an end to the present task.

First, accordingly, the sermon is expanded through agreement of authorities. Such agreements are threefold: of the Bible, of sacred authorities, and of the moral philosophers. So also they are taken up in three ways: from a same, from a like, and from a contrary. Take the passage: "The righteous shall flourish like the palm tree."[64] From a same: "The righteous shall flourish like the lily." From a like: "The righteous has these blessings: he is brave and prudent. And since he performs good works, he will be rewarded." From a contrary: "The unrighteous, on the other hand, do evil and so are punished."

Secondly, a sermon is expanded through discussion of words, as I have said above. There should be a discussion of the words present both in the theme and in the authorities adduced. When the preacher wishes to discuss the words of Christ in some authority, he should first consider how many *clausulae* the authority contains, and the order of the *clausulae* or of the words. For when the authority has several *clausulae*, the preacher should consider whether he can adapt some one of them to the number of virtues and vices, or to the parts of penitence. This discussion of words can also be performed through a definition or description of an appellative taken up in the theme. Take [again] for illustration the Psalmist's, "The righteous shall flourish like the palm tree in the home of the Lord." In discussing, I can inquire, who is the righteous? And I can answer: he who renders to each his own—to God, to prelates, to masters, and to men. To God, an act of grace; [to prelates,] due reverence; to masters, obedience; and so on.

Again, I can extend the discussion of the words, and ask, why the home? why the palm? why the Lord? why the home of the Lord? In the same way, what is good? what is honorable? and so with other words. These apply in the discussion of all themes or of other authoritative passages adduced in the sermon.

In like manner let this theme (Luke 21[:19]) be used: "In your patience possess ye your souls." Now in discussing, I can

---

[64] Vulg. Ps. 91:13.

ask, who is patient? and, what is patience? I can answer, patience is the disregarding of hostility incurred; and the disregarding is forbearance of the mouth from murmurings and dark speech, and is the repose of the heart from hate and rancor. Likewise take the passage: "All men are liars,"[65] and: "They are all gone aside . . . [There is none that doeth good, no,] not one."[66] In discussing, I can ask, who are these? I can answer: lay brothers, prelates, members of the flock, cloistered monks, secular clergy, and so forth. And the discussion can be made quantitative, that is, by distribution of the whole authority into parts, as above: lay brothers, prelates, members of the flock, cloistered monks, and so on.

Words can also be discussed through argumentation—for example, through reasoning from the greater or the less; from analogy; from opposites, as affirmation of the contrary, or denial; or from relative condition, as privation or possession. Similarly, from praise or blame, and here with respect to all the dialectical and rhetorical commonplaces which find a place in the sermon projected. For an example of reasoning from the greater, take the passage: "God spared not the angels that sinned."[67] Therefore He will not spare sinful men, the greater ingrates, as it were. Again, He did not spare Adam and Eve, whom He created with His own hand, nor Judas, His apostle and disciple. Therefore neither will He spare others who sin in their own way. For if that which seems the more to be an inherent quality is not present, then that which seems the less to be inherent will not be present.

In the same way from a discussion of words the preacher can bring out for himself the *effects* of the terms taken up in the theme. Choose this theme (Luke 18[:14]): "He that humbleth

[65] Vulg. Ps. 115:11.
[66] Vulg. Ps. 13:3 and 52:4.
[67] II Pet. 2:4.

himself shall be exalted." In discussing the effects of the terms
of this authority, I can say: The causes of humility are many.
Job 14: "Man that is born of a woman"—thus, with guilt—
"is of few days"—thus, transitory—"and full of trouble"[68]—
thus, of weeping.

The discussion of words can likewise be developed, and the
sermon expanded, through considering the effects of vices and
virtues. For example, man is exalted through humility. So we
should humble ourselves. Conversely, the opposite applies.
So we should therefore beware of exalting ourselves.

The words of some authority can also be discussed through
the fourfold combination of copulative and disjunctive parts
in the theme taken up—from the part of subject or of predicate.
For example, take this passage: "The voice of rejoicing [and of
salvation] is in the tabernacles of the righteous,"[69] and the
rest. I can discuss it as follows. Voice is manifold in the hearts
and consciences of different persons. There is the voice of
rejoicing in the tabernacles, but of damnation, not of salvation,
in the tabernacles of the sinners, who here have your consola-
tion. And there is the voice of salvation, not of rejoicing, in
the tabernacles of the penitent. And there is a third voice,
neither of rejoicing nor of salvation, in the tabernacles of the
damned. And there is a fourth voice of both rejoicing *and*
salvation in the tabernacles of the saved. In the same way discuss: "I have done judgment and justice."[70] Some do judgment
and not justice; others, the opposite; some, both; others,
neither. Or this: "I will sing of mercy and judgment: unto
thee, O Lord, will I sing."[71] So discuss other themes, which
are virtually infinite in number.

---

[68] Job 14:1.
[69] Vulg. Ps. 117:15.
[70] Vulg. Ps. 118:121.
[71] Ps. 101:1. The text of the treatise erroneously reads *sileam* for *psallam*.

The *third* kind of expansion can be made through the properties of things. A sermon can be expanded and amplified through the properties of things with reference to the praise of someone—of his moral conduct. For example, in the Psalms it is written: "God, thy God, hath anointed thee with the oil of gladness above thy fellows,"[72] and the rest. This may be discussed as follows. Grace is conveniently denoted by oil, for oil has a sanative virtue. Thus grace cures the wounds of the soul by destroying sins. This method the Savior used (Matthew 22[73] and Mark 12) in the parable of the husbandmen who slew the heir; it was also used by the prophet Nathan,[74] and in Romans 12. Let punishment be administered them whom the oil of grace does not avail. Similarly, "As the lily among thorns,"[75] for a lily is white and fragrant, and so on, whereas a thorn is such and such. All these things concerning the good can be set forth also in relation to wickedness—concerning the wicked, hypocrites and the like, for example.

Fourthly, a sermon is expanded through multiple interpretation. If the passage bears a number of meanings or significations, the preacher should accordingly examine how through them the sermon can be expanded. It should be noted that these senses are fourfold; and that since the Old Testament is a prefiguration of the New, the New Testament is explained of itself.

(1) First, following the historical or literal sense. In accordance with this sense Jerome speaks.[76] It is the simple explanation of the words, as when we set a thing forth as it was seen or

[72] Vulg. Ps. 44:8.
[73] Matt. 21.
[74] II Sam. 12.
[75] Song of Sol. 2:2.
[76] See J. Forget, "Jerome (Saint)," *Dict. de théol. Catholique*, 8 (1924), 958 ff. Jerome's emphasis on the literal interpretation is perhaps best exemplified in his commentary on Jeremiah.

done. For example, in the *Gesta Romanorum*[77] it is stated: "David ruled in Jerusalem." Following that sense, we explain simply according to the primary meaning of the words as they sound.

(2) Secondly, following the tropological or moral sense. In accordance with this sense Gregory speaks.[78] We use this sense when we discuss a matter from the ethical point of view, looking to moral instruction or correction. We use it mystically or openly. Mystically, as: "Let thy garments be always white";[79] that is, at all times let thy deeds be clean. Openly, as in [Epist. I] John [3:18]: "My little children, let us not love in word, nor in tongue, but in deed and in truth." Or we explain tropologically when we convert what has been done into what should be done, as: "Just as David conquered Goliath, so ought humility to conquer pride." And this sense is in another way called the moral sense because it regards the habits of men, to wit, virtues and vices. In the use of the tropological or moral sense, the ways of the world should be introduced, vices dissuaded against, and habits corrected, and the conclusion ought to be made with the authority from which the theme has been drawn. There are three characters of men: the spiritual, the noble, and the common. Hence correction should be made one way in regard to the spiritual, and otherwise in regard to the noble.

(3) Thirdly, a sermon can be expanded by following the allegorical sense. In accordance with this sense Ambrose speaks.[80] Exposition by the allegorical sense is exposition by a sense other than the literal one. "David reigns in Jerusalem"

---

[77] I have not found the citation there; cf. Vulg. III Kings 2:11 and II Kings 5:3 and 5.

[78] [See pp. 95 and 144, and cf. pp. 100 f.] below.

[79] Eccles. 9:8.

[80] See the Preface to his *In Psalm. XXXVI Enarratio;* his allegorical method is well evident, for example, in the treatise *De Noe et arca.*

means that Christ, who is signified through David, reigns, in the faith of believers, in Jerusalem, that is, in the Church Militant. In the use of this sense, exemplification should always be made through a simile, as when there is introduced the life of Christ, of the Blessed Virgin, or of another holy person. Their virtues are always wanting in us. So we, too, should act like to them. Since every act of Christ is our instruction, so too, whatever good the saints have done and whatever ill they have borne, have been entirely for our improvement and example, in order that we may follow in their footsteps.

(4) Fourthly, a sermon can be expanded according to the anagogical (text: *anagoricus*) sense. It is the anagogical sense when we speak of supernal or celestial things, mystically or openly. Mystically, as: "Blessed are they that wash their robes in the blood of the Lamb that they may have right to the tree of life."[81] That is, blessed are they who purify their thoughts so that they may see Jesus Christ, who says: "I am the way, the truth, and the life."[82] Openly, as in saying: "Blessed are the pure in heart, for they shall see God." With this sense the minds of the hearers are to be stirred and exhorted to the contemplation of heavenly things. Conclude with the authority from which the theme derived.

Fifthly, a sermon is expanded through analogies and natural truths. For illustration, posited that in the theme or in some other authority used in the sermon the discussion is upon the love of God, why God is to be loved. Then the preacher can expand his sermon through some natural truth like the following. It is natural for every creature to love its parents. How much the more ought we to love God, from Whom it becomes natural for us to love our parents. Then *a fortiori*, we should

---

[81] Vulg. Rev. 22:14.
[82] John 14:6. The verse next cited is from Matt. 5:8. [Cf. p. 95 below.]

love Him from Whom our parents and we come. Amplification of the sermon can be accomplished also through analogies. For example, posited that in some part of the sermon the discussion is upon the love of one's neighbor and compassion for him. Then I can draw an analogy with irrational creatures, let us say, sows. When one sow squeals, all rush together for mutual aid. If irrational animals act thus, then *a fortiori*, we rational beings ought in time of need to pity and help those near to us. So in a like manner can a sermon be expanded by other analogies.

Sixthly, the sermon is expanded through marking of an opposite, to wit, correction.

Let the marking of an opposite be used when some people act in a way contrary to that in which a thing should rightly be done. The Lord God, on account of His goodness, which He reveals to us in creation, recalling, and redemption, is to us like a good father to his sons, in that He provides for us in all necessary things, and recalls us to Himself through many and diverse happenings, so that we can yet approach to Him and possess eternal life. This He does, not for His own sake, since He is sufficient unto Himself, but from pure goodness. Therefore deservedly should the acts of grace be performed. Nothing displeases the Lord God more than ingratitude, for where this is present, grace does not find access or footing, because ingratitude dissipates merits, destroys rewards, dries the fount of divine mercy, and obstructs the days of grace.

The opposite signification is in the form of correction. It should be used in every sermon in order that evil deeds committed may not be deemed likely to prove other than evil, and not be defended as though they were lawful.

Two principles through which a sermon can be expanded apply in the marking of an opposite: confirmation and refutation.

In confirmation there should be mentioned the extrinsic advantages which accrue to the possessor of a thing, or which can accrue if the thing is in itself good. If the thing is bad, the advantages which accrue to its opposite should be mentioned, to wit, by setting forth various virtues and aptitudes for good works. But in the contrary method of refutation, there should be set forth the evil losses which follow or can follow the possessor of a thing, or follow the thing, if it is evil in itself. But if it is a good thing, what will follow its opposite should be declared, to wit, the various inclinations to evil and the different vices caused by evil in a man. Finally, conclude therefrom how good or how evil the thing is, and who are the persons that will as a result be rendered censurable or praiseworthy.

Seventhly, the sermon is expanded through comparisons.

Expansion of sermons by comparisons occurs when an adjective is used in some authority. Then it of itself can become a subject of treatment through its positive, comparative, and superlative, and conversely, from its superlative to the other grades of comparison. For example, the Psalmist writes: "Thou art great and doest wondrous things."[83] This may be discussed as follows. Great has God appeared in the creation of things, greater in the re-creation of man, but greatest in the glorification of the saints. Again, in Matthew 19[84] it is written: "He that hath delivered me unto thee hath the greater sin." Discuss as follows. Judas was guilty of a great sin, because from greed he coveted a great reward; of a greater sin, because he betrayed his Master; of the greatest sin, because he despaired of the mercy of God.

Note, too, an example from the superlative: Be ye imitators of God as his dearest children, because ye are dear on account of the image of creation, dearer on account of the reward of

[83] Vulg. Ps. 85:10.
[84] Wrong reference. John 19:11.

redemption, dearest on account of the inheritance of heavenly bliss. So on Ephesians 2[:4]: "But God, [who is rich in mercy,] with His great love wherewith He loved us," say: "The charity of God was great for us in creation, greater in guidance, greatest in redemption. But it will be exceeding in glorification." Similarly, on the Psalmist's: "Gird thy sword upon thy thigh, O most Mighty,"[85] the discourse may run as follows. They girt themselves, mighty in guarding their husbands, more mighty as continent widows, most mighty as continent virgins. Likewise, Wisdom 39: "The mighty shall be mightily tormented."[86] Thus the mightier more mightily, the mightiest most mightily shall be tormented, and so on. Also Galatians 6[:10]: "As we have therefore opportunity, let us do good unto all men." So do good to subordinates, peers, and superiors. And there are many more examples of this kind.

In the same fashion the discourse can be developed through consideration of differences. Take for example Romans 23: "[These are the names of the valiant men of] David. Seated in the seat, the wisest captain among the three."[87] Declare who the wise are—they who have practical experience; the wiser, they who have wisdom in things human; the wisest, they who have wisdom in things divine. So the discourse can be carried on through various kinds of reception, as with: "Then took Simeon Him up in his arms."[88] Discuss this as follows. Simeon received Him into his arms; Mary conceived Him in the womb; Martha received Him into her home; the Father received Him into heaven. Or in I Matthew 2[89] it is written: "Take heed to the precepts of the law." Some take heed to the precepts of God through contemplation, some

[85] Vulg. Ps. 44:4.
[86] Actually 6:7.
[87] Wrong reference. Cf. II Sam. (Vulg. II Kings) 23:8.
[88] Luke 2:28.
[89] Wrong reference. I Macc. 2:68.

through anxious care; some through hypocrisy scorn to do so, and some through malevolence.[90] Observe that this method is more beautiful in Latin than in the vernacular tongue.

The sermon can also be developed through consideration of the various parts played. For instance in John 8[:26] it is written: "I have many things to say to [and judge of] you." Christ speaks *to* us as a judge, as an advocate. He speaks *in* us as an inspirer. He speaks *with* us as a teacher. And so with the like. In this method things which are "for an end" are often multiplied. In illustration, "for that end" which is remaining in sin, different people conduct themselves differently. Some propose to remove the sin. Some seem partly to confess their sins, and partly not. Some beware of committing sins but do no penance for sins committed. Some repent of having committed sins but do not beware of committing sin. Take up the authority in Romans 6[:1]: "What shall we say then [,brethren]? Shall we continue in sin, that grace may abound [in us? God] forbid." Then say: some remain in sin, and so on, as above.

Eighthly, the sermon is expanded through interpretation of a name. For example, when a name appearing in some authority needs interpretation, this can so be accomplished that the material will be better understood and received. Just as God is explained as giving eternal life to His own, so Israel is interpreted as man seeing God, or as a prince or hero with God. Whoever then wishes to expand a sermon through this means should assume the interpretation which he sees is useful for achieving his purpose. If now in some authority this name, Israel, appears, and the preacher is preaching on bravery, let him supply a meaning to some saint in accordance with this interpretation, especially if he uses definition or description. Take the passage: "Blessed are they that dwell in thy

[90] I have perforce here rendered *emulatio* in its bad sense (malevolence).

house, O Lord!"[91] The definition of blessedness is subjoined, as follows: "Blessedness is the perfect state of all good congregations." Then show for whom in the house of heaven the gift will be perfected—for him first in whose vision there is truth; secondly, the state of blessedness will be perfected through the fruition of supreme goodness; and thirdly, the desire for all wishing and yearning will be calmed. This is how the sermon is expanded through interpretation and definition.

Ninthly, the sermon is expanded through multiplication of synonyms, particularly when the matter in hand is reproving, laudatory, or exhortative. When reproving, thus: "It is the word of blessed Job[92] that man born of a woman is of few days and full of trouble." Amplify by synonyms as follows: Man is filled with woes in that he is oppressed by cares, beset by worries, irritated by adversity, choked by perils, and the like.

Expand in this way also in eulogy: "Truly was this saint a light to the erring, a torch to the unknowing, a lamp to the wandering." Or if in someone's praise we speak of virtue, we may say: "This virtue decorates the mind, adorns the soul, dignifies our manner of living, and magnifies grace."

Likewise in exhorting to emulation of the examples of our ancestors: "Let us emulate the good, let us imitate the saints, let us follow the righteous, let us give heed to the examples of our fathers." This use is clear in the passage of the Psalms: "O come, let us sing unto the Lord, let us make a joyful noise,"[93] and so forth. A similar expression of good will is: "We praise Thee and glorify Thee,"[94] and the like.

If you commit to memory, retain, and resort frequently to

[91] Vulg. Ps. 83:5.
[92] See note 68 above.
[93] Vulg. Ps. 94:1.
[94] Cf., e.g., Vulg. Dan. 3:51 ff., 4:31; Luke 2:20.

the nine ways just treated, you will find no themes, or very few, to which two or three or more of the methods are not applicable. You should from them select that method which is most convenient to time, place, and audience. "Meditate upon these things . . . [For in doing this thou shalt both save thyself, and them that hear thee],"[95] says the Apostle to Timothy. All of Scripture, divinely inspired, is useful for teaching, arguing, educating, and arresting injustice, so that man is perfected by instruction in every good work of God.

Now finally we must see what precautions the foresighted preacher should maintain in the pulpit.

First precaution: No preacher should fear to show reverence of the Lord, Jesus Christ, and the Glorious Virgin Mary, His Mother. Thus, for example, do the ambassadors and the household of princes make salutation by saying: "Our Master and Glorious Prince," and bowing. In similar fashion, when the people of the court and the canons of cathedral churches receive papal bulls, they lay down their birettas and reverently kiss the feet of his Holiness. All the more, and *a fortiori*, ought we to show reverence to our Lord, Jesus Christ, our Creator and Redeemer, and the Glorious Virgin, His Mother.

Second precaution: A preacher should never pronounce the name of God, the Blessed Virgin, or another holy person, without an adjoining attribute. Thus, say: "Our Lord, Jesus Christ, His Glorious Mother, the Virgin Mary," and so forth.

Third precaution: The preacher should never in the pulpit frivolously or presumptuously put any belief to the test as, for example, with reference to the Conception of the Blessed Virgin, and the like. For example, while some people say that she was conceived in original sin, some say the contrary. On this subject it must be said that it better befits the honor and

---

[95] I Tim. 4:15–16, paraphrased in the text of the treatise.

praise of the Glorious Virgin piously to believe that she was not conceived in such sin, than to defend her frivolously. Since everything is possible with God, it was possible for Him to choose the holy and immaculate womb in which He wished to be incarnated. Though scholars sometimes disagree on this and the like kind of questions, to do so is yet not contrary to faith. But where it is a matter of faith, no one disagrees with another.

Fourth precaution: When the preacher brings up doubts and disputed questions in the pulpit, he should not retire without settling the point. For the people, being simple, and ignorant how to distinguish ordinary writings from Sacred Scripture, may doubt, and even stumble and fall. So they should by no means be left unsatisfied. Therefore let the preacher solve the question, or rather, as I say, not propose it.

Fifth precaution: He should take proper care to express the last syllable of each utterance as sharply and completely and fitly as the first, that is, he should end a phrase as vigorously as he begins it. Thus the matter will be easier to grasp and understand. You will perceive this more clearly in the ensuing precaution.

Sixth precaution: The preacher should speak complete words, intelligibly, and slowly. And especially he should not repeat a thing two or three times, or change the words. Multiplying words in this fashion does not sound well; rather it often creates tedium and laughter in the hearers, unless, for the sake of better impressing difficult or unusual material, it is at times necessary to reiterate or repeat.

Seventh precaution: The preacher should conduct himself and speak with as great gravity as he should maintain in speaking of Christ in His presence, and in that of other princes and kings. Thus the preacher should show earnestness to the limit of his power, for on this do the guidance and care of souls in preaching rest. If he wishes to show earnestness in the presence of princes, let him do likewise in the presence of the simple, or in respect to the sheep entrusted to him, for the care of souls is equal, and a prince's soul is no better than a pauper's. So the preacher should show himself in full degree solicitous and diligent in caring for souls on God's behalf, since from concern of this sort great merit accrues to him.

Eighth precaution: Above all, the preacher should beware of passing on too hastily to things beyond—as is the spirit compelling men to haste. It impedes the speaker and confounds the gravity and meaning of the discourse.

The ninth precaution is restraint in looking about. This is very important in preaching, because objects disturb the senses, and through an object the natural memory is scattered and thus the order of memory confused.

Tenth precaution: That in grave matters of correction, the preacher should not resort to specific or personal allusion. As a wounded horse does not willingly permit touching his wound, so, by nature, sinners dread being corrected, since every virtue is natural and every vice is against nature, according to the Blessed Bernard.[96] One shrinks from a crime committed, because nature, from which, by ordination of God, it is at variance, attests that one should not commit evil. So, conversely, no one shrinks from virtue. Therefore every virtue is natural and every vice unnatural. The preacher should also note that correction has a threefold state. The correction of the spiritual is one thing, that of the noble another, that of the common still another.

Eleventh precaution: The preacher should with greatest care avoid prolixity in a sermon, lest the people begin to weary and henceforth shun other sermons. Wherefore the

[96] For example, *In Psalm.* "*Qui Habitat*" *Sermo* X (Migne, *Pat. Lat.* 183. 223), *peccatum* is termed *malum animae.*

preacher should zealously seek to collect more useful and fruitful material, and reduce it to a brief and compendious summary, in order that the people may be better able to commit
it to memory when he ends. If the preacher leaves them, so
to speak, unsated, quite willingly will they hear more of the
same substance. If any of his material remains unsaid, let it
serve for the next ensuing holy day. So let the preacher watch
the hour, and when it is over, cease his sermon.

Twelfth precaution: In the method of using the vernacular
language, the preacher should not shackle himself to the following difficulty: he should not seek to translate the words in
the very, and special, order in which they stand in the Latin.
Let him translate in a better and clearer way. He must at
times help his material, that is, express it otherwise than in the
precise order of the words. Often he must use circumlocution,
as in the passage which defines male as that "that openeth
the matrix."[97] It is not fitting thus grossly to express what he
should rather term woman's vessel or gate of birth. And so
with the like.

In bringing to an end the material I have presented, dear
brethren, [let me say that] to earn eternal life the Word of
God is not enough, unless each strives to fill his mind there-
with, in order to be able to escape the horrible peril of the
unprofitable servant.[98] Our Savior orders him to be cast into
the outer darkness with hands and feet bound. For a servant
who knows the will of his Master and does not fulfil it will be
flogged with many blows. Through the holy apostles and other
learned men and prophets the Lord God gave us the Sacred
Scriptures, in which He teaches us His will and the true way by
which we can come into the kingdom of heaven. Our Lord

[97] Exod. 13:15.
[98] Matt. 25:30.

Jesus Christ in the Gospels instructs us like a schoolmaster how to arrive at eternal life. Therefore let us in deed fulfil what we are shown we must do and emulate.

This is the end of the Art and True Method of Preaching, composed by St. Thomas Aquinas, and illustrated from the works of other holy doctors. One who diligently studies it will surely be great in that art.

It remains only to form a tree, which I do in the following fashion, adding an explanation of its meaning. Preaching is like a real tree. As a real tree develops from root to trunk, and the trunk puts forth main branches, and the main branches multiply into other branches, so in preaching the theme develops into the protheme or prelocution as root into trunk. Then the prelocution or protheme grows into the principal divisions of the theme as the trunk into the main branches. And the principal branches should, beyond, multiply into secondary divisions, that is, subdivisions and subdistinctions, and finally expand as the example in the tree below shows. Its theme is divided into three parts; each part is divided into three members; each member can be amplified by several of the nine methods above described, as will stand out more clearly on the tree below.

Now note that the method of preaching is threefold.

In the first kind, the preacher should, after taking up his theme and setting forth its text,[99] proceed to the consummation of his sermon, at the beginning merely by expounding the Gospel. It is the ancient method, well exemplified by the homilies of Gregory and other holy doctors. After the exposition of the Gospel, the preacher should advance to the division and subdivision of his theme and the main substance of his

[99] The Latin reads: *dicto dimisso.*

sermon. And that is how the sermon is set into form. Then he should make invocation of the Holy Spirit, since without assistance he could not express such thoughts. And he implores the blessed Virgin by the *Salutantes* together with the *Ave Maria*, or through some other invocation. This method is the lay, or popular and beautiful, method. The decrees prescribe the elucidation of the Gospel on Sundays to the simple in heart.

In the second method, the preacher should, after setting forth his theme and its text,[100] proceed to the development of his sermon—to the division or distinction, without, however, dividing the words of the theme. For example, if he should take this theme on the dead, "O death, how bitter is the remembrance of thee,"[101] without dividing these words, he would add: "We must know that the remembrance of death is bitter to lovers of the world for three reasons: first, on account of the world which they leave; secondly, on account of the future punishment they will receive; thirdly, on account of the delights of the flesh which they lose." Note that it advances to distinction from a theme that has not been divided. This is the light and simple method. No prelocution is formed from the theme; the exposition of the Gospel is not introduced; nor is there a division of the words of the theme.

The third method, and according to our plan: first the preacher should in the silence pronounce his theme in Latin, then introduce one prayer[102] in the vernacular tongue, to wit: "May our Lord, Jesus Christ, give to living men grace and mercy, to His church peace, and to us sinners after this life eternal life." Then he should resume his theme, expressing it in the vernacular. And after this he can draw or elicit from his theme one prelocution, in place of the Gospel, and can

[100] The Latin reads: *themate et dicto dimisso.*
[101] See note 54 above.
[102] The Latin reads: *dictum.*

form this prelocution through similes, moralizations, proverbs, or natural truths, or sometimes also by adducing definite authorities. Another name for the prelocution is the protheme, because it is expressed before the division of the theme and the main substance of the sermon. Mark that the prelocution or protheme should not be overlong, so that the theme, together with its chief sermon-materials, can have place for expression. Further, when the prelocution has been premised, resume the theme and its division. After this comes the invocation of the Holy Spirit, as earlier. Next comes the treatment of the members in order: first, the first main part of the theme with its divisions; next, the second main part of the theme with its subdistinctions; and so likewise with the third. And when all the members, main and subordinate, have been discussed, the preacher can make a practical recapitulation of his sermon, so that if the hearers have not attended to the beginning, they may know on what the sermon is effectively based. Thereby, and with other relevant considerations, the material of the sermon can be better grasped.

This method is the more common one among modern preachers and is suitable to intelligent men and hearers.[103] As was above mentioned, an example of it appears in the tree below.[104]

[103] The Latin reads: *et viris intelligentibusque auditoribus utilis.*

[104] The diagram of the tree, missing from the Cornell copy of the tractate, is here reproduced, in the original Latin, from a manuscript in the Bayer. Staatsbibl., Munich (*Cod. Lat. Monac.* 23865, fols. 19ᵛ–20).

IV
Rhetorical Invention in Some Mediaeval Tractates on Preaching[*]

PROFESSOR ETIENNE GILSON has aptly said that no other epoch was so conscious of the ends it pursued and the means required to attain them as the mediaeval period.[1] It had its poetry and its arts of poetry, its eloquence and its arts of rhetoric. If you seek the key to its art of oratory, you must search in its *Artes Praedicandi*.[2] Now if one sets out to study the sacred rhetoric of the Middle Ages, one does well to note what the great classical rhetoricians selected to emphasize as rhetorical essentials, and to heed what their sense of rhetorical values dictated. We need not belittle the importance of attention to *elocutio*, which for the literature of the mediaeval period happily has begun to fare well at the hands of scholars,[3] but at present I intend rather to accept the logic which prompted Cicero to adopt the title *De Inventione* as representing the whole field of rhetoric. Invention was to him the most important

[*] Reprinted from *Speculum*, II (1927), 284–295.
[1] This article is part of a paper read before the Mediaeval Latin Section of the Modern Language Association, Cambridge, Massachusetts, Dec. 29, 1926.
[2] Etienne Gilson, "Michel Menot et la technique du sermon médiévale," *Revue d'histoire franciscaine*, II (July, 1925), 303.
[3] See, e.g., M. B. Ogle, "Some Aspects of Mediaeval Latin Style," *Speculum*, I (1926), 170 ff.

element of the art.[4] We respect the prominence which the principle of invention has in his *De Oratore*, and we observe that his *Topica* is a tract on inventional method. We note the care the author of the *Ad Herennium* bestows upon invention. Aristotle bases his first two books upon the processes of invention; in fact, some critics[5] believe that his original plan may well have excluded Book III, the book which he devotes to style. The *De Inventione*, Cicero's *Topica*, and the *Rhetorica ad Herennium* were well known throughout the Middle Ages. The contributions of Boethius, whose works were also very influential (notably upon St. Bonaventure)—the Commentary on the *Topica* of Aristotle, the Commentary on the *Topica* of Cicero, and the *De Differentiis Topicis*[6]—were likewise in the field of invention. And, finally, we may regard it as highly significant that Augustine gives first place to invention in oratory.[7] In the following pages I purpose, therefore, to subordinate the *quo modo* (*orator dicat*) to the *quid*.

One may confidently assert of classical rhetoric in the mediaeval period that it was by no means neglected. The persistence of the rhetorical discipline as an integral part, however modified, of the school curriculum, is well attested.[8] And R. Cruel[9] and other students of mediaeval preaching do not think to question the influence of classical rules on preaching. Despite the fact that Gregory opposed theatrical preaching,

[4] See E. M. Cope and J. E. Sandys, eds., *Rhetoric of Aristotle* (Cambridge, 1877), I, 28.

[5] See J. E. Sandys, Introduction to Jebb's translation of Aristotle's *Rhetoric* (Cambridge, 1909), p. xxi.

[6] Gilson, p. 207, points out the great debt St. Bonaventure's Rhetoric in the *Collationes in Hexaemeron*, iv, 21–25 (*Opera Omnia*, V, 353) owes to Boethius' *Speculatio de Rhetoricae Cognatione* (Migne, *Pat. Lat.*, LXIV, 1217 ff.).

[7] *De Doctr. Christ.* IV. 1. 1. See M. Roger, *L'enseignement des lettres classiques d'Ausone à Alcuin* (Paris, 1905), p. 142; A. F. Ozanam, *La civilisation au cinquième siècle* (Paris, 1862), p. 160.

[8] See T. Haarhoff, *Schools of Gaul* (Oxford, 1920), pp. 157 ff.

[9] *Geschichte der deutschen Predigt im Mittelalter* (Detmold, 1879), p. 244.

and that Augustine[10] thought it necessary to defend the use of rhetoric by a Christian teacher, the view of St. Thomas that eloquence and secular learning could profitably be used by a preacher[11] must be regarded as more generally characteristic of the mediaeval attitude towards pagan rhetoric. If the Fathers did try to check the rhetorical tendency in themselves, it was merely to subordinate eloquence to the main, and high, purpose of preaching. In some cases the classics were directly and consciously influential, in others indirectly, even though the winning of souls was a different end from the usual ends of deliberative, epideictic, or forensic oratory. The effect of tradition is often too subtle to detect. In any event, preaching had a rhetorical function in the clear exposition of Scripture, with the persuasive purpose of winning souls to God—a function and a purpose germane to the universal uses of rhetoric. With the aid of rhetorical criteria, then, preaching can be studied in the treatises we are now considering. In them we find the characteristic distrust of the ornaments of rhetoric, but, as well, a live awareness of and regard for classical rhetorical authorities.

William of Auvergne writes: "A simple sermon, unpolished, unadorned, moves and edifies the more." He despises the preacher "who, with ornate words, casts naked truth into the shadow."[12] Humbert de Romans: "They who seek adornment are like those who care more for the beauty of the salver in which food is carried than for the food itself."[13] Alain de Lille: "Preaching ought not to contain scurrilous or puerile words, or rhythmic melodies, or metric consonances. These contribute

---

[10] *De Doctr. Christ.* IV. 1 and 2.

[11] See J. Walsh, "St. Thomas on Preaching," *Dominicana*, V (1921), 6–14.

[12] A. de Poorter, "Un manuel de prédication médiévale," *Revue néo-scolastique de philosophie*, XXV (1923), 202.

[13] *Maxima Bibliotheca Veterum Patrum*, ed. M. de la Bigne (Lyons, 1677), XXV, 432.

rather to soothing the ear than to instructing the mind. Such preaching is theatrical, and therefore should be unanimously contemned. . . . Yet though preaching should not shine with purple verbal trappings, neither should it be depressed by bloodless words. Rather a middle course should be pursued."[14]

So much for the attitude towards embellished style; on the attitude to classical rhetoric the following outline of opinions and practice will be informative.

William of Auvergne has modeled his *Rhetorica Divina*, a rhetoric of prayer, upon Plato, Aristotle, and Cicero.[15] Humbert would like the preacher to know pagan history as well as Christian, and makes use of Seneca, Horace, and Cicero. The author-compiler of the "Aquinas"-tractate quotes Tully in recommending the art of preaching, and approvingly offers William's argument: "Since so many volumes of rhetoric have been written by the band of rhetoricians, is it not more just and worthy that their own art and doctrine should enjoy treatment by the band of preachers, so that they will be divine rhetoricians?"[16] Alain: "It will be possible on occasion to insert the sayings of Gentiles, just as Paul in his Epistles inserts philosophers as authorities."[17] Alain has called Rhetoric the daughter of Cicero, and named her Tullia;[18] nor in the present tractate does he think it necessary to exclude profane authors—in fact he uses pagan myths, and quotes from Plato, Cicero, Seneca, Lucretius, and Persius. But one need only glance in the works of Cruel[19] and Lecoy[20] at the long list of pagan, Arabic, and Jewish authors used by mediaeval

---

[14] *Summa de Arte Praedicatoria*, Migne, *Pat. Lat.*, CCX, 112.
[15] A. Lecoy de la Marche, *La chaire française au moyen âge* (Paris, 1886), p. 68.
[16] See "A Late Mediaeval Tractate on Preaching" [p. 54 of this volume].
[17] *Summa de Arte Praedicatoria*, Migne, *Pat. Lat.*, CCX, 114.
[18] *Anticlaudianus*, iii. 2, Migne, *Pat. Lat.*, CCX, 513.
[19] P. 463.
[20] Pp. 472–473.

preachers to conclude that more than one preacher must have accepted the old saying. "It is no sin to be taught by the enemy, and to enrich the Hebrews with the spoils of the Egyptians."[21]

The secret of rhetorical invention lies in the conscious artistic use of the topics or commonplaces. The τόπος[22] is the head under which arguments fall, the place in the memory where the argument is to be looked for and found, ready for use, the storehouse or thesaurus,[23] the seat,[24] the haunt[25] (as if the argument were the game to be captured), or the vein[26] or mine where arguments should be sought. One recalls how Cicero in his *Topica* applies eleven categories to the establishment of legal proof,[27] and how the author of the *Ad Herennium*, also with a forensic case in mind, uses the following ten commonplaces of amplification[28]—*adaugendi criminis causa:* (1) Consider authority and precedent; remind the jury how weighty this matter has been held to be by our ancestors. (2) Consider to whom the charge appertains; if it affects every one, then the action is most atrocious. (3) Ask what would

---

[21] E.g., John Bromyard in the Prologue of his *Summa Praedicantium*, cited by G. R. Owst, *Preaching in Mediaeval England* (Cambridge, 1926), p. 304.

[22] Aristotle, *Rhetorica* 2. 26. 1. See H. H. Hudson, "Can We Modernize the Theory of Invention?," *Quarterly Journal of Speech Education*, VII (1921), 325–334.

[23] Cicero, *De Finibus* 4. 4. 10; cf. Quintilian, 5. 10. 20–22.

[24] Cicero, *Topica* 2. 7: "Ut igitur earum rerum quae absconditae sunt demonstrato et notato loco facilis inventio est, sic cum pervestigare argumentum aliquod volumus locos nosse debemus; sic enim appellatae ab Aristotele sunt eae quasi sedes e quibus argumenta promuntur. Itaque licet definire locum esse argumenti sedem."

[25] Cicero, *De Oratore* 2. 34. 147; cf. *De Inv.* 1.7, where he calls invention the most important of the divisions of rhetoric.

[26] Cicero, *De Oratore* 2. 174. See E. M. Cope, *Introduction to Aristotle's Rhetoric* (Cambridge and London, 1867), pp. 124 ff.

[27] Relationship; similar derivation; species; similarity; difference; contraries; adjuncts; antecedents, consequents, and contradictories; efficient cause; what has been done; authority.

[28] 2. xxx. 47–49.

happen if the same concessions were made to all; if we neglect this matter, we shall undergo great dangers. (4) Show that, if you indulge this defendant, you will encourage others, to whom his summary punishment would serve as a deterrent from crime. (5) Prove that nothing can remedy this wrong. Other things can be cured by time; this crime cannot. (6) It was premeditated; there can be no just excuse. (7) This is a foul crime, cruel, infamous, tyrannical. From such crimes comes harm to women, from such arise causes for wars that are fought to a finish. (8) This is not a common crime, but a singularly base one, for which vengeance must be quick and drastic. (9) Compare crimes: this is not a pardonable, necessary crime, but one committed through intemperate arrogance. (10) Sharply, incriminatingly, and carefully, review the crime and its consequences. Or, for an example in epideictic oratory, the two treatises ascribed to Menander of Laodicea develop topically a number of varieties, including the types used in praise of a sovereign, in praise of a city, the farewell speech to one departing, and others. Or notice in the index to Halm's *Rhetores Latini Minores* the long list (pp. 664–665) of *loci communes argumentorum* used by the authors he collected.

The extension of the method from deliberative, forensic, or epideictic rhetoric to sacred rhetoric is not difficult. We shall see how this method functioned in preaching.

In this paper on invention, I regret that I cannot consider sermons nor even *"homiletische Hilfsmittel"* other than treatises on preaching.[29] I do not consider, I mean, the collections of homilies, of text-materials for sermons, of sermons for each day, of commentaries, Biblical glosses in alphabetical order,

---

[29] See Cruel, pp. 244 ff., 451 ff.; Owst, chap. 7; A. Linsenmayer, *Geschichte der Predigt in Deutschland* (Munich, 1886), pp. 168 ff.; Ch.-V. Langlois, "L'éloquence sacrée au moyen âge," *Revue des deux mondes*, CXV (1893), 194 ff.

theme-sentences, concordances, moralities, comparisons, image-books, anecdotes, tracts on vices and virtues, *exempla* and bestiaries, chrestomathies, natural histories, parables, and homiletical lexicons—the preachers' helps and anthologies that were common in European libraries, the preachers' store-houses from which the less competent drew. These were, if anything, aids to invention. But on grounds of relative avail-ability, I limit myself to representative tractates on the art of preaching of the twelfth and thirteenth centuries, to wit: the *Liber Quo Ordine Sermo Fieri Debeat*[30] of Guibert de Nogent (early twelfth century), the *Summa de Arte Praedicatoria*[31] of Alain de Lille (end of twelfth century), the *Liber de Eruditione Praedicatorum*[32] of Humbert de Romans (thirteenth century), a manual of preaching[33] attributed to William of Auvergne (thirteenth century), and a late Dominican tractate[34] profess-ing the influence of St. Thomas Aquinas. They appeared at an important juncture in the course of the history of oratory, when both general culture and preaching had reached a high level—the period of the rise of new orders,[35] the spread of mysticism, and the growth of scholasticism. In these tractates we discover a highly developed rhetoric of invention, particularly in the method of applying commonplaces.

The Dominican Humbert's extensive work is divided into two books. The first, entitled *"De Eruditione Religiosorum Praedicatorum,"* does not especially interest us except for the very instructive chapter (6) dealing with the difficulty of

---

[30] *Prooemium ad Commentarios in Genesim*, Migne, *Pat. Lat.*, CLVI, 21–32.

[31] Migne, *Pat. Lat.*, CCX, 110–198.

[32] *Max. Bibl. Vet. Pat.*, XXV, 426–567.

[33] De Poorter, 192–209.

[34] See "A Late Mediaeval Tractate" [pp. 40–78 of this volume].

[35] Lecoy de la Marche, p. 201, in enumerating the preachers of the thirteenth century, points out that, of 318, 98 were Dominicans and 53 Franciscans. The preëminence of Dominicans, the *Ordo Praedicatorum*, makes particularly interest-ing the Dominican Aquinas-tractate.

preaching well. Therein Humbert compares the incompetent preachers who yet disdain to study other, good, preachers, with bad bakers who insist on making bread; and considers as terribly vicious the practice of those who multiply distinctions, authorities, reasons, examples, synonyms, prothemes, and the manifold exposition of words. This is in striking contrast to the inventional procedure of the treatise on preaching assigned to William of Auvergne and to that of the Aquinas-tractate. But it is no indication that Humbert generally opposed inventional method, for his second book comprises two treatises with the ambitious titles: (1) *De Modo Prompte Cudendi Sermones circa Omne Hominum Genus*, and (2) *De Modo Prompte Cudendi Sermones ad Omne Negotiorum Genus.* Humbert industriously goes about this work of supplying ready materials for address to many kinds of men, in every diverse field of the preacher's operations, and in accordance with every variety of seasons and holidays. He says: "Concerning sermon materials, note that it is often much more difficult to invent useful matter out of which to compose a sermon than to weave together a sermon from the material already invented" (p. 457). So in one hundred chapters he tells the preacher what kind of special thing to say: to all men, to all ecclesiastical people, to all the pious of a good life and of a bad life, to every kind of monk, to converts, to all scholars, to the laity, to all nobles, bad and devout, to paupers, boys, lepers, and harlots. The scholar in grammar, for example, should be admonished to remember that letters without a good life do not bring salvation; he should be told: "Multae litterae te faciunt insanire" (cf. Acts 26:24). Scholars in philosophy should be warned against seduction by philosophy. And in the second tractate of Book II, Humbert completes his inventional plan of preparing the preacher for one hundred types of *negotia*, advising him what to say, for example, at councils, synods, elections of secular priests, solemn confirmations, solemn communions, solemn obsequies for the dead, solemn condemnations of heretics.

In the Introduction to his edition of the tractate[36] which he ascribes to William of Auvergne, de Poorter mentions a *De Faciebus* by William, which furnished an inventional list of images and allegories for the preacher to use at his need. Indeed, the manual which de Poorter has edited is also on invention. It employs the usual dialectical commonplaces for Scriptural explication—*quis, quibus, ubi, quando, quomodo,* and *quid*—and aims, typically, to adapt the preacher to different classes of hearers—*ad varios status*. But, and most important, in Part II appear twenty paragraphs setting forth repertories of ideas, where the preacher can get themes for artistic development. Thus the author fulfils his purpose of furnishing not only *modum praedicandi* but also *copiam loquendi*. The commonplaces[37] are to be worked out in the usual fashion. If you develop by *contraries*, and are discussing gluttony, contrast it with abstinence. If you seek *exemplification* of various virtues, recall these types: David stands for humility and kindness, Job for patience, Stephen for charity, Susanna for continence and bravery, Anthony for discretion, John the Baptist for sobriety, Katherine for virginity.[38] If you use *division*, discuss the kinds of sin. If you use *derivation*, know that Christ is *Sol* because He shines *solus*. *Monachus* is derived from *monos ischos*, *Dominus* is analyzed into *dans minas*, and, one is astonished to read, *mulier* into *molliens herum*.

---

[36] See n. 12 above.

[37] Resemblances, relative notions, contraries, cause and effect, vices, virtues, heaven, hell, exemplification, anecdotes, continuation, definition, distinctions, observation of the issue or end of a thing, setting forth the essential weight of a word, kind, species, interpretation of Hebrew names, etymology, parts of speech.

[38] Cf. Philo's similar practice, discussed by F. W. Farrar, *History of Interpretation* (London, 1886), p. 146.

Of Eloquence

Alain de Lille's *Summa* does not contain much theory; it gives general advice, but pursues its inventional aim largely through examples and sermon materials, in the form of forty-seven sketches of homilies on ordinary subjects, varied, again, according to the audience. Both Alain and Humbert had composed separate collections of *sermones ad status*, and Alain had also written both a *Summa Quot Modis*,[39] a preacher's dictionary, and a *Liber Sententiarum*, a book of aphorisms for preachers. But the *Summa*, although it has undertaken to teach the *qualis*, *quorum*, *quibus*, *quare*, *et ubi* of preaching, succeeds in discussing only the first three. Alain's definition of preaching is the one that is later used by the author of the Aquinas-tractate: "Preaching is open and public instruction in morals and faith, devoted to the informing of men, and proceeding along the path of reasoning, and from the source of authorities."[40] The preacher's sources are, *par excellence*, the Gospels, the Psalms, the Epistles of Paul, and the Books of Solomon. Thirty-seven chapters[41] are devoted to the subjects of preaching: to sermon-sketches against luxury, arrogance, and other vices; and to sketches upon such virtues as peace, mercy, obedience, spiritual joy, and the love of God. Alain's method can be seen in the plan of Chapter 2, on the subject: *De Mundi Contemptu*. The theme is Vanity of Vanities. The general topic of division is used to set forth vanity in its three aspects, the vanity of change, of curiosity, of falsehood, each with a Biblical authority: further, the dialectical *ubi* is applied in turn to *vanitas*, *vanitatum vanitas*, *omnia vanitas*. Next is explained wherein all three vanities apply to wealth, in the fears, suspicions, and greed attending it. The same is done with honors, and with mundane pleasures. Then the ancient Fathers are called to

[39] Lecoy de la Marche, p. 496.
[40] [See p. 55 above.]
[41] Chaps. 2–38.

[88]

witness as authorities upon the contempt of riches, and a vigorous exhortation ends the homily. The last ten chapters deal with the audience of preaching: soldiers, doctors, prelates, princes, widows, maidens, and others. For example, in *Ad Oratores seu Advocatos* (41) the orator is eloquently exhorted to seek truth and justice, follow charity and bring aid to the needy, spurn greed and the popular favor, and avoid venality.

The compiler of the Aquinas-tractate points out that the material for all sermons is found in ten topics: God, the devil, the heavenly city, the inferno, the world, the soul, the body, sin, penitence, and virtue. But the author's main contribution to a theory of invention consists in his treatment of sermon-*dilatatio*. If you wish to expand a sermon, you will find nine methods of amplification. (1) Through concordance of authorities. (2) Through discussion of words. On the theme (Vulg. Ps. 91:13): "The righteous shall flourish like the palm-tree in the house of the Lord," ask "why the house?" "why the palm?" "why the Lord?" "why the house of the Lord?" (3) Through the properties of things. "God, thy God, hath anointed thee with the oil of gladness above thy fellows" (Vulg. Ps. 44:8). Grace is conveniently denoted by oil, for oil has a sanative virtue. Thus Grace cures the wounds of the soul by destroying sins. (4) Through a multiplication of senses, in four ways:[42] (*a*) according to the *sensus historicus* or *literalis;* (*b*) the *sensus tropologicus;* (*c*) the *sensus allegoricus,* (*d*) the *sensus anagogicus.* "David rules in Jerusalem," according to the literal sense, is to be explained exactly as the words sound; allegorically, by a "sense other than the literal," it means "Christ reigns in the Church Militant." "Let thy garments be always white" (Eccles. 9:8) tropologically is explained: "At all times

---

[42] [See pp. 64–66 above; on Guibert's use of the four senses, pp. 93 and 95 below; for the "Henry"-tract, pp. 141–145, 155 ff. below. This popular mediaeval method of hermeneutics is treated on pp. 93–104 below.]

let thy deeds be clean." With the anagogical sense "the minds of the hearers are to be stirred and exhorted to the contemplation of heavenly things." So, "Blessed are they who wash their robes in the blood of the Lamb that they may have right to the tree of life" (Vulg. Rev. 22:14) means "Blessed are they who purify their thoughts so that they may see Jesus Christ." (5) Through analogies and natural truths. It is natural for every creature to love its parents; how much more ought we to love God, from Whom it becomes natural for us to love our parents; then *a fortiori*, we should love Him from Whom our parents and we come. (6) Through marking of an opposite, to wit, correction. The Lord God in His goodness is to us like a good father to a son, in that He provides for us, and recalls us to possess eternal life. Therefore the acts of Grace ought to be performed. (7) Through comparisons, when an adjective is used in some authority. "He that delivered me unto thee hath the *greater* sin" (John 19:11). Continue as follows: Judas was guilty of a sin, because from greed he coveted a great reward; of a *greater* sin, because he betrayed his master; of the *greatest* sin, because he despaired of the mercy of God. (8) Through interpretation of a name. If in some authority the name 'Israel' appears, interpret it as man seeing God. (9) Through a multiplication of synonyms. "Man that is born of a woman is of few days and full of trouble" (Job 14:1). Amplify by synonyms. Man is filled with woes in that he is oppressed by cares, surrounded by worries, irritated by adversity, choked by perils. And the author-compiler leaves the treatment of amplification with the assurance that if you commit these topics to memory, retain them, and resort frequently to them, selecting such as are most convenient to time, place, and audience, you will well use Scripture to teach, to argue, to arrest injustice, and by instruction you will perfect man in every good work of God.

I include for brief consideration Guibert's work, not because it is actually a homiletical manual in plan or in effect. It has not, like the others, a developed scheme of invention. Guibert does advise the employment of the four senses of exposition, and accepts the moral as the most salutary for his purpose. Indeed, this work is the *Prooemium* to his *Libri Moralium in Genesin*, which was designed to supply the preacher with sermon-material. His discussion of the senses of explication does not appear in an organized theory of amplification, yet in his general theoretical observations on the spirit of the preacher, the sermon, and the hearer, he serves clearly to show us that the mediaeval preacher did not confine himself to considerations of sermon-structure only. Guibert is interested largely in the *grandis animi fervor;* and counsels an inner, psychological study as a means to learning the vices and virtues, in order that the preacher may be able to show forth man himself objectively. Conviction and belief are not sufficient; persuasion and action are required.

One is struck by the failure of all the authors, and especially the later ones, to formulate a clear-cut treatment of the *exemplum*. I do not think Alain has in mind *exempla* in the stricter sense when he briefly says: "In fine vero debet uti exemplis ad probandum quod intendit, quia familiaris est doctrina exemplaris."[43] And although Lecoy[44] says that Humbert also recommends the use of *exempla*, I have been unable to discover the reference. In two passages[45] Guibert advises the use of illustrative material, but he does not employ the technical term *exempla*.

In accordance with these treatises, then, the sermon was

---

[43] Migne, *Pat. Lat.*, CCX, 114.

[44] P. 301, citing *Max. Bibl. Vet. Pat.*, XXV, 433. See T. F. Crane, *The Exempla of Jacques de Vitry* (London, 1890), p. xix.

[45] Migne, *Pat. Lat.*, CLVI, 23 and 29. See T. F. Crane, "Mediaeval Sermon-Books and Stories and Their Study Since 1883," *Proceedings of the American Philosophical Society*, LVI (1917), 382, n. 11.

based on Scripture, the Fathers, and the moral philosophers. The method was to unfold truth for instruction's sake, by expounding the text and developing the sermon from that as a centre. Perhaps partly because it was useful against the failure of inspiration, and certainly because it could be an artistically effective means of invention, accredited by the rhetorical theory of centuries, the preachers filled out the analytical design of organization with a topical system of amplification. It is not for us here to judge how banal could be the whole scheme of diversified members, definitions, divisions, dialectical inquiries, or how over-refined and trivial it could be; yet one may affirm that, when allied to talent, it must have been highly effective. As we have seen, invention concerned not only the *quid*, but also the *quibus*. The tractates therefore show a careful study of the psychology of audiences, even as Jacques de Vitry's discourses consider one hundred and twenty categories of hearers. Since these tractates circulated all over Europe, no doubt a great many preachers, through "the sermon of the Lord, the food of the mind," as the Aquinas-author defines it, were successfully taught "how to recall men from error to truth, from vices to virtues, how to change depravity to rectitude, how to provide faith, raise hope, enkindle charity, dislodge the injurious, implant the useful, and foster the honorable."[46]

[46] [Page 53 above.]

V

The Four Senses of Scriptural Interpretation and the Mediaeval Theory of Preaching*

Guibert de Nogent, in his *Liber Quo Ordine Sermo Fieri Debeat*, which forms his *Prooemium ad Commentarios in Gene-sim*, a work designed to supply the preacher with sermon materials, urges[1] the preacher to use for his moral aim any or all of the four senses of Scriptural interpretation. A late Dominican tractate[2] professing the influence of St. Thomas Aquinas, which is a complete and highly organized *Ars Praedicandi* and a more representative manual than Guibert's *Prooemium*, contains the same precept in its natural place in a topical system of amplification, such as mediaeval preachers used in order to fill out the analytical design of their sermons. As a means of *dilatatio*, and even in its own topical division into four, the principle of employing the kinds of explication may be considered to belong in a theory of rhetorical *inventio*, as understood and applied by the classical rhetoricians.[3]

* Reprinted from *Speculum*, IV (1929), 282–290.

[1] Migne, *Pat. Lat.*, CLVI, 25, 26.

[2] See "A Late Mediaeval Tractate on Preaching" [pp. 40–78 of this volume] for a discussion and translation of this tractate; and especially pp. 60 ff.

[3] See "Rhetorical Invention in Some Mediaeval Tractates on Preaching" [pp. 79–92 of this volume].

The compiler of the Aquinas-tract offers nine methods of expanding a sermon: (1) through concordance of authorities, (2) through discussion of words, (3) through explanation of the properties of things, (4) through a multiplication of senses, (5) through analogies and natural truths, (6) through marking of an opposite, (7) through comparisons, (8) through interpretation of a name, (9) through multiplication of synonyms. At present we are concerned only with his development of the fourth method.

Senses are multiplied in four ways: (1) according to the *sensus historicus* or *literalis*, by a simple explanation of the words; (2) according to the *sensus tropologicus*, which looks to instruction or to the correction of morals. It is well to introduce the ways of the world, in order to dissuade the hearers from vice. This sense may be used either mystically or openly. Openly: "Just as David conquered Goliath, so ought humility to conquer pride." Mystically: "Let thy garments be always white" (Eccles. 9:8) is explained: "At all times let thy deeds be clean"; (3) according to the *sensus allegoricus*. Exposition by this sense is exposition by a "sense other than the literal." "David rules in Jerusalem," which according to the literal sense is to be interpreted exactly as the words sound, by the allegorical sense signifies that "Christ reigns in the Church Militant." The *sensus allegoricus* uses exemplification by simile, as when the life of Christ, or lives of the Saints, are introduced, with an injunction that the hearer follow in their footsteps. With (4) the *sensus anagogicus*, used mystically or openly, "the minds of the listeners are to be stirred and exhorted to the contemplation of heavenly things." So, "Blessed are they that wash their robes in the blood of the Lamb that they may have right to the tree of life" (Vulg. Rev. 22:14), in the mystic use of this sense, means "Blessed are they who purify their thoughts that they may see Jesus Christ, who says: 'I am the way, the truth, and the life'" (John 14:6). Openly, explain it as "Blessed are the pure in heart, for they shall see God" (Matt. 5:8).

In similar fashion Guibert illustrates how to interpret the word "Jerusalem." Literally, it is the city of that name; allegorically, it represents the Holy Church; tropologically, it signifies the faithful soul of whosoever aspires to the vision of eternal peace; anagogically, it denotes the life of the dwellers in Heaven who see God revealed in Zion.

Considering how common this method of hermeneutics was in the exegetical theory of the Middle Ages, one as a matter of course expects to find its rôle in the theory of preaching equally important. The purpose of a multiple exposition was for the most part so obviously persuasive that its adoption into oral discourse was a very natural procedure. Thus Gregory the Great justifies the multiple method (in his case, tripartite) by its effect upon the hearer:

First we lay the foundations in history; then by following a symbolical sense, we erect an intellectual edifice to be a stronghold of faith; and lastly, by the grace of moral instruction, we as it were paint the fabric in fair colors. . . . For the word of God both exercises the understanding of the wise by its deeper mysteries, and also by its superficial lessons nurses the simple-minded. It presents openly that wherewith the little ones may be fed; it keeps in secret that whereby men of loftier range may be rapt in admiration.[4]

Even in the schools—surely this was true in the twelfth century—these multiple senses were used as separate artistic

---

[4] I use the excellent translation by F. H. Dudden, *Gregory the Great: His Place in History and Thought* (New York, 1905), I, 193, of Gregory, *Epist.* v. 53a (the dedication of his lectures on the Book of Job, the *Magna Moralia*, to Leander of Seville).

disciplines, the tropological or moral being considered as the especially useful instrument of the preacher. In his system of instruction Hugh of St. Victor utilized the arts of the trivium and the quadrivium in support of his larger principle of the threefold criticism of divine science.[5] Should an extended study of mediaeval sermons be made, with the aim of learning how general the use of the fourfold sense of Scripture was in the actual practice of preaching, I venture to predict that the results would show a greater correlation between theory and practice than was admitted by Diestel to be true of exegetical practice in the large. Diestel says: "Doch wird in der exegetischen Praxis diese Vierfachheit selten durchgeführt."[6]

The prevalence of the multiple method is traceable to Alexandrian philosophy and theology,[7] in which, in the reconciliation of Christianity and Platonism, allegory[8] was long regarded as essential to the attainment of *gnosis.*[9] Ultimately, of course, allegory in hermeneutics must be referred to Jewish haggadic exegesis, which had had an established history of

[5] See G. Robert, *Les écoles et l'enseignement de la théologie pendant la première moitié du XIIe siècle* (Paris, 1909), pp. 103 ff., treating the method of Hugh of St. Victor; and Hugh of St. Victor, *De Sacramentis, Prologus,* chap. vi, Migne, *Pat. Lat.,* CLXXVI, 185.

[6] Ludwig Diestel, *Geschichte des Alten Testamentes in der christlichen Kirche* (Jena, 1869), p. 163.

[7] See F. W. Farrar, *History of Interpretation* (London, 1886), Lectures 2 to 5; A. Sabatier, art. "Herméneutique," *Encyclopédie des sciences religieuses,* VI, 210–219; G. Heinrici, art. "Hermeneutik," *Realencyklopädie für protestantische Theologie und Kirche,* 3d ed., VII, 718 ff.; A. Immer, *Hermeneutics of the New Testament,* tr. A. H. Newman (Andover, 1890), pp. 29 ff.

[8] Clement sought authority in Ps. 78: 2: "Howbeit we speak wisdom among them that are perfect: yet not the wisdom of this world, nor of the princes of this world, that come to naught"; and in I Cor. 11: 6: "I will open my mouth in a parable: I will utter dark sayings of old."

[9] W. Sanday, *Inspiration* (Bampton Lectures, London, 1893), p. 39, says that in the earliest known commentary on a book of the New Testament, that of the Gnostic Heracleon (*c.* A.D. 170) on St. John, the allegorical method is already full-blown.

allegorical interpretation for several generations before Philo viewed persons and things in the Old Testament as τρόποι of the soul, and sought to prove that Greek philosophical ideas, through the ὑπόνοια, underlay the story of the Old Testament; although Philo was also influenced by Stoic rules[10] of interpretation that had evolved from the study of Homer. I recall Philo[11] because of his influence on Origen. Origen, great allegorist of Christianity, brought the multiple sense of Scripture to the Christian Church, and firmly fixed the nature of Scriptural exegesis for succeeding centuries. From a double division of *sensus historicus* or *literalis*, and *sensus spiritalis*, he developed a trichotomous scheme: the literal, σωματικόν; the moral, ψυχικόν, ἡ τροπολογία; and the spiritual, πνευματικόν, ἡ ἀλληγορία, ἡ ἀναγωγή.[12] Augustine[13] and Jerome[14] continued the practice of multiple explication. Indeed, Augustine used four topics: *historia; aetiologia,* which considers causes; *analogia,* which studies a text from the point of view of congruence of the Old and New Testament; *allegoria,* which is figurative interpretation. But this was not the quadruple system we have in our treatises and which persisted in the Middle Ages. Rather, when the Augustinian topics were considered, as they were by St. Thomas Aquinas,[15] the first three topics were comprehended under the first. But, on the other hand, the quadruple method of the kind noted in our tractates on preaching was

---

[10] Such as were applied by Crates of Mallos. See D. W. Bousset, *Jüdisch-Christliche Schulbetrieb in Alexandria und Rom* (Göttingen, 1915). On Philo and Heraclides Ponticus, see Farrar, p. 138.

[11] See C. G. A. Siegfried, *Philo von Alexandria als Ausleger des Alten Testaments* (Jena, 1875), and Z. Frankel, *Über den Einfluss der palästinischen Exegese auf die Alexandrinische Hermeneutik* (Leipzig, 1851).

[12] E.g., *De Principiis* IV, 11 ff., ed. C. H. E. Lommatzsch, *Origenis Opera Omnia* (Berlin, 1849), XXI, 500 ff. Origen classed Philo with the Christian Fathers.

[13] *De Utilitate Credendi* V ff., ed. J. Zycha, *C.S.E.L.* XXV (1891), 7 ff.

[14] See n. 30 below.

[15] *Summa Theologica* I, art. 10, Reply obj. 2.

used by Cassian,[16] Aldhelm,[17] Hrabanus Maurus,[18] Bede,[19] John of Salisbury,[20] St. Thomas Aquinas,[21] Dante,[22] and many others.[23] Hugh of St. Cher compared the four senses to the four coverings of the tabernacle, the four winds, the fourfold cherubim, and the four rivers of Paradise.[24] Sabatier[25] says that the first to introduce our quadruple method, which was merely another arrangement of the same elements as appear in Origen's triple scheme, involving the separation of *anagoge* from *allegoria*—the first to set the style for the Middle Ages— was Eucherius of Lyons (died *c.* 449); but in the Preface to his *Formulae Spiritalis Intellegentiae*,[26] Eucherius writes as if others had made the same classification. We see it exemplified in his contemporary Cassian; but it must go back at least to Greek theologians of the fourth century. Alardus Gazaeus, the

[16] *Collationes* XIV, 8, *De Spiritali Scientia*, Migne, *Pat. Lat.*, XLIX, 962. Cassian's exposition is very clear. He has the usual two primary classes: historical interpretation and spiritual intelligence. The last three senses are placed under spiritual knowledge.

[17] *De Virginitate* IV, ed. R. Ehwald, *Monumenta Germaniae Historica*, XV (1919), 232.

[18] *In Epist. ad Gal.* 4: 24, Migne, *Pat. Lat.*, CXII, 330.

[19] See C. Plummer, ed. of the *Historia Ecclesiastica* (Oxford, 1896), I, Introduction, pp. lvi ff. Bede uses both a threefold (*Opp.* vii. 317), and a fourfold (*Opp.* vi. 96, 97), system of classification, and identifies "typical" with "allegorical" (*Opp.* vii. 246, 247).

[20] *Policraticus* VII, 12 (666a), ed. C. C. I. Webb (Oxford, 1909), II, 143–144.

[21] *Summa Theologica* I, art. 10, Reply obj. 3. St. Thomas accords with Cassian and the usual custom of placing the last three senses under the head of the spiritual.

[22] *Convivio*, tract. II; and the letter to Can Grande.

[23] See the very valuable article by E. v. Dobschütz, "Vom vierfachen Schriftsinn," in *Harnack-Ehrung* (Leipzig, 1921), pp. 1–13.

[24] Farrar, p. 295.

[25] P. 212.

[26] Ed. C. Wotke (Vienna, 1894); *Praefatio*, p. 5: The literal sense "ueritatem nobis factorum ac fidem relationis inculcat"; the tropological "ad uitae emendationem mysticos intellectus refert"; and "anagoge ad sacratiora caelestium figurarum secreta perducit." "Sunt etiam qui allegoriam in hoc scientiae genere quarto in loco adiciendum putent, quam gestorum narratione futurorum umbram praetulisse confirment."

seventeenth-century editor of Cassian, gives these verses, still extant in his day (but made famous by Nicolas of Lyra and perhaps used by others before him), which are characteristic of the scholastic method, and no doubt served as a mnemonic aid to invention:

> Littera gesta docet, quid credas allegoria,
> Moralis quid agas, quo tendas anagogia.[27]

Thus also Hugh of St. Cher in the thirteenth century taught: "historia docet quid factum, tropologia quid faciendum, allegoria quid intellegendum, anagoge quid appetendum."[28]

Now one can readily see that multiple distinctions, by their subjective nature, could, in the practice of arbitrary preachers, easily breed confusion. Nor is a wide reading of mediaeval sermons necessary to prove as true of that era Farrar's indictment:

Homiletics have been to an incredible extent the *Phylloxera Vastatrix* of exegesis, and preachers, with their habit of thrusting into texts an endless variety of commonplaces which have no connection with them, have become privileged misinterpreters. They have ploughed with the unequally-yoked ox and ass of science and sermon-making, and made texts an excuse for saying this or that as it pleased them, with no thought of the real meaning of them.[29]

That the categories of allegorical and tropological, and allegorical and anagogical, might overlap was known to some observers in the Middle Ages;[30] but that ambiguity and

---

[27] Cassian, *op. cit.*, p. 962. *Speres* sometimes appears for *tendas;* see v. Dobschütz, pp. 1 ff.

[28] See v. Dobschütz, p. 12, n. 12.

[29] P. 246, n. 1.

[30] Gazaeus discloses this in studying the method of Jerome, *Epist. ad Hedibiam, quaest.* 12, *Ezech.* 16, and *Amos* 4. See Cassian, *Collat.* XIV, 8, p. 962.

equivocation were created by the multiplicity was denied by St. Thomas Aquinas:

> The multiplicity of these interpretations does not cause ambiguity or any sort of equivocation, since these interpretations are not multiplied because one word signifies several things, but because the things signified by the words can themselves be types of other things.[31]

We might perhaps grant St. Thomas the truth of his contention with regard even to a fourfold interpretation, yet a denial of ambiguity and equivocation would surely seem of little avail concerning the "septem sigilli" of Angelom of Luxeuil[32] (ninth century): (1) *historialis;* (2) *allegorialis;* (3) a combination of *historialis* and *allegorialis;* (4) with respect to the intimation, proper or tropical, of Deity; (5) *parabolaris,* when one thing is written in Scripture, and something else is meant; (6) with respect to the two comings of the Savior, when either the first or the second is prefigured, or both are; (7) the method (allied to the *allegorialis,* but differing from it in serving morals proper rather than faith in general) which possesses a twofold preceptive quality, in that it both points a definite moral to correct living, and also carries a figure of a larger life meant to be foreshown. And Martin Marrier, seventeenth-century editor of Odo of Cluny, studies[33] that abbot's work through eight senses of interpretation: (1) *litteralis,* or *historicus* (as used by Jerome); (2) *allegoricus,* or *parabolicus* (as used by Gregory); (3) *tropo-*

---

[31] *Summa Theologica* I, art. 10, Reply obj. 3.

[32] *Enarrationes in Libros Regum, Praefatio Apologetica,* Migne, *Pat. Lat.,* CXV, 245 ff. Angelom does admit that an original triplicate division is the source of his seven "sigilli." The *Zohar* has as secondary to the four senses an additional three: numerical value of the letters, mystical allegory, higher inspiration. See Louis Ginzberg, art. "Allegorical Interpretation," *Jewish Encyclopedia,* I.

[33] Introduction to Odo's *Moralium Epitome S. Greg. in Job,* Migne, *Pat. Lat.,* CXXXIII, 105 ff.

logicus, or *etymologicus* (as used by Ambrose); (4) *anagogicus*, or *analogicus* (as used by Augustine); (5) *typicus*, or *exemplaris* (as used by Basil and Bernard). Thus Christ refers to John the Baptist as *Elias* (Matt. 11:14); (6) *anaphoricus*, or *proportionalis* (as used by Pope Clement), based on temporal relativity. The story of Isaac and Ishmael portends the relations between the Church and Synagogue; (7) *mysticus*, or *apocalypticus* (as used by Gregory of Nazianzus), *sensus totus divinus . . . atque ineffabilis;* (8) *boarcademicus*,[34] or *primordialis* (as used by Jewish Cabalists), in which the point of view is that of eternal bliss and salvation. No conscious use of these eight senses is observable in Odo's works (indeed one may not expect cabalistic influences in Christian works at a time when the Cabala was not yet in being), nor does Marrier suggest such a conscious use in Odo's method. Yet this extension towards over-refinement is worth noting. We may, on the other hand, be certain that the belief in an unlimited sense of Scripture by John Scotus Erigena represents on the part of that great allegorist rather a refusal to yield to the mechanism of a formula than a desire to extend the number of *topoi*. To Erigena "the sense of the divine utterances is manifold and infinite, just as in a single feather of the peacock one sees a marvelous and beautiful variety of innumerable colors."[35] We may compare, in Jewish exegesis, the *Zohar*'s seventy aspects of the *Torah*.[36]

It is not surprising that the attitude of the Reformation was

[34] In reply to a request for information concerning this unusual word, which I have found nowhere else, Professor Louis Ginzberg of the Jewish Theological Seminary of America suggests that it must represent בְּאוּר קַדְמוֹן (*beur cadmon*), almost literally: *sensus primordialis*.

[35] *De Div. Nat.* IV. 5, Migne, *Pat. Lat.*, CXXII, 749 c. Cf. Henry Bett, *Johannes Scotus Erigena* (Cambridge, 1925), pp. 152 ff.; and R. L. Poole, *Illustrations of the History of Mediaeval Thought* (London, 1884), p. 67.

[36] See W. Bacher, "L'exégèse biblique dans le *Zohar*," *Revue des études juives*, XII (1891), 35.

antipathetic to the use of the four senses. Melanchthon[37] regards it as the trifling and vicious recourse to a monstrous metamorphosis on the part of inept illiterates, who have no science of speaking, and who do not even appreciate that ἀναγωγία, meaning *petulantia*, may not be used for ἀναγωγή.

Philo's rôle in the history of Christian exegesis is characteristic of the relations between Jewish and Christian hermeneutics through the long and rich histories of both, especially in the Middle Ages. In Jewish Biblical hermeneutics, there was a Midrashic, homiletical, type of interpretation which aimed at moral instruction. There was a similar long quarrel as to stress upon the *peshat* or primary sense, or upon the *derash*, or Midrashic sense. There were, especially from the thirteenth century on, Jewish scholars who drew upon Christian exegetical methods,[38] and works criticizing Christian methods.[39] There was prevalent[40] the fourfold interpretation: *peshat*, *derash*, rational-philosophical, and cabalistic-mystical, and in the Zohar[41] (which first appeared in the thirteenth century in Spain) there are found the almost exact equivalents of the patristic four senses: פשט *peshat,* דרש *derash,* רמז *remez* (allegori-

---

[37] *Elementa Rhetorices, De Elocutione II, De Quatuor Sensibus Sacrarum Scripturarum:* "Sed has nugas commenti sunt homines illiterati, qui cum nullam dicendi rationem tenerent, et tamen uiderent scripturam plenam esse figurarum non potuerunt apte de figuris iudicare. Itaque coacti sunt nouam quondam rhetoricam comminisci." "Errant autem in hac uoce cum dicunt ἀναγωγίαν pro ἀναγωγή, significat enim ἀναγωγία petulantiam, seu feritatem morum, ab ἀνώγαγος, quod est intractabilis et petulans." "Et hoc modo omnes uersus prodigiosa metamorphosi quadrifariam interpretabantur, quantumuis interdum dictum aliquod repugnaret illi metamorphosi." Cf. pp. 145–146 below; ἀναγωγή = ἀνά + ἄγω.

[38] E.g., Isaac Abravanel (end of fifteenth century).

[39] E.g., Abraham Ibn Ezra's (twelfth century) Commentary on the Pentateuch (*Sefer ha-Yashar*).

[40] E.g., the Commentary on the Pentateuch by Bahya ben Asher (Saragossa, end of thirteenth century). See P. Bloch-K. Kohler, art. "Bahya," *Jewish Encyc.*, II.

[41] I. Broydé, art. "Zohar," *Jewish Encyc.*, XII, calls *remez* "the sense for allusion," *derash* "anagogical," and *sod* "mystical."

cal), and סוד *sod* (mystical), which W. Bacher[42] thinks were probably modeled upon the Christian arrangement.[43] On the other hand, it was seen above, in regard to Odo's editor, that one sense-topic was borrowed from the Jewish Cabala.[44]

In the light of this interrelationship in Biblical exegesis and of the natural use of preaching as a general medium of hermeneutical practice in the religious activity of both Christians and Jews in the Middle Ages, more information than we have on mediaeval Jewish rhetoric, sacred and secular, would be very welcome.[45] We know there were scholars among the Jews who used rhetoric derived from Arabic sources,[46] and scholars who applied rhetoric to sacred eloquence.[47] Great homiletical collections were extant, and highly elaborated sermons expounding the Pentateuch text were delivered by the Darshanim, among whom several great figures appeared in the thirteenth and fourteenth centuries, particularly in Spain. Such considerations, as well as the frequent intercourse between Jewish and Christian scholars in the Middle Ages, and the attention generally given by Jewish philosophy to

[42] See art. "Bible Exegesis," *Jewish Encyc.*, III; and also D. Philippson, art. "Homiletics," *ibid.*, VI.

[43] On the *pardes*, see W. Bacher, "Das Merkwort Pardes in der jüdischen Bibelexegese," in D. B. Stade, *Zeitschrift für die alttestamentliche Wissenschaft*, XIII (1893), 294–305. See also A. Schmiedel, *Studien über jüdische Religionsphilosophie* (Vienna, 1869), p. 229; W. Bacher, "Die Bibelexegese (Vom Anfange des 10. bis zum Ende des 15. Jahrhunderts)" in J. Winter and A. Wünsche, *Geschichte der rabbinischen Literatur* (Trier, 1894), II, 239–339. For Jewish-Christian interrelationship in Biblical exegesis, see L. I. Newman, *Jewish Influence on Christian Reform Movements* (Columbia University Oriental Studies, XXIII; New York, 1925), p. 183, n. 27; for Jewish influence upon Nicolas of Lyra, *ibid.*, pp. 71 ff.

[44] See A. Jellinek, "Christlicher Einfluss auf die Kabbala," in *Beiträge zur Geschichte der Kabbala* (Leipzig, 1852), pp. 51–56; Newman, *op. cit.*, pp. 176 ff.

[45] So also, for a later period, one would like to see a comparison of Judah Messer Leon (the *Nōpheth Ṣuphim*, ed. A. Jellinek; Vienna, 1863) and his contemporary Reuchlin in their dependence on the rhetorical theory of Aristotle, the *Rhetorica ad Alexandrum*, the *Rhetorica ad Herennium*, Cicero, and Quintilian.

[46] E.g., Abulwalid Ibn Janah (ninth century).

[47] E.g., Moses Ibn Ezra (twelfth century) in his *Kitab al-Muhadarah*.

alien thought, suggest that there was an interaction between these two religious systems, not only in hermeneutics, but also in other departments of sacred rhetoric.[48] A comparative study of Jewish and Christian preaching in that epoch would prove fruitful.

[48] See S. Maybaum, *Jüdische Homiletik* (Berlin, 1890), pp. 1–22.

VI

Classical Rhetoric and the Mediaeval Theory of Preaching*

A MONG the sculptures on the *portail royal* of Chartres Cathedral, that mediaeval *summa* of chiseled stone, one may see
the seven liberal arts personified in female form.[1] And under
these one may perceive the outstanding representatives of all
the arts. There, symbolized in its place in mediaeval life, is
Rhetoric, and at her feet is Cicero. From Carolingian times
well into the Renaissance, rhetoric as one of the liberal arts
was figured in church sculptures, murals, mosaics, manuscript
miniatures, the ornamentation of library rooms, fountains,
table-tops, bronze vessels, windows, tapestry, altars, and
gravestones; in one form or another at Auxerre, Bourges,
Clermont, Laon, Rheims, Rouen, St. Omer, Sens, Soissons,
Freiburg Münster, the Abbey of St. Gall, Rimini, Florence,
Siena, the Vatican; the handiwork in the earlier period most
often of unknown artists, but later also of Giotto, the brothers
Pisani, Pollaiuolo, Botticelli, Melozzo da Forli, Pinturicchio,

---

* Reprinted as revised for *Historical Studies of Rhetoric and Rhetoricians*, edited by
Raymond Howes (Ithaca, N.Y., 1961), pp. 71–89. Originally published in
Classical Philology, XXVIII (1933), 73–96.
[1] Part of this paper was read before the Classical Association of England and
Wales at Cardiff on April 9, 1929.

and Raphael.[2] Cicero is almost always her attendant, and she appears with attributes that vary with the imagination of the artist. At times she holds a pose perhaps intended to be faithful to Capella's striking portrait[3] of the omnipotent queen, a woman of sublime and radiant beauty and regal poise, helmeted, and bearing her flashing weapons in her hands; her robe girt about her shoulders in the Latin way, embroidered with a multitude of figures, and her breast bejeweled in most exquisite colors. Thus she appears with a sword and shield; or, again, she makes an oratorical gesture, or carries a scroll, a tablet and stilus, or a golden nugget. The motive was persistent in the fine art of the period.

This prominence of rhetoric in art is a reflection of her importance in literature. Almost consistently throughout the Middle Ages—from the works of Capella to those of Vincent of Beauvais, from the fifth century to the thirteenth and beyond—rhetoric as one of the liberal arts played a significant part in mediaeval life. The classical rhetoric survived in many forms. In the first place, manuscripts of some of the chief classical authors themselves were plentiful in European libraries. Secondly, there were the works of the minor rhetoricians[4] of later date, who, following the relatively compendious fashion of an isagogic work or encyclopedia, preserved the general principles and terminology of the ancient rhetoric—writers like Fortunatianus, Marius Victorinus, Martianus Capella, Cassiodorus, Isidore, Alcuin, Notker, and Anselm of Besate. Thirdly, there were commentaries on, and translations of, Cicero, commentaries on and adaptations of the *Rhetorica ad*

---

[2] Karl Künstle's *Ikonographie der christlichen Kunst* (Freiburg im Breisgau, 1928) supplies most of the information at present available in this field. See his Bibliography, pp. 145 ff., and also W. Molsdorf, *Christliche Symbolik der mittelalterlichen Kunst* (Leipzig, 1926).

[3] *De Nuptiis Philologiae et Mercurii*, sec. 426; ed. A. Dick (Leipzig, 1925), p. 211.

[4] See Carolus Halm, *Rhetores Latini Minores* (Leipzig, 1863).

Herennium, and several commentaries on Capella, notably by John Scot, Dunchad, and Remigius of Auxerre. In the tradition of Alcuin and others that rhetoric is fundamentally a juridical art,[5] concerned with speaking well in civil questions, there arose a group of works like the *Ecclesiastica Rhetorica*[6] of the second half of the twelfth century, virtually a forensic rhetoric for canon law, and professedly developed in accordance with rhetorical doctrine. Also in this tradition, and maintaining the alliance of rhetoric and law in the schools, there grew up from Carolingian times well into the later period a huge mass of tracts, *Artes Dictaminis*, devoted to letter-writing and legal administration. These were designed to prepare students for positions in the ecclesiastical and state chanceries; the *artes*[7] assumed the name of rhetoric, and the teachers often called themselves "rhetors." Almost universally such tracts

[5]   "Qui Retoricque bien sauroit
Il connistroit et tort et droit"

says Gossuin of Metz (*saec.* xiii) in *L'image du monde;* see Ch.-V. Langlois, *La vie en France au moyen âge* (Paris, 1927), III, 161.

[6] E.g., Cod. Lat. Monac. 4555 (*saec.* xiii), fols. 87 ff.; 22271 (*saec.* xii), fols. 143 ff.; ed. Ludwig Wahrmund in *Quellen zur Geschichte des römisch-kanonischen Prozesses*, I, Heft 4 (Innsbruck, 1906). See Eilbert, *Ordo Judiciarius*, ed. Wahrmund, in *Quellen*, I, Heft 5 (1906); Heinrich Siegel, "Über den *Ordo Iudiciarius* des Eilbert von Bremen mit Berücksichtigung der *Ecclesiastica Rethorica*," *Sitzungsb. der Kaiserl. Akad. der Wiss.*, LV (Vienna, 1867), 531–553; Albert Lang, "Rhetorische Einflüsse auf die Behandlung des Prozesses in der Kanonistik des 12. Jahrhunderts," *Festschrift Eduard Eichmann* (Marburg, 1941), pp. 69–97.

[7] The works of Ludwig Rockinger are the most important for this branch of learning. See especially his *Briefsteller und Formelbücher des 11ten bis 14ten Jahrh.* (Munich, 1863–1864); cf. also L. J. Paetow, *The Arts Course at Mediaeval Universities* (Urbana-Champaign, Ill., 1910); C. H. Haskins, *Studies in Mediaeval Culture* (Oxford, 1929), pp. 170–192; André Wilmart, "L'*Ars Arengandi* de Jacques de Dinant," *Analecta Reginensia* (*Studi e Testi*, 59; Vatican City, 1933), pp. 113–154; E. H. Kantorowicz, "Anonymi *Aurea Gemma*," *Medievalia et Humanistica*, I (1943), 41–57; Helene Wieruszowski, "*Ars Dictaminis* in the Time of Dante," *Med. et Hum.*, I (1943), 95–108, and "Arezzo as a Center of Learning and Letters in the Thirteenth Century," *Traditio*, IX (1953), 351 ff.; P. O. Kristeller, "Matteo de' Libri, Bolognese Notary of the Thirteenth Century, and his *Artes Dictaminis*," in *Miscellanea G. Galbiati*, II (Milan, 1951), 283–320.

borrowed their *introductio* and stylistic from rhetoric, added *salutatio* and *petitio* to the Ciceronian divisions of *exordium*, *narratio*, and *conclusio*, frequently used the principles of invention, disposition, and *captatio benevolentiae*, and discussed *clausulae*, colors, and the modes of expanding material. Boncampagni pictures[8] this kind of rhetoric as empress of the liberal arts, adorned with gold and precious stones, moving among roses and lilies of the valley. His fancy at least reflects the high esteem in which the rhetors held their art. And, finally, there were many special tracts on rhetorical colors.

Rhetoric then, as always, was in close kinship with grammar, and with that other member of the trivium, of which she is traditionally the ἀντίστροφος, dialectic. The rhetorical use of the dialectical τόποι, developed by Aristotle, the *Auctor ad Herennium*, and Cicero, and for the Middle Ages especially by Boethius, in his *De Differentiis Topicis*, became of particular importance with the increased interest in dialectic that after the year 1200 attended the growth of scholasticism. To Alcuin,[9] Roger Bacon,[10] and Gerson,[11] rhetoric was a branch of logic; while Brunetto Latini,[12] Dante's teacher, placed rhetoric under politics. And lastly, there was the usual interaction between rhetoric and poetry. In his study of the theories of poetry[13] of the twelfth and thirteenth centuries, Professor Edmond Faral includes works just as properly belonging to the field of rhetoric, for example, the *Ars Versificatoria* of Matthew of Vendôme and the *Poetica* of John of Garland.

[8] Cf. Rockinger, pp. 128 ff.

[9] See his treatise in Halm, pp. 525–550.

[10] *Opus Tert.*, LXXV, in *Opera*, ed. J. S. Brewer (London, 1859), p. 309.

[11] *Opera* (Antwerp, 1706), IV, 214 ff. and 571–582.

[12] Francesco Maggini, *La rettorica di Brunetto Latini* (Pubblicazioni del R. istituto di studi superiori: sezione di filosofia e filologia, XXXVIII; Florence, 1915); and also his *La "rettorica" Italiana di Brunetto Latini* (Florence, 1912), p. 65; Helene Wieruszowski, "Brunetto Latini als Lehrer Dantes und der Florentiner," *Archivio Italiano per la Storia della Pietà*, II (1957), 186–189.

[13] *Les arts poétiques du xii⁰ et du xiii⁰ siècles* (Paris, 1924).

Now, while there are signs that in the tenth and eleventh centuries the interest in rhetoric had in some places somewhat abated, in the period we are now considering, from the twelfth century on into the fifteenth, its popularity is again unquestionable. The rhetorical education flourished in the schools[14] of Europe, and especially France. With grammar it was a fundamental subject in cathedral schools, monasteries, and city schools, although in the new universities it had not yet won the influence that a great deal later it was to enjoy. And as one of the *artes sermocinales* it was included in the *studium artium* of the religious orders. Late in this period an anonymous rhetorician can with bold assurance maintain that "rhetoric is the science which refreshes the hungry, renders the mute articulate, makes the blind to see, and teaches one to avoid every lingual ineptitude."[15]

What I consider significant in mediaeval literature, as in the cathedral sculptures, is the theological environment of rhetoric. It is not strange that men of vision, like Roger Bacon, saw the value of rhetoric in moral philosophy. Nor is it surprising that William of Auvergne should write a *Rhetorica*

---

[14] On rhetoric in mediaeval education see particularly Paetow; F. A. Specht, *Geschichte des Unterrichtswesens in Deutschland* (Stuttgart, 1885); F. H. Denifle, *Die Universitäten des Mittelalters bis 1400* (Berlin, 1885); F. A. Eckstein, *Lateinischer und griechischer Unterricht* (Leipzig, 1887); J. L. Clerval, *L'enseignement des arts libéraux à Chartres et à Paris* (Paris, 1889); Hastings Rashdall, *The Universities of Europe in the Middle Ages* (Oxford, 1895); Hilarin Felder, *Geschichte der wissenschaftlichen Studien im Franziskanerorden* (Freiburg im Breisgau, 1904); H. Holzappel, *Handbuch der Geschichte des Franziskanerordens* (Freiburg im Breisgau, 1909); Martin Grabmann, *Die Geschichte der scholastischen Methode* (Freiburg im Breisgau, 1909); Friedrich Paulsen, *Geschichte des gelehrten Unterrichts* (Leipzig, 1919); C. S. Baldwin, *Medieval Rhetoric and Poetic* (New York, 1928); Richard McKeon, "Rhetoric in the Middle Ages," *Speculum*, XVII (Jan., 1942), 1–32; E. R. Curtius, *European Literature and the Latin Middle Ages*, tr. W. R. Trask (New York, 1953); Dorothy Grosser, "Studies in the Influence of the *Rhetorica ad Herennium* and Cicero's *De Inventione*" (unpub. Ph.D. diss., Cornell University, Ithaca, N.Y., 1953); R. R. Bolgar, *The Classical Heritage and Its Beneficiaries* (Cambridge, 1954).

[15] An anonymous *Rhetoric* published at Memmingen, 1490–1495; see *Gesamtkatalog der Wiegendrucke*, No. 2671.

Divina,[16] a rhetoric of prayer. I paraphrase slightly an introductory poem addressed to William:

When you teach suasion to the lowly, how to pour out words to God, the Creator becomes gentler toward the sin, and for your guidance grants pardon to the sinner. Quintilian, these are not your oratorical colors, nor are they yours, Marcus, glory of eloquence. Nor did he give them forth, the admired of Athens. Lost, vain, and treacherous was your wisdom, which taught only how to move the heart of a human judge. Whereas our lofty art teaches by prayer to mollify the just wrath of that great Judge, even God. Ah, how much better with words to placate the puissant and eternal Father than to dispense the words of human law!

This is an echo of chapter 1, in which the author establishes an art of "spiritual oratory in causes and affairs of the soul. . . . If secular *oratio* has deserved so many works of laborious care, how much more worthy and just that sacred *oratio*, with which in fruit and utility the secular cannot compare, should have its artists and scholars?" William's art of prayer, like the Roman oration, embraces *exordium, narratio, confirmatio,* and *conclusio,* and adds *petitio.*

But obviously the widest field for rhetoric in the Middle Ages was in preaching, the dissuasion from vice, and the persuasion to virtue, the winning of souls to God. With the spread of scholasticism and the rise of the great preaching orders, the Dominicans and the Franciscans, preaching flowered in practice and theory. In the twelfth century for the first time, and continually thereafter, the theory received treatment in special manuals—the *Liber Quo Ordine Sermo Fieri Debeat* of Guibert de Nogent (*saec.* xii),[17] the *Summa de Arte Praedicatoria* of Alain de Lille (end *saec.* xii),[18] the *De Eruditione Praedicatorum* of Humbert de Romans (*saec.* xiii),[19]

---

[16] The copy I have consulted is in the Bibliothèque Nationale, Paris, Rés. D. 15239 (Hain-Copinger, No. 8305).

[17] *Prooemium ad Commentarios in Genesim,* Migne, *Pat. Lat.,* CLVI, 21–32.

[18] Migne, *Pat. Lat.,* CCX, 110–198.

the Franciscan *Ars Concionandi* wrongly attributed to St. Bonaventure,[20] *Artes Praedicandi* professing falsely the authorship of
Albertus Magnus[21] and Henry of Hesse (fl. *saec.* xiv),[22] and
claiming the influence of St. Thomas Aquinas.[23] Among the
many other writers of *Artes Praedicandi* were the following:[24]

[19] *Maxima Bibliotheca Veterum Patrum*, ed. M. de la Bigne (Lyons, 1677), XXV,
426–567.

[20] *Opera Omnia*, Suppl. III (Trent, 1774), cols. 385–417.

[21] *Gesamtkatalog der Wiegendrucke*, Nos. 590–591. See R. Stapper, "Eine angeblich von Albertus Magnus verfasste Ars praedicandi," *Römische Quartalschrift*,
Suppl. XX (Freiburg im Breisgau, 1913), pp. 388–402, and H. Kuhle, "Zur
angeblich von Albert d. Grosse verfassten Ars praedicandi," *Röm. Quart.* (1928),
pp. 324–328. The *incipit*, "Veritas ewangelica predicatoribus", is the same as that
of William of Auvergne's *De Faciebus*, and these incunabula are regarded as copies
of that tract of William's; see Th.-M. Charland, *Artes Praedicandi* (listed in n. 24
below), pp. 21–22. In the present paper I refer to this tract as the Albertus-tract.

[22] See Hain, Nos. 8397, 8398, 8399, and " 'Henry of Hesse' on the Art of
Preaching" [pp. 135–159 of this volume].

[23] See "A Late Mediaeval Tractate on Preaching" [pp. 40–78 of this volume].

[24] In the case of several names in the list the authorship of tracts is as yet not
definitely certain. Until the problems are thoroughly investigated I tentatively
accept the attributions of the MSS themselves, knowing full well from many of
the cases above that have been studied how often such assignments are false.
Furthermore, as regards several others in this list, references to tracts of their
authorship are known, but as yet no MSS have been found by me. The enumeration here is not exhaustive, especially as to the fourteenth and fifteenth centuries;
and where I have not made a personal examination of the MSS I may have
inadvertently included other than strictly technical treatises.

Since the original publication of this list, in 1933, a great deal of additional
information has become available. For much fuller lists of authors, problems of
authorship involved in certain instances, information about the many anonymous
tracts, and other pertinent studies of mediaeval homiletical theory, see: M. M.
Davy, *Les sermons universitaires parisiens de 1230–1231* (Paris, 1931); Th.-M.
Charland, *Artes Praedicandi* (Paris-Ottawa, 1936); W. O. Ross, "A Brief *Forma
Praedicandi*," *Modern Philology*, XXXIV (May, 1937), 337–344, and *Middle
English Sermons* (London, 1940); Mary F. Boynton, "Simon Alcok on Expanding
the Sermon," *Harvard Theol. Rev.*, XXXIV (July, 1941), 201–216; J. de
Ghellinck, *L'essor de la littérature latine au xiie siècle* (2d ed.; Brussels, 1954), n. 35,
pp. 206–208; Dorothea Roth, *Die mittelalterliche Predigttheorie und das Manuale
Curatorum des Johann Ulrich Surgant* (Basel, 1956); Heinrich Fichtenau, *Arenga*, in
Mitteilungen des Instituts für Osterreichische Geschichtsforschung, Ergänzungsband, XVIII
(Graz-Cologne, 1957). [See also Caplan, the two Hand-Lists, *Mediaeval Artes
Praedicandi*, and the lists of doctrinal and historical studies in different languages
entered in the Bibliography, pp. 271–272 below.]

THIRTEENTH CENTURY	FOURTEENTH CENTURY	FIFTEENTH CENTURY
Alexander of Ashby (?)	Symon Alcok	St. Antoninus of Florence, O.P.[29]
William of Auvergne[25]	Fr. Astazius, O.M.	Thomas von Cleve, O.P.[30]
Arnoldus de Podio, O.P.	John Avonius, Carm.	John Felton (?)
Jean de la Rochelle, O.M.	Robert of Basevorn	Jacques le Grand, O.S.A.
Richard of Thetford, O.S.B.	Alphonsus Bononiensis	John of Guidernia
John of Wales, O.M.[26]	Franciscus Fabrianensis, O.M.	Gozewijn Haeks, Carm.
	Philippus Florentinus, O.M.	Stephanus Hoest[31]
	John Folsham, Carm.	Magister Koburck
	Jacobus Fusignani, O.P.[27]	Paul Kölner of Ratisbon
	Ranulph Higden, O.S.B.	Martinus Alphonsus of Cordova, O.S.A.
	Robert Holcoth, O.P.	Michael of Hungary, O.M.[32]
	Hendrik Aeger van Kalkar, Carth.	Fridericus de Nuris
	Henry of Langenstein (Henry of Hesse, the elder)[28]	Thomas Penketh, O.S.A.
	Jean de Châlons	Ludovicus de Rocha, O.M.
	Raymond Lull, O.M.	Silvester de Marradio, O.P.
	Martin of Amberg	Hugo de Sueth, O.P.
	Nicolas Oresmius	Thomas of Salisbury
	Hermannus Teutonicus, O.P.	
	Thomas de Tuderto, O.S.A.	
	Baldo degli Ubaldi	
	Thomas Waleys, O.P.	
	Olivier de Went, O.P.	

[25] A. de Poorter, "Un manuel de prédication médiévale," *Revue néo-scolastique de philosophie*, XXV (1923), 192–209. See also n. 21 above.

[26] Published anonymously as *Ars Praedicandi sive Informatio Notabilis et Praeclara de Arte Praedicandi* and as *Ars Praedicandi;* see *Gesamtkatalog der Wiegendrucke,* Nos. 2669 and 2670, and Pellechet, Nos. 313 and 314. The manuscripts are also anonymous, except two that are pertinent: Mazarine 569, fols. 80ᵛ–86ᵛ, bearing

Add a goodly number of anonymous *Artes Praedicandi* or *Sermocinandi*, and also numerous small tracts on methods of expanding a sermon. These systematic, carefully developed treatises are quite different from the rare, sketchy, and rudimentary attempts of the earlier period to give outline to the art. For example, a ninth-century manuscript (Cod. Lat. Monac. 22053, fol. 93) progresses as far as to list seven *modi* of preaching: (1) by teaching disciples; (2) by persuading people; (3) by chiding the haughty; (4) by refuting the contrary-minded; (5) by terrifying the lukewarm; (6) by assuaging the wrathful; (7) by promising life everlasting to the good and torments everlasting to the wicked. The manuals were scattered plentifully over the libraries of Europe. A catalogue of the year 1500 of the library of Tegernsee Abbey (Benedictine),[33] numbering from fifteen hundred to two thousand manuscripts, lists over fifty on rhetoric, and twelve *Artes Praedicandi;* but this is perhaps a special instance. Tracts on rhetoric and preaching were indeed extremely popular, though I cannot prove that an art of preaching was ever so highly esteemed as the two *Artes Dictaminis,* by Peter de Vineis and Thomas of Capua, which the usurious wardrobe clerk, John of Ockham,

---

the name of John of Wales, and Troyes 1922, fols. 87–95, bearing that of Humbert of Prully. The ascription, then, of this tract to John of Wales (throughout the present study) is merely tentative.

[27] Hain, Nos. 7399, 7400, 8162, 8168.

[28] Erfurt (Amplon.) MS Qu. 151 (end *saec.* xiv), fols. 155–156ᵛ, regarded as genuine by F. W. E. Roth, "Zur Bibliographie des Henricus Hembuche de Hassia dictus de Langenstein," in *Beihefte zum Centralblatt für Bibliothekswesen* (Leipzig, 1888), II, 15. [Cf. n. 22 above, and pp. 138–139 below.]

[29] *Summa Moralis, Pars* III, *Tit.* XVIII, chaps. 3–6 (Venice, 1582), fols. 326–339.

[30] See n. 63 below.

[31] *Modus Predicandi Subtilis et Compendiosus* (Strassburg, 1513).

[32] *Evagatorium, Modus Predicandi* (Cologne, 1503).

[33] Cod. Lat. Monac. 1925 (=21).

lent to a friend—at a charge of a goose per week.[34] These tracts are perhaps over two hundred in number, the great majority still in manuscript form, unpublished.[35] I have examined only a fair proportion of them, but feel confident that the general conclusions of this paper will be borne out when this attractive and unplowed field of research has been exhaustively worked. Further study of these documents is bound to throw light on a great cultural activity.

Having reviewed the different aspects of mediaeval rhetoric, I shall now indicate the attitude of theologians and preachers to rhetoric, consider briefly the acknowledged dependence of these *Artes* on classical rhetoric, and from a brief survey of their technique point out the general lines of the inheritance.

Even when regarded as different from preaching in origin, material, or purpose, rhetoric has been admitted to close kinship with it. In their view of pagan learning the Middle Ages show differences of opinion that warn us against generalization, but it is safe to say that the distrust of rhetoric as a profane study was not as anxious in the later period[36] as often in earlier times. One is tempted even to decide that the repeated expression of antipathy to secular learning was often more a convention than a proof of genuine belief or feeling.

Let us select for a spokesman that fierce opponent of the liberal arts, the Spaniard Paulus Albarus of the ninth century:

"In the beginning was the word and the word was with God and God was the word. The same was in the beginning with God (John 1:1)." This the learned Plato knew not, of this the eloquent

[34] T. F. Tout, *Chapters in the Administrative History of Mediaeval England* (Manchester, 1920), II, 226.

[35] The manuscripts of which we have knowledge must number almost five hundred.

[36] See Grabmann, "Wertung und Verwertung der antiken Klassiker in der Literatur des 12. Jahrhunderts," *op. cit.*, II, 59 ff., for a discussion of the position of scholasticism with regard to profane studies.

Tully had no thought, into this fiery Demosthenes never inquired. The tortuous briar-bushes of Aristotle have it not, nor is it found in the sinuous subtleties of Chrysippus. The art of Donatus has not searched into this by the rules of art, nor yet the rank discipline of all the grammarians. The geometricians, named after the earth, follow what is earthly and dusty. The rhetoricians, wordy and redundant, have filled the air with empty wind. The dialecticians, bound fast by rules and entangled on all sides by syllogisms, crafty and cunning, are deceitful spinners of words rather than builders of the art of speech.[37]

The state of mind herein exposed must not be regarded as by any means universal. To be sure, St. Augustine, former teacher of rhetoric, in his *Confessions* looks back with misgivings upon the days when, as he says, he "used to sell the talkativeness that emphasizes victory [*victoriosam loquacitatem vendebam*]"; furthermore, one learns how flagrant he judged this offense to be from the fact that his next words refer to the lustful passion of his early years—so that the editors of a recent book of selections from this work are quite justified in stressing the collocation when they head the chapter as follows: "In my teaching of rhetoric and keeping a mistress I yet showed traces of faith in Thee."[38] But the more significant tradition was set by St. Augustine in the *De Doctrina Christiana*, Book IV, in which he depends heavily on Cicero's *Orator*, joins eloquence to religion, and proclaims the value of such profane wisdom for theology. This point is echoed by countless writers through the Middle Ages. Three quotations expressing the dominant attitude to pagan erudition recur: Proverbs 9:1: "Wisdom has

[37] M. L. W. Laistner, *Thought and Letters in Western Europe, A.D. 500–900* (rev. ed.; London, 1957), pp. 212–213. For an excellent discussion of education and the seven liberal arts in the Carolingian period one should read all of chap. 8 in this book.

[38] J. M. Campbell and M. R. P. McGuire, *The Confessions of St. Augustine* (New York, 1931), p. 116.

builded her house; she hath hewn out her seven pillars [of the liberal arts]"; from St. Augustine: "It is no sin to despoil pagan thought of the gold of wisdom and the silver of eloquence, as by God's precept the Hebrews despoiled the Egyptians";[39] from the marriage law in Deuteronomy 21:12–13: "If the hair of the beautiful captive woman [pagan learning] shall be shorn and her nails pared, after that 'thou shalt go unto her, and be her husband, and she shall be thy wife.'"[40] In the influential *De Clericorum Instructione*,[41] Hrabanus in effect writes: "Rhetoric, by which I understand the art of speaking well in civil questions, which seems to belong to mundane science, still is not extraneous to ecclesiastical discipline, for skill in this art is useful to the preacher for fluent and proper teaching, as well as for apt and elegant writing, and for delivering a sermon. He does well who learns it fully, and so fits himself to preach God's word." Then, borrowing from St. Augustine (*De Doctr. Christ.*, IV. 2): "For although rhetoric can sway to either truth or falsehood, who dares say that truth should be unarmed and defenceless, that only the false persuader should make his hearer *benevolus*, *intentus*, and *docilis*, should speak briefly, clearly, with verisimilitude, and, on the other hand, dares condemn the speaker of truth to a tedious, unintelligible, and incredible discourse?" To be sure, Robert of Melun (*saec.* xii), inspired by Plato, bids philosophers spurn rhetoric, which makes the false appear true and the true false, which emphasizes the *inanis suavitas verborum* instead of the *fructuosa virtus sententiarum*, which aims to delight rather than profit, and feeds the ear rather than the soul.[42] Yet in the same century John of Salisbury, praising eloquence, declares that he who

[39] *De Doctr. Christ.*, II. 60. See p. 83, n. 21, above.

[40] Doubtless through Jerome, *Epist.*, No. 70.

[41] *De Rhetorica*, in *De Clericorum Instructione*, III, 19, ed. A. Knoepfler (Munich, 1900), pp. 225–226.

[42] Quoted from the *Sententiae* by Grabmann, II, 350.

condemns so great a good is manifestly a fool.[43] Honorius Augustodunensis (*saec.* xii) in the striking work, *De Animae Exilio et Patria*,[44] conceives the soul, which is traveling in search of the fatherland, the wisdom of Scripture, as first passing through the ten cities of the liberal arts, the third of which is Rhetoric, where Tully teaches the Roman virtues by ornate speech. The suburbs to this metropolis are History, Fable, and Books on Oratory and Ethics. Vincent of Beauvais (*saec.* xiii), who outlines well the traditional rhetoric in civil questions, using Cicero's *De Oratore*, Quintilian, Isidore, and Boethius, would not in his *Speculum Doctrinale* pass over the dignity and excellence of rhetoric; in preaching, however, he prefers the Christian, who acknowledges Holy Writ is paramount, to the Ciceronian.[45] St. Thomas Aquinas (*saec.* xiii): "Eloquence and learning can profitably be used by a preacher."[46] In the same century, Ranulphe d'Homblières,[47] and in the next, John Bromyard,[48] oppose secular literature when read for pleasure's sake, for the delight in poetic adornments and verbal ornamentation, but approve it when the useful therein is turned to Holy Writ. The "Aquinas"-tract, echoing William of Auvergne: "So many works have been written by rhetors on their art. How much worthier that the art and doctrine of sacred rhetoric should receive attention from the preacher-company."[49]

The preacher does well to consider the cock, we read in a thirteenth century manuscript of Bruges (546, fol. 42[vb]), if he would learn his various duties, and chiefly the duty he owes

---

[43] *Metalogicon* I. 7 (835 a), ed. C. C. I. Webb (Oxford, 1929), p. 23.
[44] Migne, *Pat. Lat.*, CLXXII, 1243–1244.
[45] *Speculum Majus* (Venice, 1591), II. 3. 99; IV. 1. 55; IV. 17. 52.
[46] See J. Walsh, "St. Thomas on Preaching," *Dominicana*, V (1921), 6–14.
[47] See P. C. L. Daunou in *Hist. litt. de la France*, XX (1842), 14.
[48] *Summa Praedicantium*, Prologue and II. 12. 32.
[49] [See p. 54 above.]

the liberal arts. The cock and the good preacher have seven qualities in common:

(1) Before crowing, the cock beats his sides. Before preaching, the preacher must mortify himself.
(2) To crow, the cock stretches his neck. So must the preacher lift his head; he must preach of heavenly things, and not mundane.
(3) The cock crows only at certain hours. So does the preacher preach.
(4) The cock shares his grain with his hens. The preacher must willingly communicate his wisdom to others.
(5) The cock attacks his rivals. The preacher should attack all heretics.
(6) The cock shuts his eyes before the sun. The preacher must shut his eyes to the blaze of success.
(7) At nightfall the cock mounts to his wooden roost, and comes down only at daybreak. The preacher must at time of temptation climb to his perch—that is, consider the cross and the passion of Christ, and descend only when all danger has vanished.

But the cock possesses another "virtue." Before lifting his head to crow he bends a bit. So at times the preacher must incline to the liberal arts—not always, for he must lift his head—that is, must climb towards the higher wisdom, must *ad universitatem vel theologiam ire*, and not do as those who are so charmed by logic or grammar as never to be able to part from it, in the manner of the husband who knows not how to leave his wife.

Thus, even though we remember that in some cases rhetoric found a welcome place in civil matters but was not admitted in theology; even though occasionally the Psalter was considered sufficient to train a monk for his career;[50] and even though at times there was legislation within the religious orders against recourse to the profane arts, yet rhetoric clearly had an accepted place in theology and preaching. To be sure, the art did not in the Middle Ages attain to the full flower of its

[50] Felder, p. 382.

great days in classical civilization, when there existed a free environment for deliberative oratory. When scholars pass this judgment,[51] they cannot be gainsaid. Yet it is equally true that rhetoric in the mediaeval period flourished far more than is generally believed. It is incorrect to say, as Gröber does, that the Middle Ages were averse to it,[52] or to say, as Specht does,[53] that the art of speaking well could not concern a clerk or monk because his interest did not rest in this world.

What distrust there was for rhetoric was distrust for embellished style, because rhetoric was an art of adornment. "*Ornatu florum sermonem reddo decorum,*" speaks Rhetoric in a mediaeval chart of the liberal arts.[54] Elegance is neither necessary nor fitting for truth; elegance is reserved for *dictamen.* Alain opposes scurrilous and puerile words, and rejects rhythmic melodies and metric consonances, because they soothe the ear rather than inform the mind; he would steer a middle course between purple trappings and bloodless words.[55] "Albertus" has no faith in the sublimity of words, nor in the learned words of human science, as so much meretricious adornment, but desires verbal simplicity.[56] The preacher's discourse should be neither scorned for rusticity nor suspected for a counterfeit grace and beauty. Humbert emphasizes content; to seek adornment is to prefer the beauty of the salver in which food is carried rather than the food itself.[57] The Franciscan *Ars Concionandi:* "Use ordinary words; do not coin words, or you will be ridiculous." William of Auvergne: "The more simple and unadorned a sermon is, the more it moves and

---

[51] E.g., Paetow, chap. III.
[52] M. G. Gröber, *Grundriss der romanischen Philologie* (Strassburg, 1902), p. 252.
[53] P. 115.
[54] Cod. Lat. Monac. 2689 (*saec.* xiv), fol. 173ᵛ.
[55] Migne, *Pat. Lat.,* CCX, 112.
[56] See Stapper, *art. cit.*
[57] *Max. Bibl. Vet. Pat.,* XXV, 432.

edifies."[58] Even Surgant, writing in 1502: "Divine Rhetoric has no need for polished language."[59]

What is noteworthy in these judgments is the rhetorical nature of the critique. Style was indeed studied, even *clausulae* were not neglected, and special tracts on rhetorical colors for use in sermons were common; but, as in classical theory, λέξις did not have equal importance with εὕρεσις. Style was subordinate to content.

Now what influence of the ancient rhetoric do we find acknowledged in these tractates? The Albertus-tract uses Isidore's rhetoric. The Franciscan author of the *Ars Concionandi* uses St. Augustine and Cicero, adopting their rhetorical aims —*docere, delectare, flectere*—and finding that divisions, through *proprietas*, fulfilled the purpose *docere*, that distinctions through *lenitas* served the aim *delectare*, and expansions through *utilitas* achieved the end *flectere*. He thus sets the thematic form of preaching, the unique contribution of mediaeval theory, squarely upon the basis of classical rhetoric. The Aquinas-tract, using Cicero's name, but really paraphrasing a passage in Aristotle's *Rhetoric*, Book III, insists that it is not enough to have something to say, but it is necessary also to know how to say it. Humbert uses Seneca, Horace, and Cicero, and suggests that pagan history as well as Christian should be read by preachers. Alain, who in the treatment of rhetoric in *Anticlaudianus* cites Cicero, Quintilian, Sidonius, and Symmachus, in the *Summa de Arte Praedicatoria* quotes from Cicero, Plato, Seneca, Lucretius, and Persius; he approves of inserting the sayings of Gentiles. The dependence, then, on ancient authors and classical rhetoric is often highly conscious, and we are not in all cases left to infer the subtle effects of indirect influence.

[58] De Poorter, p. 202.
[59] Ulrich Surgant, *Manuale Curatorum* (completed in 1502; 1st printed ed., Basel, 1503), Book I, *Consideratio* 19.

Indeed, the studies of Cruel, Linsenmayer, and Lecoy de la Marche would lead a reader to believe that in the actual practice of preaching recourse to the classics was more general a habit than even the theories indicate. For one example, Ovid is extensively used for moralization, even though, so far as I now know, the name of Ovid is absent from these *Artes*. The preacher would learn so to use Ovid from consulting the moralities, the tracts on vices and virtues, the collections of *sententiae, exempla,* and the like mediaeval books designed expressly for his aid, themselves rich in classical lore. With these I am not here concerned.

When we look at the pertinent classical works that were available for the formation of a theory of preaching, we find the logical works of Aristotle, which were the strongest basis of scholastic science, and lent themselves to rhetorical application; the *Categories* and *Topics,* directly or indirectly, seem to have contributed most. Add such rhetorical and dialectical works as Cicero's *Topica, De Inventione,* and *De Oratore;* Horace's *Ars Poetica;* the *Rhetorica ad Herennium* (regarded as Cicero's *Rhetorica Nova*), which had a wide influence, as did the *Commentaries* which Boethius wrote on Aristotle's *Categories* and *Topics,*[60] and Boethius' own *De Differentiis Topicis.* Quintilian was perhaps used to a lesser degree.[61] One should note that in these classical works the emphasis is upon invention. And, indeed, I would say that the richest legacy bequeathed to mediaeval rhetoric from the ancient period was the principle

[60] See Grabmann, "Boethius als Vermittler des Aristotelismus an das abendländische Mittelalter," *op. cit.,* I, 149–160.

[61] For a *Fortleben* of Quintilian in this period, see F. H. Colson, *M. Fabii Quintiliani Institutionis Oratoriae Liber I* (Cambridge, 1924), Introduction, pp. xliii–lvi; also Paul Lehmann, "Die *Institutio Oratoria* des Quintilianus im Mittelalter," *Philologus,* LXXXIX (1934), 349–383; A. Mollard, "L'imitation de Quintilien dans Guibert de Nogent," *Moyen Age,* V (1934), 81–87; Priscilla S. Boskoff, "Quintilian in the Late Middle Ages," *Speculum,* XXVII (Jan., 1952), 71–78.

of the inventional use of the *topos* or commonplace, the artistic finding of the right argument communicable to the right audience in the right circumstances. Developed in ancient theory for the three types of secular oratory—judicial, epideictic, and deliberative—it was admirably suited to the scholastic method and to the fourth kind of oratory, preaching. In accordance with classical doctrine the method was used in selecting the text and materials of discussion; further, as the peculiar sermon form demanded, in applying the very weighty principle of amplification; and, finally, in the study of the audience.[62] Neither before nor since has the method been carried out in such a systematic yet varied way.

The topical method operated at once in the enumeration of the proper materials of preaching—usually ten, as with "Aquinas" and "Albertus": God, the devil, the heavenly city, hell, the world, the soul, the body, sin, penitence, and virtue. "Albertus" (William of Auvergne, *De Faciebus*) studies each of these by seven *loci* of disputation. In Part II of his *Ars Praedicandi* William devotes twenty chapters to repertories of ideas which should serve the preacher as themes for artistic development.

The tracts are not all concerned with only one type of preaching; they vary in content, treatment, and, occasionally, point of view. They vary, too, in their definitions. Alain's is often quoted: "Preaching is open and public instruction in faith and morals, devoted to the informing of men, and proceeding along the path of reasoning and from the source of authorities." The Aquinas-tract borrows this and offers also: "Preaching is the fitting and appropriate dispensation of God's word." "Henry of Hesse" supplies the following curious sentence: "The art of preaching is the science which teaches how to say something about something," but proceeds to

---

[62] See "Rhetorical Invention in Some Mediaeval Tractates on Preaching" [pp. 79–92 of this volume].

explain that the subject of the art is the Word of God. And John of Wales provides this: "Preaching consists in invoking God's aid and then suitably, clearly, and devoutly expounding a proposed theme by means of division and concordance; its aim being the catholic enlightenment of the intellect and the enkindling, with grace, of emotion."[63] Guibert's treatise is an inner psychological study of the preacher rather than a technical manual. The author of the "Henry"-tract knows four kinds of preaching: the *postillatio* (by mystic interpretation of the terms of a text), the modern method (thematic), the *antiquus* (homily), the *subalternus* (a mixture of homily and modern). "Albertus" discusses three: the *tractatus* (homily), preaching through syllogisms and distinctions (equivalent to the modern and thematic), and preaching through poetic fictions. John of Wales treats four variations of the type developed by concordances. The author of the Aquinas-tract knows three kinds: the *antiquus* (called also the lay, or beautiful and popular); the smooth and simple, a variation of the thematic, with divisions but without distinctions; and the modern or thematic. And St. Antoninus offers seven methods of procedure.

Despite the outstanding opposition of such tracts as Humbert's, the thematic, in its varied forms and modifications, was the most popular method. It comprised a theme from Holy Writ; a protheme,[64] also from the Bible, which should lead to

---

[63] Mazarine MS 569, fol. 81va, or Basel A VIII. 1. fol. 148[r]. Florenz Landmann, *Das Predigtwesen in Westfalen* (Münster in Westphalia, 1900), p. 122, n. 1, gives this as also Thomas von Cleve's definition, Münster Paulin. MS 476, fol. 139. On p. 121, n. 8, he recognizes the close resemblance of the tract going under the name of Thomas von Cleve (*saec.* xv) and the anonymous treatise represented by *Gesamtkatalog*, Nos. 2669, 2670. This last is really a version of the thirteenth-century treatise now attached to the name of John of Wales (cf. n. 26). A study of Paulin. 476.139–155 would be desirable.

[64] See Etienne Gilson, "Michel Menot et la technique du sermon médiéval," *Revue d'histoire franciscaine*, II (July, 1925), 301 ff. This paper provides an excellent treatment of sermon-method.

a prayer invoking God's aid, and yet recall the theme; and divisions and subdivisions of the theme, by means of authoritative passages, from the Bible, the Church Fathers, and the philosophers, arranged largely in an artistic syllogistic order. This scheme was of course not inherited from classical rhetoric, which could not have had such special needs in view. The Middle Ages are to be credited with inventing it. But the contribution of the principles of Aristotelian logic is evident in its form, so that a title of a tract may, like Jean de Châlons', read *De Modo Praedicandi et Syllogizandi*,[65] and preaching be defined as an "exposition of Holy Writ by division and subdivision." Were the modern student, fortified by a knowledge of Aristotle's *Rhetoric*, to contend that the rhetorical enthymeme, not the syllogism, is proper to the art of rhetoric, the mediaeval preacher would perhaps reply that sacred eloquence differs from secular in that its subject matter lies not in the realm of opinion and probability, but in truth and divine science; that it is as sound a procedure to use a dialectical method in the demonstration of truth as in the investigation of it; and, further, that in Aristotle and Cicero and Quintilian he had precedents for the policy of adapting to rhetorical purposes the methods of the allied art of dialectic. Petrus Cantor (*saec.* xii) makes clear this relationship of dialectic and rhetoric, so peculiar to scholasticism, in his idea of the edifice of the spirit. This is formed of *lectio*, the foundation, and *disputatio*, the wall, supporting *praedicatio*, the roof, which protects the faithful from the surge and whirl of vices.[66]

In these tracts the part played by what one might term "purer" rhetoric was in the means of division and subdivision,

[65] Cod. Lat. Monac. 17290 (*saec.* xiv–xv), fols. 136–146 ("ars . . . faciendi sermones secundum artem (formam) syllogisticam"); also Bibl. Nat. 173 (*saec.* xiv), fols. 12–24ᵛ; Cod. Lat. Monac. 14580 (*saec.* xv), fols. 152 ff.; Vat. Ottob. 396 (*saec.* xv), fols. 14–29; Angers 324 (*saec.* xv), fols. 128 ff.

[66] *Verbum Abbreviatum*, chap. 1, Migne, *Pat. Lat.* XXV, 25.

namely, amplification, as a principle of both invention and disposition.

In examining a number of *artes* I note the following topics of expansion:[67] (1) Concordance of authorities, Biblical, patristic, philosophic. (2) Questioning and discussion of words and terms, often with division—*Dominus illuminatio mea et salus.* Ask, why *dominus*, why *illuminatio*, why *mea?* (3) Discussion of the properties of things. Psalms 44:8: "God hath anointed thee with the oil of gladness." Oil betokens grace, for it has a sanative virtue. (4) Analogies and natural truths. You love your parents. Your parents come from God. Therefore you must love God. (5) Ratiocination and argument. This might be from simile, example, the topic of the greater and less, or from opposites, often with confirmation, refutation, and conclusion. In the later period argument could be presented by any of the following means: *syllogizando, inducendo, exemplificando,* or *enthymematizando.* In the favorite argument from opposites, vices might be set against virtues. St. Antoninus offers also an epideictic method of expansion, the praise or blame of the matter in hand. (6) Comparison, a play upon adjectives or verbs. A play on the topic of the greater and less: Judas' sin was great in that he was greedy; it was greater in that he betrayed his master; it was greatest in that he despaired of God's mercy. Or, following Richard of Thetford, the preacher could ring the changes upon *qu(a)eritur,* **re***quiritur,* **ex***quiritur,* **in***quiritur.*[68] (7) Similitudes. Among the mediaeval books which "Henry of Hesse" advises for supplementary use by the preacher is the *Book of Similitudes,* the *Summa de Exemplis*

---

[67] There are several tracts outlining eight methods—the favorite number. "Henry of Hesse," on the other hand, offers only three: division, question, and digression. This list is rather a composite (superficial, I am aware) of topics of *dilatatio* that are not necessarily distinct and separate, but obviously overlap.

[68] Paris, Bibl. Nat., Nouv. Acq. Lat. 280 (*saec.* xiii–xiv), fol. 1; *Inc.:* "Octo modis potest aliquis habundare in themate."

et Rerum Similitudinibus Libris Decem Constans (*c.* 1300) of Joannes Gorinus of San Gimignano, which supplies the preacher with every kind of material for moralistic comparison. (8) Explication by hidden terminology. Here perhaps may be found the source of the practice still operative today, of orating by the interpretation of initials—to which, no doubt, we must ascribe the high success of an alumni secretary who pleads with all elements that make up the university to hold FAST: *F*, the faculty; *A*, the alumni; *S*, the students; and *T*, the trustees! (9) Multiplication of synonyms. "Ah, man's woes! He is oppressed by cares, surrounded by worries, vexed by adversity, and choked by perils." (10) Any or all of the dialectical topics like species and genera, whole and parts, and the categories: *quid, de quo, quare, quale, quantum, quando, ubi.* (11) Explication of scriptural metaphors. (12) Cause and effect, in the moral realm. (13) Anecdotes. The place of *exempla* in these tracts is yet to be investigated. (14) Observation of the end or purpose of a thing. (15) Setting forth the essential weight of a word. Sermons devoted to the mere word *et* were not unknown. (16) Interpretation of Hebrew names. (17) Etymology. Since *mulier = molliens herum* (William of Auvergne), one may see how unlimited was the service of this science to tropology. Yet of such fancies was born the beautiful legend of Veronica[69] —not Berenice (φερενίκη), victory bearer, but Vera Icon, true image. (18) Parts of speech. (19) Rhetorical colors, as with Surgant,[70] at the end of this period (1502). (20) The use of the four senses of scriptural interpretation—historical or literal, allegorical, tropological—which is especially important in preaching because it looks to the correction of morals—and anagogical, which is explication from the point of view of

[69] Dante, *Paradiso* XXXI. 104 and *Vita Nuova* XLI. 2–5. [For etymologies in Alanus' commentary on the *Rhetorica ad Herennium*, see pp. 257–258 below.]
[70] See n. 59 above; cf. Roth, p. 173 ff.

heavenly things. A great proportion of the anonymous tracts, and also Bromyard, Guibert, the Aquinas- and Henry-tracts, and the *Ars Concionandi* employ these senses as a means of prolonging a sermon in developing a theme; I have elsewhere discussed the history and popularity of the "four senses."[71] The method is perhaps not quite lost to us even today,[72] and apparently was still popular in England well into the eighteenth century. I here offer what I fear is an unworthy illustration, from an account[73] of a sermon allegedly delivered by the notorious Dr. Dodd of Samuel Johnson's day, which I coalesce with a seventeenth-century version, somewhat different, in a letter of Sir John Suckling.[74] It will be noticed that this sermon illustrates also explication by hidden terminology, and, at the end, the principle of multiplying synonyms:

Certain drunken students of Cambridge, returning from a merry meeting at a country alehouse, by the way overtook Dr. Dodd, who in a sermon he had lately made on temperance, among other reproofs, as the sweet-sugared fellows constructed it, had termed them "malt-worms." Wherefore they by violence took him and compelled him to preach a sermon upon the theme "Malt." The reverend gentleman commenced: "Let me crave your attention, my beloved. I am a little man, come at a short warning, to preach a short sermon, upon a short subject, to a thin congregation, in an unworthy pulpit. Beloved! My text is 'Malt.' There is no teaching without a division. I cannot divide my text into syllables, it being

[71] See "The Four Senses of Scriptural Interpretation" [pp. 93–104 of this volume]. Since that paper was written, it has become abundantly clear that the principle of the use of these senses was extremely popular in the tracts on preaching. A very interesting treatise, *Compendium de Sensibus Sacrae Scripturae*, by Hermann von Schilditz, O. S. A. (*saec.* xiv) appears in MS A VII. 45, fols. 133–147, of the Universitätsbibliothek at Basel.

[72] The Jesuit Polcari, as late as 1859, gives careful attention to the four senses in his influential *Universae Eloquentiae Institutiones* (Naples), pp. 245 ff.

[73] A. C. Bombaugh, *Gleanings for the Curious from the Harvest Fields of Literature* (Philadelphia, 1876).

[74] *A Book of Seventeenth-Century Prose*, ed. R. P. R. Coffin and A. M. Witherspoon (New York, 1929), pp. 456–457, from Bodl., Ashm. MS 826, fol. 102ᵛ.

but a monosyllable. Therefore I must divide it into letters, which I find in my text to be four: *M-A-L-T*. *M*, my beloved, is moral; *A* is allegorical; *L* is literal; *T* is theological.

"First, the moral teaches such as you drunkards good manners; wherefore *M*, my masters, *A*, all of you, *L*, listen, *T*, to the theme; and therefore, *M*, my masters, *A*, all of you, *L*, leave off, *T*, tippling.

"Secondly, the allegorical is when one thing is spoken, and another meant. The thing here spoken is malt, the thing meant the oil of malt, which you rustics make *M*, your masters, *A*, your apparel, *L*, your liberty, *T*, your treasure.

"Thirdly, the literal sense hath ever been found suitable to the theme, confirmed by beggarly experience: *MA*, much ale, *LT*, little thought.

"Fourthly, the theological is according to the effects it works, which are of two kinds: the first in this world, the second in the world to come. The effects it works in this world are *M*, murder, *A*, adultery, *L*, looseness of life, and *T*, treason. In the world to come the effects of it are *M*, misery, *A*, anguish, *L*, lamentation, *T*, torment. And thus much for my text, 'Malt.'

"A word of caution, take this: A drunkard is the annoyance of modesty, the spoiler of civility, the destroyer of reason, the brewer's agent, the ale-wife's benefactor, his wife's sorrow, his children's trouble, his neighbor's scoff, a walking swill-tub, a picture of a beast, a monster of a man. But I much fear that I lose my labor, my theme showing that it is *M* to *A*, a thousand pounds to a pot of ale, that one knave of *L*, fifty, will ever leave to love potting."

By this time the ale and his persuasion had so wrought as they fell asleep, and the preacher closely crept away.[75]

The *doctrina localis* is employed throughout in *dilatatio*. To the author of the *Ars Concionandi* it is a *clavis* method, a "Key to the Scriptures," for it opens and closes the sense of a scriptural passage.

[75] The story of a sermon recently delivered at Yale University is doubtless apocryphal. A student, deeply affected by an hour's varied exposition, in this style, of the true meaning of the monosyllable *Y-A-L-E*, is alleged to have piously expressed his thankfulness that he was not attending the Massachusetts Institute of Technology.

It is clear, then, that the sermon was studied from the point of view of *elocutio*, *inventio*, and *dispositio*. The preacher and the hearer were likewise not neglected.

The saying of Gregory, that whose life is despised so is his preaching, is often quoted. The Aquinas-tract recognizes preaching by deed as well as by word. Much attention is paid to the speaker's personality and habits. For example, St. Bonaventure sets down nine desirable qualities. He must be of the right age, not far from thirty; he must not be boyish either in appearance or in habits; he must have no bodily deformities; he must be strong, and of competent eloquence, well trained at least in grammar and Holy Writ, and able to speak without error or confusion; for his persuasive purpose he must be irreproachable in life and habits, industrious, prudent, and not contentious.[76] Evidently these sacred rhetors had a lively consciousness of the power of ethical persuasion.

These divine rhetors give as much thought to *pronuntiatio* as did the Roman authorities. A Berlin manuscript (Theol. Fol. 287 [*saec.* xv], fol. 310) offers, in verse form, the following aids to delivery: regulate your gestures; neither drag along nor run too fast; be very patient; keep the people in order happily; avoid shouting; suppress a cough; refrain from spitting; let your words be clear, not harsh, and never vile. The Henry-tract suggests a *vox acuta* in exposition, a *vox austera* in correction, a *vox benevola* in exhortation. The Aquinas-treatise sets forth specific gestures to express the emotions appropriate to different Biblical verses: admiration, horror and excitement, irony and derision, elation, weariness and indignation, joy and hate. *Venite ad me omnes* must be uttered with gracious countenance and holding up of the hands. And the preacher should imitate the gestures he thinks Christ used in a given case. William's *Rhetorica Divina* (chap. xxv) considers even the

[76] *Opusc.*, XIII, 360 b ff.

gestures of prayer and the part played in prayer by such *adjutoria* as blushing, weeping, groaning, and sighing. Among the preacher's vices listed in the Henry- and Aquinas-tracts are ignorance, lack of facility, excessive pointing of the fingers, tossing of the head, closing of the eyes, too much noisiness, remote digression.[77] The Aquinas-treatise also sets forth precautions: proper reverence, the clear and intelligible enunciation of every syllable; the avoidance of tedium and laughter by avoiding repetition or a deviation from the original plan of the sermon; an adequate summary to aid the hearer's memory; the comporting of one's self as if in Christ's presence; watching the hour and shunning prolixity, lest the people do not return.

The soundness of rhetorical judgment in these precepts arises from the close study that the theorists made of their audiences. But for the profound treatment of the emotions in Aristotle's *Rhetoric*, I would say that the classical rhetoricians never so thoroughly analyzed affections as the mediaeval theorists did the vices and virtues. Numberless tracts on this subject were purposely designed for the preacher's aid. Humbert has one hundred chapters on different audiences (*ad varios status*) with topical hints as to what they should be told—scholars, nobles, paupers, boys, harlots. St. Bonaventure studies the commonplace vices of certain audiences: if you address merchants, you must discuss fraud and mendacity; if soldiers, rapine and arson.[78] With audience in mind, he protests against involved sentences, and demands easy words within the capacity of the hearers to understand.[79] Jacques de

---

[77] Surgant (Book I, *Consideratio* 23) adds: voluntary baring of the teeth, uncontrolled features, indecent gestures, sleepy delivery, excessive briskness or speed. Petrus Cantor (*Verb. Abbrev.*, chap. 1): "Excessive speed is the mother of oblivion and the stepmother of memory."

[78] *Opusc.*, XIII, 359 b.

[79] *Ibid.*, XVI.

Vitry had 120 categories of hearers.[80] The *Ecclesiastica Rhetorica* reminds the speaker that there are seven primary emotions: fear, pain, sadness, shame, indignation, wrath, and hate of sin. Even the psychology of communication between speaker and audience is nicely imaged forth by "Albertus'" figure of preaching as a *desponsatio* or *matrimonium* of gospel truth; the bride is decked out with simple diction, and the witnesses to the alliance are arguments, examples, and parables.[81] But long before our period Gregory in his *Pastoral Rule* (Part III, Prologue) had asked the preacher to remember, when weighing the condition of his hearers, that some herbs nourish some animals and kill others, that a soft whisper quiets a horse but excites a puppy, that bread which gives the strong their strength afflicts children, and that in the ideal state the hearer's attention resembles the tense strings of the cithara. The sick, the simple, the rich, the sad—all kinds of people and all affections were examined by these preachers, and a therapeutic by opposites was artistically employed. They followed the rule: *sermo coaptandus qualitati auditorum*,[82] and therein they well followed ancient precept. ἦθος, πίστις, and also πάθος—all were studied in this "art of arts, and science of the sciences."[83]

The theory of thematic preaching had its critics. Humbert considers vicious the current multiplication of distinctions and authorities.[84] Gerson (*saec.* xiv–xv) calls the preachers of his day "sophists" because they use naught but crude logic, devoid of verbal adornment.[85] Obviously to him they were

[80] See the *Prooemium* to his *Sermones* (Antwerp, 1575).

[81] See Stapper, *art. cit.*

[82] E.g., so suggests the Franciscan author of the *Ars Concionandi*. See n. 20 above.

[83] So called in Aquinas-tract [p. 54 above]; cf. Gregory, *Pastoral Rule*, Part I, i.

[84] Chap. 6.

[85] *Lectio 2 super Marcum, op. cit.*, IV, 217.

incomplete artists, and insufficient rhetoricians. Roger Bacon's (*saec.* xiii) opposition also rests on rhetorical grounds: in the divisions, consonances, and verbal concordances, he finds neither sublimity nor great wisdom, but an infinite childish dullness and a cheapening of God's word; "of which ostentatiousness may God himself rid his Church; . . . it is perverse vanity lacking every rhetorical ornamentation and persuasive virtue."[86] Bacon desired beauty, emotion, and the study of such works as Seneca *On Wrath;* this he recommended as a thesaurus for special persuasive topics. Joly, eighteenth-century historian of preaching, consistent with the spirit of his times, savagely attacks the bizarre and ridiculous taste of these scholastics, their false subtleties, the tissue of texts, the exaggerated allegories, the excessive divisions and minute reasonings, and the insipid monotony of thoughts.[87] But while acknowledging the pedantry and concentrated formalism, we can find much to praise in the methodical ordering of the thematic sermon (the *arbor picta* is a favorite suffix to these tracts);[88] we can find much to laud, too, in the inventional scheme, and in the dexterity and practical variety of treatment, and can appreciate that the theory served its day well.

The influence of classical rhetoric on mediaeval preaching was therefore definite and considerable. Furthermore, from the nature of the preacher's education, from the wide interest in rhetoric in this period, from the persistence of the rhetorical tradition, and from the quality of some elements that we have considered in the mediaeval theory, I regard it as legitimate to assume an even greater contact and influence than one finds expressed or recognized. This is a safe assumption, even when

[86] *Opus Tert.*, chap. LXXV.

[87] J. M. E. Joly, *Histoire de la prédication* (Amsterdam, 1767), p. 201.

[88] Such an *arbor* appears at the end of the Aquinas-tract in some editions. [See pp. 76 and 78 of this volume.]

one allows for the possibility that need and experience often create the development of a practice which is not always to be identified with conscious art, nor is to be referred to rules derived from an alien source. But the Middle Ages never achieved that complete synthesis of homiletics and classical rhetoric that we begin to find in the Renaissance. It is only in that period and later that manuscripts appear in which the classical authors are fully searched and carefully excerpted for the specific use of preachers.[89] Then, as in Chytraeus' *Praecepta Rhetorica*,[90] Cicero, Pericles, and Demosthenes are studied together with St. Basil and St. Paul. Then appear such descriptions as Reuchlin's in his *Liber Congestorum de Arte Praedicandi* (1503):[91] a preacher is a *vir religiosus dicendi peritus*, which converts the elder Cato's famous definition of the orator as a *vir bonus dicendi peritus;* and the matter of preaching is everything offering itself to make us daily better, on which the preacher knows how to speak well. Then appears the rhetorically scientific division of the kinds of preaching into the didactic, epitreptic (devoted to inducing belief), and paraenetic (directed to persuading men to a course of conduct), which Melanchthon devised in a system of sacred rhetoric firmly based on classical rules.[92] It is much later when, in *Polyhistor*,[93] Morhof, a severe critic of what he terms the barbarous preaching of the scholastic period, insists that there is no distinction between civil and sacred oratory except in subject matter; that the precepts and method are the same in both, and all

[89] Cf. Cod. Lat. Monac. 18635, fols. 67–123 (*saec.* xv–xvi): "Tractatus de rhetorica ex Tullio, Quintiliano, aliis excerptus in usum praedicatorum."

[90] Ed. Leipzig, 1562.

[91] In *De Arte Concionandi Formulae* . . . *Ioanne Reuclino, anonymo quodam rhapsodo, Philippo Melancthone, D. Ioanne Hepino autoribus* (London, 1570), fols. 2–19ᵛ.

[92] *De Officiis Concionatoris*, in *De Arte Concionandi Formulae*, fols. 54–61.

[93] *De Rhetoribus atque Oratoribus Sacris*, in *Polyhistor* VI, 4 (Lübeck, 1747), I, 983–1000.

inspiration is to be drawn from Aristotle. But, although the greatest of all oratorical theories, Aristotle's *Rhetoric*, was known in translation in the thirteenth century, mediaeval preaching had no demonstrable first-hand contact with it. The first direct quotation from this book that I have thus far found in any of these *artes* is in Surgant (1502),[94] and it is more than a century later when Peacham in the *Compleat Gentleman* (1622)[95] refers offhand to the reputation enjoyed by Aristotle's *Rhetoric* as a book sufficient to make both a scholar and an honest man. So far as I know, it is only in modern times that to the three classical types of oratory, forensic, deliberative, and epideictic, the sacred has been added as a fourth,[96] thus gaining a rightful place among its fellows within the rhetorical art. And indeed, only quite recently has been developed the systematic classification of the *ars praedicandi* itself into its genera, the *concio*, the *laudatio*, the *homilia*, the *enarratio sacrarum litterarum*, and the *oratio funebris*, as by the Jesuit Polcari.[97] The preaching of the Renaissance and modern times drank more deeply, yet mediaeval theory also tasted more than superficially at the fount of classical rhetoric.

[94] Book I, *Consideratio* 6.
[95] Ed. G. S. Gordon (Oxford, 1906), p. 45.
[96] E.g., D. Ferrari, *L'arte di dire* (Milan, 1907).
[97] Pp. 217 and 239 ff.

VII

"Henry of Hesse" on the Art of Preaching[*]

IN THE present state of our knowledge it is best to assign the *Tractatulus Eximii Doctoris Henrici de Hassia de Arte Praedicandi* to an *auctor incertus*. The name Henry of Hesse[1] was borne by two scholars in the fourteenth century; but we have no proof that this is the work of either. They were both professors of theology, both brilliant preachers, and practically contemporary; and the works of one have in the past often been attributed to the other.

The better-known Henry, of Langenstein (near Marburg), called Henry of Hesse the elder[2] (1325–1397), studied and later taught philosophy at the Sorbonne, where he was made Vice-Chancellor. In the Schism he supported Urban VI; after Clement's victory he returned to Germany (1383), and became

[*] Reprinted from *PMLA*, XLVIII (1933), 340–361.

[1] In the eighteenth century it was thought that there had been five different Henrys of Hesse, four of the fourteenth century. Cf. Casimir Oudin, *Commentarius de Scriptoribus Ecclesiasticis* (Leipzig, 1722), III, 1256 ff. And the problem was further complicated by the confusion of these with Henry of Oyta, Henry of Frimaria, and Jean Gerson, whose writings have been assigned now to one, now to another.

[2] See Joseph Aschbach, *Geschichte der Wiener Universität* (Vienna, 1865), pp. 366–402; B. Bess, art. "Heinrich von Langenstein" in *Realencyclopädie für protestantische Theologie und Kirche;* H. Hurter, *Nomenclator Literarius Theologiae Catholicae* (Innsbruck, 1906), II, 690 ff.; R. Cruel, *Geschichte der deutschen Predigt* (Detmold, 1879), pp. 575–576; Anton Linsenmayer, *Geschichte der Predigt in Deutschland* (Munich, 1886), p. 461; Otto Hartwig, *Untersuchungen über die Schriften Heinrichs von Langenstein* (Marburg, 1857).

Professor of Theology, Dean of the Theological Faculty, and finally Rector, at the University of Vienna. There he taught dogmatic theology, exegesis, and canon law; but he is known also as an astronomer and mathematician, and as an opponent of astrological superstition and of corruption in the church. Indeed, the list of subjects treated in the works regarded as genuinely his shows a wide diversity—astronomical, historical-political, theological-polemical, exegetical, dogmatic, medical; and, besides works on these subjects, there are his sermons, letters, and prophecies. The younger Henry of Hesse[3] (died in 1427) was also a student at Paris, and later became Dean of the Philosophical Faculty in the new University of Heidelberg, where he taught Aristotelian dialectic ánd Biblical exegesis. After 1414 he retired to the Carthusian monastery at Monik-husen (near Arnheim in Geldern). His literary works include Biblical commentaries and several religious tracts. Apparently no one has had enough evidence even to think of assigning the *Tractatulus* to the younger Henry—whose personality and works have, in any case, been but imperfectly known. It has generally been associated with Henry of Langenstein. At present, however, virtually all reputable authorities[4] follow Hartwig[5] in denying Henry of Langenstein's authorship, on the ground that the principles laid down in the tract fail to correspond with the arrangement of the authentic sermons that we have from him.[6] The last treatment of his works, by Roth,[7] does not so much as refer to this tractate on preaching.

"Henry's" tract and the *Tractatulus Solemnis de Arte et Vero*

[3] See especially Hartwig, pp. 1 ff., and Hurter, II, 691, n. 1.

[4] Cruel, p. 597; Linsenmayer, p. 102; Hurter, II, 692 (*"si ipsius est"*).

[5] P. 19.

[6] Aschbach, p. 393. We have *sermones de tempore* and other sermons by Henry of Langenstein; see F. W. E. Roth, "Zur Bibliographie des Henricus Hembuche de Hassia, dictus de Langenstein," in *Beihefte zum Centralblatt für Bibliothekswesen* (Leipzig, 1888), II, 111–113.

[7] Roth, pp. 97–118.

Modo Predicandi,[8] compiled by an unknown Dominican profess-
ing the influence of St. Thomas Aquinas, were among the first
works of this nature to appear in printed form in Germany.
The two are in every respect representative of the mediaeval
theory of homiletics, and especially because they reveal the
variety in the methods of preaching employed in that period.
Yet I may add that a study of many unpublished *artes*, manuscripts of which are to be found in a great number of European
libraries, shows that there was even greater diversity than is
indicated by these two tracts. A curious situation attends four
items listed in Hain's *Repertorium* of incunabula. In Nos. 1352,
1353, 1354, and 1355, the title-page announces that Henry's
manual follows the text of the "Aquinas-tract"; but whereas
the Aquinas-text appears in each, in none is Henry's treatise
actually included. At the Staatsbibliothek in Munich copies
of all four can conveniently be examined; the text of our tract
is contained neither in the exemplars of these items there
found[9] nor in copies I have seen elsewhere.

For constructing my text, therefore, I resorted only to the
separate editions, all issued before 1500. Hain lists three: Nos.
8397, 8398, 8399, all in quarto, and without name of publisher,
or date or place of publication. Of these I have succeeded in
finding, and have collated, copies of the first two only. A copy
in the Bibliothèque Nationale at Paris (Rés. D. 8046) represents No. 8397—for the sake of convenience it is called A in
my notes; and one in the Staatsbibliothek at Munich (4o Inc.
s.a. 981) represents 8398—here called B. Hurter,[10] who may
be using Fabricius[11] as a source of information, refers to an

---

[8] See "A Late Mediaeval Tractate" [pp. 40–78 of this volume]. I shall here-
after for brevity refer to this as the Aquinas-tract, and to the other as Henry's.

[9] In a letter to me, Dr. Georg Leidinger, Director of that library, verified my
observations made in 1929.

[10] II, 696.

[11] J. A. Fabricius, *Bibl. Lat. Med. et Inf. Aet.* (Florence, 1858), II, 203.

extant edition from the press of Johann Gruninger of Strassburg (1483–1528); but he fails to give its date or tell where it
can be found, and I have not found a copy.

I have used only the printed editions because the manuscripts of this tract have not been thoroughly investigated. To
use the *incipit* as the sole criterion for the identification of
manuscripts is of course a method insufficient for definite and
final conclusions; yet this procedure may serve as a preliminary
to an appropriate study. Thus far I have information of the
following manuscripts containing tracts which bear the same
incipit as the present work: Cod. Lat. Monac. 3590 (*a*. 1480),
fols. 93–99 (part of a whole entitled *Ars Contemplandi, Predicandi,
et Memorandi); 5683 (saec.* xv), fols. 255–258ᵛ; 15548 (*a*. 1469),
fols. 280–285 (*cum glossulis Germanicis); 16226 (xv), fols. 206–
221; 19670 (xv), fols. 55ᵛ–58ᵛ; 21708 (xv), fols. 303–307ᵛ (the
Henry-tract together with part, at least, of the Aquinas-tract);
23836 (xv), fols. 118ᵛ–123ᵛ; 24516 (xv), fols. 53–58ᵛ; 24539
(xv), fols. 21–29ᵛ; 24571 (xv), fols. 42–49; Vienna 4121
(*a*. 1472), fols. 137–159ᵛ [Prol. *inc.*: "Artem quivis ut faciliori";
yet cf. Einsiedeln, Benedict. Monast. MS 332 (xv–xvi), fols.
23–50, *Ars Praed.* of Fridericus de Nürx, with prologue bearing
the same *incipit*]; 13707 (xv), fols. 169–171ᵛ; Erlangen Univ.
729, fols. 117–121; 775, fols. 157–160. A cursory examination
of some of the Munich manuscripts here listed showed a
diversity indicating that there are at least two different tracts
among them; and perhaps also, in accord with the mediaeval
fashion, one treatise or more representing merely abstracts
from the Henry- and Aquinas-manuals. Three other manuscripts connected with the name of Henry of Hesse have
come to my attention. Erfurt (Amplon.) MS Qu. 151 (end
saec. xiv), fols. 155–161ᵛ, entitled *Tractatus Hassonis de Modo
Predicandi*[12] (*Inc.*: "Octo sunt modi predicandi"), however

---

[12] Wilhelm Schum, *Beschreibendes Verzeichnis der amplonianischen Handschriften-
Sammlung zu Erfurt* (Berlin, 1887), p. 415.

genuine a work it may be of Henry of Langenstein,[13] is definitely not a manuscript of our present treatise. A second,
Basel MS A. vi 4, listed by Haenel[14] as a tract on preaching
by Henry of Hesse, proves to contain no such work. And I
have not yet been able, by correspondence with the librarian,
to procure fuller information of the third: Skt. Florian,
Stiftsbibliothek MS xi. 113 (xiv), fols. 82–84, *Modus Sermon-
isandi Magistri Hainrici de Hassia cum Prooemiis et Petitionibus
(Germanice et Latine).*

I do not attempt to decide which preceded in time, A
or B, or whether the printer of one had the other before
him. If some such relation is assumed, it seems impossible to
say which represents the revision; or even to judge which is
clearly the better text. As my notes indicate, each has bad
readings and a goodly number of typographical errors, and
some of these are common to both.

In my text I have not preserved the abbreviations and suspensions of the original editions. The spelling is not consistent
in either A or B, and in many places the spelling in one does
not correspond with that in the other. I have therefore
adopted the better spelling of a word where at least one
edition justified it, and have otherwise not departed from the
originals.[15] The texts also differ at some passages in punctuation, for instance, in using or omitting parentheses. In such

---

[13] Roth lists this (No. 47), without elaboration, among the authentic religious
tracts of Henry of Langenstein.
[14] Gustav Haenel, *Catalogi Librorum Manuscriptorum* (Leipzig, 1830), col. 625.
The correction of Haenel's error was kindly supplied me by Professor Gustav
Binz, Chief Librarian of the *Universitätsbibliothek* in Basel. The references to the
Skt. Florian and Erlangen manuscripts I owe to the courtesy of Father Th.-M.
Charland, O.P., of the *Institut d'études médiévales d'Ottawa.*
[15] For example, since both texts in one place read *vicium* [p. 154 below], I
have kept that spelling there, even though they consistently elsewhere in com-
mon spell the word with a *t.*

cases, and generally, I have punctuated solely with the reader's convenience in mind.

It is obvious that Henry often quotes from memory, and gives several wrong references. The Latinity of a bare, sketchy, schematic work of this sort is of course not to be studied as if it were discursive prose of high quality and of a better period. The author is at least almost always clear, although he may use an infinitive of purpose with a verb of motion (*venit audire*), or so unusual a word as *defectuosa*. Because he in several places employs the form of a tabular chart, and the arrangement of items does not clarify their relation to one another, I have, without violence, as I trust, converted such passages into continuous prose.[16]

Henry's tract clearly shows the influence of dialectic. Most of the *Artes Praedicandi* owe as much eventually to Aristotle's logical works as to the doctrines of the art of rhetoric proper. In fact, these tracts represent a union of the sister arts that was typical of late-mediaeval homiletics (1200-1500). To be sure, the Aquinas-tract is obviously richer than Henry's in purely rhetorical principles. To illustrate, the author of that work considers the four senses of interpretation as topics of expansion in a theory of invention. He professes a frankly rhetorical view of his art and has recourse to profane rhetoricians, whereas Henry limits himself in this respect almost to a brief glance at delivery.

These two tracts are properly considered together. They have, as my notes show, some material in common, which may

[16] For example, on the last folio of B one finds the following arrangement of items:

	Ignorantia predicantis	Intollerabile vitium
	Infacundia	Naturale
Vitia	Digitorum demonstratio nimia	
	Capitis iactatio	Moralia
	Oculorum clausura	
Applicatio defectuosa		Artificialia

In A, *Moralia* appears directly under *oculorum clausura*. [See p. 157 below.]

derive from a common source. But there are also significant differences, and notably in the description of sermon-types. Henry's has four methods: (1) the oldest—the homily; (2) the modern or thematic; (3) the old, or textual; (4) the substitute, a combination or modification of (1) and (2). The Aquinas-compiler gives three: (1) the ancient, "lay, or popular and beautiful" type, inorganic in form; (2) the "light and simple," or thematic, corresponding in general to Henry's modern; (3) the modern, or textual. The correspondences between the two systems,[17] although patent, are not exact, there being various differences in detail.

The Aquinas-tract draws upon more sources, and is the richer and fuller treatise. Yet a complete idea of the art of preaching in the Middle Ages can by no means be gained from that alone; the present tract materially contributes to our knowledge. Although, to mention a defect, Henry's absurd etymologies do not commend themselves, the logical organization and compactness of the manual do indeed; the precepts are truly informative, and as a work on preaching the tract may be profitably consulted by all who wish to understand the artistic method of this important branch of eloquence.

The Aquinas-tract is Dominican in authorship and doctrine. Note how Henry also depends mainly on Dominican scholarship in the books he suggests for supplementary reference. The "moralities"[18] among these were obviously very valuable as learned aids to preachers in this period; they must have served especially well in the tropological, or moral, method of

---

[17] See Cruel, pp. 596 ff. Other theorists offer a diverse number of methods. For example, Surgant gives five in his *Manuale Curatorum;* William of Auvergne, in his *De Faciebus,* three; John of Wales, in his *De Arte Praedicandi,* four; and St. Antoninus, in the *Summa Moralis,* seven. See "Classical Rhetoric and the Mediaeval Theory of Preaching" [pp. 122 ff. of this volume].

[18] For the Aids to preaching see the valuable treatments by Cruel, pp. 451–468, and Linsenmayer, pp. 168–184.

instruction and persuasion. That all four senses of explication were important is quite evident—the theory of the whole tract is based on their use in a manner precisely consistent with that general in such *artes*.[19] Thus Henry even cites the traditional exemplars of the four senses of interpretation: Jerome, Augustine, Basil, and Gregory.

The treatise had a demonstrable influence. Many principles are drawn from it, and a direct reference is made to it, in Ulrich Surgant's authoritative and influential Art of Preaching, the *Manuale Curatorum*,[20] which is as much a summary of mediaeval homiletical method as a representative text of the Renaissance.

[The *Tractatulus* follows.]

---

[19] See "The Four Senses of Scriptural Interpretation" [pp. 93–104 of this volume].

[20] Book I, *Consideratio* 10, fols. 16ʳ–18ʳ, ed. Basel, 1507–8, on the conditions [see p. 147 below] which a theme should fulfil.

"*Henry of Hesse*"

TRACTATULUS EXIMII DOCTORIS HENRICI DE HASSIA DE ARTE PRAEDICANDI VALDE UTILIS

Tractatulus Eximii Doctoris Henrici de Hassia De Arte Predicandi feliciter incipit.

Ars predicandi est scientia docens de aliquo aliquid dicere. Subiectum artis illius est verbum Dei.

[1] Fundamentum primum: Gloriosus Hieronimus Bibliam de Greco in Latinum transtulit.

Quatuor sunt figure generales, que ideo dicuntur generales, quia omni parti sermonis conveniunt.

Prima dicitur hystoria et est simplex litteralis sensus interpretatio, ut cum Evangelium vulgarisatur. Et dicitur hystoria ab hysteron Grece, quod est[a] gesticulatio Latine, quasi geste rei narratio, unde gestum, id est, factum.

---

[a] est *om.* B.

A SHORT AND VERY USEFUL TRACT ON THE ART OF PREACHING BY THE *DOCTOR EXIMIUS*, HENRY OF HESSE

A Short Tract on the Art of Preaching, by the Distinguished Doctor, Henry of Hesse, here auspiciously begins.

The Art of Preaching is the science which teaches how to say something about something.[21] The subject of this art is the Word of God.

[1] Primary basis: The glorious Jerome translated the Bible from Greek into Latin.

The general figures are four—they are called "general" because they are suited to every part of the sermon:

The first is called *historia*, and is the simple interpretation of the literal sense, as when the Gospel is rendered in the vernacular. It is called *historia* from the Greek *hysteron*, which in Latin is *gesticulatio*, being the narration of a *res gesta* [an exploit], as it were—whence *gestum*, that is *factum* [a thing done.][22]

[21] Cf. Aquinas-tract [pp. 54–56 above].
[22] This fanciful etymology I have not found elsewhere.

[2] Gregorius moraliter.

Secunda dicitur tropologia et est sensus hystorie ad:
[a] partem hominum spiritualium; [b] hominem solum nobilium; [c] corpus hominis vulgarium; [d] animam hominis; [e] virtutes; [f] mores et vitia.
Regula generalis: Omne quod respicit[b] hominem secundum substantiam seu accidens expositione mistica spirituali comprehenditur sub tropologia.
Exemplum tropologie: David regnavit in Hierusalem, id est, Christus. Beata Virgo est mater adoptiva. Et dicitur tropologia a tropos, quod est mos, et logos, sermo, quasi sermo moralis.

[3] Ambrosius habuit curam de ecclesia.

Tercia allegoria dicitur et est sensus hystorici ad [a] Christum, [b] beatam Virginem, [c] ecclesiam militantem expositio. Regula generalis: Omne quod respicit fidem quocumque modo expositione mistica comprehenditur sub[c] allegoria.
Exemplum allegorie:[d] David regnavit in Hierusalem, id est, Christus in ecclesia militante. Dicitur autem allegoria ab alleos, quod est alienum, et gogos, ductio, quasi ad alienum ductio[e].

[4] Augustinus, quia altius scripsit aliis tribus doctoribus.

---

[b] recipit A.	[d] allegorice A.
[c] sua AB.	[e] alienum sensum ductio B.

---

[2] Gregory [interpreted Scripture] from the moral point of view.

The second figure is called *tropologia*, and is the exposition of the historical sense with reference to: [a] the realm of spiritual men; [b] man, the only noble creature; [c] the general body of mankind; [d] the soul of man; [e] the virtues; [f] morals, and the vices.
General rule: Everything that regards man according to substance or attribute by a mystical, spiritual, exposition is comprehended under tropology.
Example of tropology: David ruled in Jerusalem.[23] That is, Christ rules in Jerusalem. The Blessed Virgin is the adoptive mother. Tropology gets its name from *tropos*, character, and *logos*, discourse—an ethical discourse, so to speak.

[3] The object of Ambrose's care was the Church.

The third figure is called "allegory" and is the exposition of the historical sense applied to: [a] Christ; [b] The Blessed Virgin; [c] The Church Militant.
General rule: Everything that regards faith in some way through a mystical interpretation is comprehended under *allegoria*.
Example of allegory: David ruled in Jerusalem. That is, Christ rules in the Church Militant. Allegory derives its name from *alleos*, different, and *gogos*,[24] guidance—a guidance to something different, as it were.

[4] [The exemplar is] Augustine, because he wrote with greater profundity than did the other three doctors [above-mentioned].

[23] Vulg. II Kings 5:3 and 5; III Kings 2:11.
[24] = ἄλλα and ἀγορεύω; Isidore, *Etym.* 1. 22: *Allegoria est alieniloquium.*

Quarta dicitur anagogia, et est sensus hystorici mistica[f] ad [a] Deum, [b] ecclesiam triumphantem, [c] dyabolum, [d] infernum expositio. Partes orationis sunt duplices, videlicet: essentiales, accidentales.

Regula generalis: Omne quod respicit[g] futuram patriam expositione mistica comprehenditur sub anagogia.

Exemplum anagogie: David regnavit in Hierusalem, id est, Deus in regno celesti. Dicitur autem anagogia uno modo ab ana, quod est sursum, et gogos, ductio, quasi sursum ductio; alio modo ab ana, quod[h] est sursum, per contrarium, quia deorsum, et gogos, ductio, quasi deorsum ductio.

Nota: hoc complexum (sensus misticus) habet se ad ultimas tres figuras, ut genus respectu suarum specierum.

Cautela: Sacra scriptura, sicut Biblia, vel reducibile sicut hystorie seculares, ad cautelam[i] non in omni termino predicabili semper simul et semel debet recipere omnes tres ultimas figuras, sed quandoque unam tantum, aliquando duas, aliquotiens tres, etc.

Ratio: In celo non nisi bonum, in inferno non nisi malum, in terra reperitur utrumque, etc.

Quadruplex est modus predicandi: antiquissimus, et eo usus fuit Christus et multi sancti doctores post eum; modernus; antiquus, qui fuit post Christum et sanctos doctores, et ante modernos; subalternus, et est aggregatus ex omnibus illis predictis.

---

[f] misticus AB.   [g] recipit A.   [h] qund A.   [i] caudem B.

The fourth figure is called *anagogia*, and is the mystic exposition of the historical sense applied to: [a] God; [b] the Church Triumphant; [c] the devil; [d] hell. The parts of the discourse are twofold: essential and accessory.

General rule: Everything that regards the Future Fatherland through a mystic interpretation is comprehended under anagogy.

Example of anagogy: David ruled in Jerusalem. That is, God rules in the Heavenly Kingdom. Further, *anagogia* in one way takes its name from *ana*, upwards, and *gogos*, guidance—as though a guidance upwards; in another, from *ana*, upwards, *per contrarium*, wherefore downwards, and *gogos*, guidance—a guidance downwards, as it were.

Note: this complex (the mystic sense) is comprised of three ultimate figures, as a genus with respect to its species.

Precaution: Holy Writ, as, for example, the Bible, or a reducible thing, like the secular writings of history, for precaution should not in every predicable term, nor always at the same time, nor once for all, receive all three ultimate figures; but now one, now two, sometimes three, and so forth.

Reasoning: In heaven is naught but good, in hell naught but evil, on earth both are found, and so forth.

The method of preaching is fourfold: (1) The oldest, and this Christ used, as well as many holy doctors after him. (2) The modern. (3) The old, which flourished after Christ and the saintly theologians, and before the modern. (4) The substitute, gathered from all these methods I have mentioned.

Of Eloquence
Modus Antiquissimus

postillatio, et est plurium terminorum alicuius textus ad unum[j] sensum tendentium mistica expositio. Correlarium: postillatio fit sine aliqua divisione. Postillatio—ille terminus componitur originaliter a prepositione post et a pronomine illa; inde postillare, inde et postillatio, et sic de aliis.

Exemplum hystorie: Erat quidam Rhomanorum imperator qui habebat filium unicum cui desponsavit filiam regis Ethiopie; et sic committitur anagogia. Aliud: Exiit qui seminat seminare semen suum; et sic de aliis.

Exemplum postillationis: Imperator est Deus pater. Filius est Christus. Desponsatio est copulatio in fide. Et filia regis Ethiopie est humilis anima, dives, id est, plena virtutibus.

Modus Modernus

dicitur modernus quia incidit cum veteri arte et est facilis et subtilis. Partes sermonis essentiales, et sine istis sermo non congrue fieri potest: thema, prothema, divisio, subdivisio.

Duplex est sermo: completus, et fit ex omnibus quatuor predictis; incompletus solum fit ex duobus.

Nota: Due sunt partes sermonis necessarie, scilicet: thema, divisio. Et alie due

---

[j] unum *om.* A.

The Oldest Method

is the postillation, the mystical exposition of most of the terms of a text that aim at a single interpretation. Corollary: Postillation is fashioned without any division. The term "postillation" is originally composed of the preposition *post* and the pronoun *illa*;[25] from these comes to "postillate," and then "postillation," and so with the rest.

Example of *historia*: There was a certain Roman Emperor who had an only son; to him he betrothed the daughter of the King of Ethiopia. Thus is *anagogia* occasioned. Another example: A sower went out to sow his seed;[26] and so with the rest.

An example of postillation: The Emperor is God, the Father; the son is Christ; the betrothal is union in faith; and the daughter of the king of Ethiopia is the humble soul, rich in, or full of, virtues.

The Modern Method

is so-called because it accords with the old art and is easy and precise. The essential parts of a sermon, without which a sermon cannot suitably be formed: (1) the theme; (2) the protheme; (3) the division; (4) the subdivision.

A sermon is twofold: the complete, composed of all four above-mentioned parts; and the incomplete, composed only of two.

Note: A sermon has two necessary parts: theme and division. There are also two

[25] The phrase *post illa (verba textus)* the preacher would use as a formula for beginning his exposition. See Cruel, pp. 123 ff.

[26] Luke 8:5. Note, with respect to the first example of *historia*, the resemblance in style to that of the *Gesta Romanorum* (see pp. 483 and 386 in Hermann Oesterley's edition, Berlin, 1872); but I have not in the *Gesta* found the specific example.

sunt; debent[k] esse scilicet: prothema, subdivisio. Prothema magistralis pars est, subdivisio subtilis.

[A] Thema debet esse: de Biblia sumptum; bene quotatum; quantitatem habens; qualitatem[l] habens; non nimis breve; non nimis longum; sensum habens perfectum; conveniens dici; terminis predicabilibus ornatum. Canon qualitatis: Termini predicabiles in proposito sunt nomina pura, verba, et participia, et per hoc quod dicitur[m] pura, excluduntur syncategoremata,[n] id est, consignificativa[o] secundum dyalecticos, ut omnis, nullus, quidam, aliquis, quilibet, etc. Canon quantitatis: Ad thema maius quatuor termini predicabiles sufficere possunt; ad minus vero duo saltem deducendi.

[B] Secunda pars sermonis, scilicet, ante divisionem: Prothema est prelocutio facta pro approbatione terminorum predicabilium in themate positorum. Compositio prothematis debet esse ex auctoritatibus Biblie atque doctorum cum introductione auctoritatis philosophie, per exemplum in rerum natura declarata. Nota: Quelibet auctoritas Biblie principaliter debet respicere suum terminum predicabilem et ad minus principaliter sensum thematis. Auctoritates vero doctoris et philosophi principalius debent respicere sensum thematis quam aliquem terminum predicabilem seorsum.

Deductio prothematis: Prothema generaliter, id est, absque divisione vel distinctione, debet correspondere sensui thematis, et hoc fit dupliciter, ut infra:

| [k] de bene AB. | [m] dicit AB. | [o] significativa B. |
| [l] qualitetem A. | [n] syncategreuma A. | |

---

others; these should be protheme and subdivision. The protheme is the chief part, and the subdivision is the particular.

The theme should: be taken from the Bible; be well quoted; have quantity; have quality; be not too short; be not too long; have complete meaning; be fit for oral delivery; be adorned with predicable terms.[27] The canon of quality: Predicable terms in the text are pure nouns, verbs, and participles, and because the word "pure" is used, co-predicates, or—according to the dialecticians—consignificatives, are excluded, as *all*, *no*, *a certain*, *some*, *any*, and the rest. The canon of quantity: For a major theme four predicable terms may suffice, but for a minor at least two must be deduced.

The Second Part of the sermon or the ante-division: The protheme is the prelocution designed for the proof of the predicable terms found in the theme. It should be composed of authorities drawn from the Bible and from theologians, together with the introduction of an authority from philosophy, for example, on the demonstrated nature of things.

Note: Any authority from the Bible should primarily recall its predicable term, and secondarily the sense of the theme; but authorities from a theologian or a philosopher should rather recall the sense of the theme than some separate predicable term.

The deducing of the protheme: The protheme should generally, that is, without division or distinction, correspond to the sense of the theme; and this is accomplished in double fashion, as follows:

[27] Cf. Aquinas-tract [p. 57 above].

Of Eloquence

[1] Primo vocaliter, cum quilibet terminorum predicabilium probatur per concordantiam apertam, ut infra patet.

Thema: O mors quam amara est memoria tua (Ecclesiastici ix).

Prothema—Mors: (Psalmista) Mors peccatorum pessima; (Apocalipsis) Beatus vir qui fuerit liberatus a morte secunda, id est, eterna damnatione;[p] (Augustinus) Nihil certius morte, nihil incertius hora mortis; (Philosophus) Omnium terribilium terribilissimum mors. Amara memoria: (Regum) Amaritudo mea amarissima;[q] (Ecclesiastici vii) Memorare novissima et in eternum non peccabis.

Conclusio illius prothematis: Bene ergo dicitur Ecclesiastici: O mors quam amara est memoria tua. Hec fuerunt verba prothematis preassumpti.

[2] Secundo significative, cum prothema themati concordat per aliquem sensum misticum spiritualem vel equivalentem, id est, per synonimum,[r] ut infra.

Thema aliud: Vas electionis est mihi iste (Actuum); (Levitici) Sume vas unum et mitte in illud manna. Nota: Vas in themate significat sanctum Paulum, in prothemate significat mortariolum aureum.

---

[p] damnatio A.   [q] anarissima A.   [r] synoninum A.

[I] First, [the protheme is deduced] through the verbal expression, when some one of the predicable terms is proved by clear agreement, as is shown below. Theme: "O death, how bitter is the remembrance of thee" (Ecclesiasticus 9).[28] Protheme [on] death: The Psalmist: "The death of the wicked is very evil."[29] The Apocalypse: "Blessed is the man who hath been freed from the second death, that is, from eternal damnation."[30] Augustine: "Nothing is surer than death, nothing less sure than the hour of death."[31] The Philosopher: "Of all terrible things death is most terrible."[32] [Protheme on] bitter remembrance: Kings:[33] "[Behold, in peace is] my bitterness most bitter." Ecclesiasticus:[34] "Remember thy last end, and thou shalt never sin."

Conclusion of this protheme: Thus well expressed is the verse of Ecclesiasticus, "O death, how bitter is the remembrance of thee." These were the words of the protheme taken up beforehand.

[II] Secondly, [the protheme is deduced] through the meaning, when protheme agrees with theme through some mystic spiritual sense or the equivalent, that is, by synonym, as below.

Another theme: "He is a chosen vessel for me" (Acts).[35] "Take a vessel, and put [an omer full of] manna therein" (Leviticus).[36] Note: "Vessel" in the theme means St. Paul, in the protheme the golden spoon.

[28] Actually Ecclus. 41:1. Cf. Aquinas-tract [pp. 58 f. and 77 above].

[29] Vulg. Ps. 33:22. Cf. Aquinas-tract [p. 58].   [30] Cf. Rev. 20:6.

[31] *Sermones* 47. 2, 3, on Mark 13:32 ("But of that day and that hour knoweth no man"); tr. R. G. MacMullen in *Nicene and Post-Nicene Fathers*, VI, 412.

[32] Cf. Aristotle, *Eth. Nic.* 3. 9.

[33] Wrong reference. Isaiah 38:17.   [34] 7:40.   [35] 9:15.

[36] Wrong reference. Ex. 16:33. See Num., chap. 7, for references to the golden spoon, among the offerings made by the princes of Israel at the dedication of the tabernacle.

Misticatio illius termini vas in prothemate: Per vas intelligitur sanctus Paulus, per manna corpus Christi missum pro refectione sacramentali in animam sancti Pauli.

Conclusio illius prothematis: De quo dixit Christus Actuum: Vas electionis est mihi, ut supra. Correlarium: prothema probat thema, et themaˢ concludit prothema.

Modus concludendi prothemata: Prothema concludi debet cum themate, et hoc fit dupliciter:

[1] Primo, quod directe vocali correspondeat, cum sensus themati simpliciter correspondeat. Exemplum: ut supra, O mors, etc.

[2] Secundo, indirecte, cum similitudo vel thematis pars misticata correspondet sensui thematis de parte prothematis, ut supra, vas electionis; de similitudine, ut infra.

Thema aliud: Benedictio domini super vos (Psalmista).

Prothema: (Philosophus) Actus activorum sunt in patiente predisposito.ᵗ Exemplificatio: Patet de terra et petra tempore pluviali. Misticatio similitudinaria: Tempus pluviale designat tempus divine gratie. Per petram intelliguntur indurati et peccatores, quia ad istos minime venit benedictio Domini; et per

---

ˢ et thema *om.* A.   ᵗ impatiente predispositio A,   impatiente predisposito B.

The mysticizing of this term "vessel" in the protheme: By "vessel" St. Paul is understood; by "manna" the body of Christ sent into the soul of St. Paul as sacramental refreshment.

Conclusion of this protheme: Of him Christ in the Acts said: "He is a chosen vessel for me," as above. Corollary: The protheme proves the theme, and the theme concludes the protheme.

The method of concluding prothemes: The protheme should end with the theme, and this is accomplished in two ways:

(1) directly—let it correspond in the verbal expression, when the sense corresponds to the theme simply. Example: as above, "O death," and so forth.

(2) indirectly, when the simile or the mysticized part of the theme corresponds to the sense of the theme from the standpoint of the protheme—as above, "a chosen vessel"; from the standpoint of the simile, as below.

Another theme: "The blessing of the Lord be upon you" (The Psalmist).[37]

Protheme: (The Philosopher): An "agent" acts upon a "patient" which is predisposed [to such action].[38] Exemplification: It is manifest from land and rock in time of rain. Mysticizing by simile: The time of rain denotes the time of divine grace. By rock are understood the hardened and sinners, because to such least of all comes the blessing of the Lord. And by earth are understood the virtuous,

---

[37] Vulg. Ps. 128:8.

[38] The emendation of the text was suggested by Professors Norman Kretzmann and R. R. K. Sorabji; see Aristotle, *Physics* 3. 1 (200 b 32–33).

terram virtuosi et fructuosi et iusti intelliguntur. Conclusio illius prothematis: Ad quos dixit Psalmista in spiritu benedictio Domini super vos.

[C] Tercia pars sermonis: Divisio est cuiuslibet et alicuius termini predicabilis in membra partitio. Regula generalis: Omnis terminus verbalis dividendus est in infinitivo, casualis vero terminus in genitivo plurali poni debet. Exemplum primi: intrare (aliud); exemplum secundi: preceptorum (aliud). Signa divisionis: alius, alia, aliud.

Nota: Quod respicit hominem hoc dicitur allegoricum membrum.

Divisionum (alia): tropologica,[u] allegorica, anagogica—extra celum nihil est. Termini apti divisionibus: anagogice—spiritualis, eternalis, celestis, infernalis, penalis, gaudiosus, luctuosus; allegorice (Christi[v] ad ecclesiam)—spiritualis, supernalis, universalis, sacramentalis; tropologice (ad animam)—temporalis, corporalis, spiritualis, particularis, virtualis, moralis, vitiosus.

[D] Quarta pars sermonis: subdivisio est alicuius membri mediantibus signis divisis ulterior partitio.[w]

Exemplum divisionis: Morientium mors (alia): corporalis, spiritualis. Exemplum subdivisionis: Mors spiritualium (alia): vivorum ut religiosorum, mortuorum ut damnatorum.

---

[u] trophologia A.
[v] Christum B.

[w] divisis ulterior partitio *om.* A.

---

the productive, and the good. Conclusion of this protheme: To these has the Psalmist said in spirit: "The blessing of the Lord be upon you."

The Third Part of the sermon: Division is the partition into members of some or any predicable term. General rule: The division of every verbal term must be carried out with use of the infinitive form, but a declinable term should be put in the genitive plural. Example of the former: To enter[39] ([having the sign] *aliud*); Example of the latter: of precepts ([having the sign] *aliud*). The signs of division: *alius* [masculine], *alia* [feminine], *aliud* [neuter].

Note: The member which has regard to mankind is called the allegorical.

The divisions [genitive plural feminine, having the sign] *alia*: tropological, allegorical, anagogical—beyond heaven there is nothing. Terms suited to the divisions: [1] from the anagogical point of view: spiritual, eternal, heavenly, infernal, penal, joyful, sorrowful; [2] from the allegorical point of view, terms of Christ with respect to the Church: spiritual, supernal, universal, sacramental; [3] from the tropological point of view, terms with respect to the soul: temporal, corporal, spiritual, particular, virtuous, moral, vicious.

The Fourth Part of the sermon: Subdivision is the further partition of some member by means of signs of division. Example of division: The death (*alia*, [i.e., feminine]) of the dying: corporal, spiritual. Example of subdivision: The death (*alia*, [i.e., feminine]) of the spiritual—of the living, as the pious; of the dead, as the damned.

[39] With reference to Luke 10:38 ff., *Intravit Iesus*, discussed below.

"Henry of Hesse"
Modus[x] Antiquus

Partes essentiales sermonis: thema, prothema, distinctio, subdistinctio.

Nota: Ille sermo caret prothemate: Ecce ego venio et habitabo[y] in medio tui. Sed sume loco thematis: Dicite filie Syon, etc.

Thema: De themate in modo antiquo idem est iudicium ut in modo moderno, etc.

Prothema: Aliqui sermones antiqui prothemate carent; aliqui loco prothematis habent auctoritatem Biblie vel plures tales; aliqui vero unam auctoritatem alicuius doctoris vel plurium; aliqui autem auctoritatem philosophie vel plures tales; aliqui similitudinem aut hystoriam mundialem.

Regula generalis: Quicquid dicitur inter thema et eius divisionem vel distinctionem prothema est.

Distinctio est totius thematis aut alicuius textus punctualis discretio.

Signa distinctionum: duo, tria, quatuor; duplex, triplex, quadruplex; primo, secundo, tercio.

Nota:[z] Quadruplex est thematis distinctio:

[1] Prima, termini a termino, ut in isto themate: Regina celi letare. Notantur tria: primum, nobilitas, ibi (regina); secundum, sublimitas, ibi (celi); tercium, iocunditas, ibi (letare).

---

[x] mons AB.   [y] habito A.   [z] Nota *om.* A.

The Old Method

The essential parts of the sermon are theme, protheme, distinction, and subdistinction.

Note: This sermon lacks a protheme: "Lo, I come, and will dwell in the midst of thee,"[40] but take in place of the theme: "Tell ye the daughter of Sion,"[41] and the rest ["Behold, thy king cometh unto thee"].

The theme: With regard to the theme in the Old Method the procedure is the same as in the Modern Method, and so forth as above.

The protheme: Some ancient sermons lack the protheme; some in the place of the protheme have one or more Biblical authorities; some, indeed, have one or more authorities from a theologian; some have one or more philosophical authorities; some a simile or secular story.

General rule: Whatever is said between the theme and its division or distinction is the protheme.

Distinction is the pointed separation of the whole theme or of some text. Signs of distinction: two, three, four; double, triple, quadruple; first, secondly, thirdly.

Note: the distinction of a theme is fourfold:

1. of term from term, as in the theme, "Queen of heaven, rejoice."[42] Three things are noticed: 1. nobility in "Queen," 2. sublimity in "heaven," 3. joy in "rejoice."

[40] Zech. 2:10.   [41] Matt. 21:5.

[42] Marian antiphon concluding the final service at Easter-time.

[151]

Of Eloquence

[2] Secunda, clausule a clausula, ut in isto themate: Regina Saba venit a finibus terre audire sapientiam Salomonis, etc. Notantur tria: primum, domus regine specificatio, ibi (regina Saba venit); secundum, eius fatigiosa itineratio, ibi (a finibus terre); tercium, sapientie Salomonis anhelatio, ibi (audire sapientiam Salomonis).

[3] Tercia, termini a clausula,[aa] ut in isto themate: Hic currite ut comprehendatis. Notantur duo: primum, cursio, ibi (sic currite); secundum, comprehensio, ibi (ut comprehendatis).

[4] Quarta, clausule a termino, ut in isto themate: Resurrexit Dominus. Notantur duo: primo, Christi ab inferis resurrectio, ibi (resurrexit); secundo, deitatis potencia et eius ascensio, ibi (Dominus).

Exemplum distinctionis: Duplex est mors—corporalis, spiritualis.

Distinctio textus[bb]: Numerus partium alicuius constituendus est secundum numerum personarum de quibus tractatur ibidem. Gratia exempli, in isto evangelio: Intravit Ihesus in quoddam castellum, agitur de tribus personis, scilicet: Ihesu, Martha, et Maria. Presens igitur evangelium distinguitur in tres partes:[cc] in prima tractatur de Ihesu, in secunda[dd] de Martha, in tercia de Maria.

Subdistinctio est alicuius membri mediantibus signis distinctivis ulterior partitio.

[aa] clusula A.
[bb] textuum B.

[cc] partes *om.* A.
[dd] secundo A.

---

2. of clause from clause, as in the theme: "The Queen of Sheba came from the ends of the earth to hear the wisdom of Solomon,"[43] and so on. Three things are noticed: 1. the specifying of the Queen's home, in "The Queen of Sheba came"; 2. her wearisome journey, in "from the ends of the earth"; 3. the inspiration of Solomon's wisdom, in "to hear the wisdom of Solomon."

3. of term from clause, as in the theme, "So run that ye may obtain."[44] Two things are noticed: 1. the running in "so run," and 2. the obtaining in "that ye may obtain."

4. of clause from term, as in the theme, "The Lord has risen."[45] Two things are noticed: 1. Christ's resurrection from hell in "has risen," and 2. the power of Deity and His ascension in "the Lord."

Example of a distinction: Death is twofold, corporal and spiritual.

Distinction of a text: The number of parts of a text is to be determined according to the number of persons treated therein. For example, in that passage of the Gospel: "Jesus entered into a certain village,"[46] three persons are concerned: Jesus, Martha, and Mary. The present Gospel, then, is distinguishable into three parts: the first dealing with Jesus, the second with Martha, the third with Mary.

Subdistinction is the further partition of some member by means of signs of distinction.

[43] Cf. Vulg. III Kings (Auth. Vers. I Kings) 10:1 ff.
[44] I Cor. 9:24.
[45] On this trope see C. Blume and G. M. Dreves, *Analecta Hymnica Medii Aevi* XLIX (Leipzig, 1906), 56.
[46] Luke 10:38 ff.

Exemplum subdistinctionis: Duplex est mors spiritualis—vivorum ut religio-sorum, mortuorum ut damnatorum.

Regula generalis: Divisio et distinctio similiter et subdivisio et subdistinctio differunt solum ratione signorum.

Subdistinctio textus: Volens distinguere textum aliquem cuilibet persone attribuat suam actionem et passionem.

Exemplum: Ex parte Ihesu quinque notantur:

    primum, castellum introibo [sic], ibi (intravit)

    secundum, attenta predicatio, ibi (audiebat verbum)

    tercium, benigna responsio, ibi (respondens)

    quartum, Marthe increpatio, ibi (turbaris)

    quintum, unius boni commendatio, ibi (porro unum).

Ex parte Marthe notantur sex:

    primum, hospite Christi specificatio, ibi (et Martha)

    secundum, Christi Ihesu hospitatio, ibi (excepit)

    tercium, sedula ministratio, ibi (Martha autem satagebat[ee])

    quartum, ab opere cessatio, ibi (que stetit et ait)

    quintum, sororis accusatio, ibi (domine, non est tibi)

    sextum, adiutorii postulatio, ibi (dic ergo illi).

Ex parte Marie notantur quatuor:

    primum, ab extris vacatio, ibi (sedens secus)

[ee] Martha autem etc. A.

Example of a subdistinction: Spiritual death is twofold—of the living, as the pious; of the dead, as the damned.

General rule: Division and distinction, and likewise both subdivision and sub-distinction, differ only in the kind of signs.

Subdistinction of a text: When you wish to apply the principle of distinction to some text, assign to each person his own action and emotion.

Example: With reference to Jesus five things are noticed:

    1. "I shall enter the village" ("entered")

    2. The preaching listened to ("heard his word")

    3. The kindly reply ("and Jesus answered")

    4. The chiding of Martha ("thou art troubled")

    5. The praise of a single good ("but one thing is needful").

With reference to Martha six things are noticed:

    1. The signifying of Christ by the guest ("and [a certain woman named] Martha")

    2. The reception of Christ Jesus ("received him")

    3. Her diligent service ("but Martha was cumbered with much serving")

    4. The ceasing from work ("and came to him and said")

    5. The accusation against her sister ("Lord, dost thou not care")

    6. The demand for help ("bid her therefore").

With reference to Mary four things are noticed:

    1. Her withdrawal from others ("sat at Jesus' feet")

secundum, devota[ff] contemplatio, ibi (verbum illius)
tercium, eterni gaudii adoptio, ibi (elegit)
quartum, beatitudinis duratio, ibi (non auferetur).

Modus Subalternus

est antiqui atque moderni commixtio, ut infra.

Figura subalterni modi: divisio, subdivisio, distinctio, subdistinctio.

Autorizatio: Quodlibet membrum postillationis, divisionis, subdivisionis, distinctionis, subdistinctionis, ad minus una auctoritate probari debet, vel duabus, ut primam sumendo de Biblia, secundam alicuius doctoris vel decreti vel sic. Auctoritatem primam sumendo ex Biblia, ecce scripta sacra; secundam ex decreto, iura; terciam ex philosophis, natura.

Applicatio: Sensus verborum mediorum inter approbandum et approbans debet convenire utrique. Approbans est auctoritas mediante qua dicta confirmantur; approbandum autem est terminus predicabilis in prothemate aut sensus thematis, ibidem ut supra in modo moderno, seu aliquod membrum sermonis cuiuscumque modi predicandi.

Partes accidentales sermonis: deductio dicitur affirmativa, vicium negativa. Deductio est magistralis sermonis elocutio, dilatatio atque conclusio.

[ff] denotat A.

---

2. Her devout contemplation ("heard his word")
3. The choice of joy everlasting ("hath chosen")
4. The continuance of blessedness ("shall not be taken away").

The Substitute Method

is a combination of the old and the modern, as below.

Scheme of the substitute method: division, subdivision, distinction, and subdistinction.

Use of authorities: Each member of a postillation, division, subdivision, distinction, or subdistinction should be proved by at least one or two authorities, as by taking the first from the Bible, the second from some theologian or decree, or the like. For taking the first authority from the Bible, you have Holy Writ; for taking the second from a decree, you have the laws; for taking the third from the philosophers, you have nature.

Application: The sense of the mediate words between the "thing to be proved" and the "thing proving" should be suitable to both. The "proving thing" is the authority by means of which what is said is confirmed. The "thing to be proved," however, is the predicable term in the protheme or is the sense of the theme, the same as above in the modern method; or it is some sermon-member of either type of preaching.

Accessory parts of a sermon: the execution, called the affirmative part, and defect, the negative.

The execution of a master-sermon includes the oral delivery, the expansion, and the conclusion.

Elocutio debet habere vocem acutam in proferendo, austeram in corrigendo, benivolam in exhortando.

Dilatatio et conclusio: Sermo tribus modis dilatatur, scilicet: divisione, questione, et digressione. Hi tres modi fiunt tantum circa terminos predicabiles.

[I] Prima regula generalis: Primo in sensum tropologicum[gg] est propinque digrediendum. Et hoc fit duplici proposito.

[A] Ut cum in auctoritate ponitur terminus significans vitium, procedendum est ut infra. Primo, introducatur cursus mundi; secundo, corrigantur mores vitiosi; tercio, persuadeatur virtus opposita; quartum, concludatur cum auctoritate a qua est digressum, ut infra.

Auctoritas: Avaricia est idolorum servitus (Apostolus).[hh]

Cursus mundi: Huic dyabolice servituti sunt astricti usurarii et omnes falsificantes pondera vel mensuras.

Correctio: Ve istis quia ab eo cui serviunt pro mercede sua sine fine puniendi sunt.

Persuasio: Si de hac servitute dyabolica liberari cupiunt studeant elemosinis usuras abjiciendo, et sic de aliis.

Conclusio: Quia avaricia est idolorum servitus, ut supra.

[B] Secundo, per oppositum, ut cum in auctoritate ponitur terminus significans virtutem. Introducatur tunc oppositum, ut infra.

[gg] tropologico B.   [hh] Auloritas apostoli: Avaricia est ydolorum servitus A.

The oral delivery should be characterized: in exposition, by a sharp voice; in correction, by an austere voice; in exhortation, by a kindly voice.

Expansion[47] and Conclusion: The sermon is expanded in three ways: division, question, and digression. These three methods are used only in connection with predicable terms.

[I] First general rule: Digression is to be made into the tropological sense near at hand. This is effected by means of a double argument:

[A] For example, when in an authority there is present a term signifying a vice, the procedure should be as follows. (1) Let the way of the world be introduced. (2) Let vicious habits be corrected. (3) Let persuasion to the opposite virtue be used. (4) Let the sermon conclude with the authority from which the digression was made, as follows.

Authority: "Covetousness is slavery to idols"[48] (the Apostle).

The way of the world: To this devilish slavery are bound usurers and all who falsify weights and measures.

Correction: Woe to such, since by him whom they serve they are, for their reward, to be punished without end.

Persuasion: If they yearn to be freed from this slavery to the devil, let them cultivate charity and eschew usury; and so with the like.

Conclusion: Because covetousness is slavery to idols, as above.

[B] Secondly, [digression into tropology is made] through an opposite, as when a term signifying a virtue is found in an authority; then let the opposite be introduced, as follows.

[47] Cf. the much fuller treatment of expansion in the Aquinas-tract [pp. 60 ff.].
[48] Eph. 5:5.

Of Eloquence

Auctoritas: Humiliamini sub potenti manu dei (Petri).[ii] Introducatur cursus de superbis et postea procedatur ut supra in primo modo.

[II] Secunda regula generalis: in sensu allegorico procedendum est ut infra. Primo, introducatur vita Christi vel alicuius sancti; secundo, persuadeantur eis virtutes; tercio, corrigantur vitia opposita; quarto, concludantur cum auctoritate a qua fuit digressum, ut infra.

Auctoritas: (Mathei xi) Discite a me quia mitis sum et humilis corde.

Introductio: Christus introduxit per se mansuetudinem et humilitatem, etc.

Persuasio: Has virtutes Christi quisquis fidelis imitari debet.

Correctio: Contrarium faciunt iracundi et elati. Prochdolor, eternis ignibus tradendi non advertentes Christi virtutes.

Conclusio: Qui dicit[jj] Mathei xi, Discite a me quia mitis, etc.

[III] Tercia regula generalis: In sensu anagogico procedendum est ut infra. Primo, exclamatio debet fieri per O in hortando, per Ve in corrigendo; secundo, exhortandi sunt bona agentes per propositionem[kk] eternorum gaudiorum; tercio, terrendi sunt peccatores per propositionem futurorum suppliciorum; quarto, concludatur cum auctoritate a qua fuit digressum, ut infra.

Auctoritas:[ll] (Apostolus) Iherusalem mater nostra que sursum est.

[ii] Autoritas Petri: Humiliamini sub potenti manu dei A. [kk] appositionem A.
[jj] dixit B. [ll] autcoritas B.

Authority: "Humble yourselves [therefore] under the mighty hand of God"[49] (Peter). Let the way of the world concerning the haughty be introduced, and after that let the sermon proceed as in the first method [A].

[II] Second general rule: in the allegorical sense the procedure should be as follows. (1) Let the Life of Christ or some saint be introduced. (2) Let the hearers be persuaded to virtues. (3) Let the opposite vices be corrected. (4) Conclude with the authority from which the digression was made, as below.

Authority: Matthew 11: "Learn of me for I am meek and lowly in heart."[50]

Introduction: Christ has through himself introduced kindness and humility, and so on.

Persuasion: These virtues of Christ any of the faithful can imitate.

Correction: The wrathful and exalted do the contrary. Alas, the sorrow! For not heeding the virtues of Christ, they are to be given to the eternal fires.

Conclusion: Wherefore says Matthew 11: "Learn of me for I am meek," and so forth.

[III] Third general rule: In the anagogical sense the procedure should be as follows. (1) Exclamation should be made by *Oh* in exhorting, and *Alas* in correcting. (2) Doers of good are to be exhorted through setting before them the eternal joys. (3) Sinners are to be frightened by the setting before them of future punishments. (4). Conclude with the authority from which the digression was made, as below.

Authority: The Apostle: "But Jerusalem which is above [is free, which is] the mother of us all."[51]

[49] 1 Pet. 5:6.
[50] 11:29.
[51] Gal. 4:26.

Exclamatio: O felices devoti; ve vobis iniusti.

Exhortatio: Agite devote, devoti, quod agitis. Iniusti, iniusta et peccata relinquite.[mm]

Proportio:[nn] Nam premia devotos prestolantur eterna, peccatores autem pene infernales.

Conclusio: Peccatores non possunt dicere cum apostolo, sed solum iusti, Hierusalem mater nostra, ut supra.

Cautela: Uni sermoni sufficiat una correctio, una exemplificatio, una cohortatio, una diffinitio, una questio.

Vitia moralia, artificialia: ignorantia praedicantis—intollerabile vitium; infacundia—naturale; digitorum demonstratio nimia; capitis iactatio; oculorum clausura; applicatio defectuosa.

Casus summarius[oo] totius artis: compositio se habet tanquam forma; auctorisatio proba; modus copula; applicatio multiplicatio; accidens deductio.

Libri amminiculativi artis presentis: Concordantie Auctoritatum Biblie; Auctoritas Decreti; Lumen Anime,[pp] per ordinem alphabeti; Similitudinum Liber; Compendium Theologice Veritatis; Summe Sancti Thome.

Finis feliciter adest.

[mm] relinquete AB.	[oo] summarinus A.
[nn] propositio B.	[pp] amime B.

Exclamation: Oh, happy ye devout. Alas, ye unjust.

Exhortation: Do devoutly, ye devout, what ye do. Ye unjust, abandon sin and injustice.

Comparison: For eternal rewards await the devout, but the punishments of hell await sinners.

Conclusion: Sinners cannot—only the just can—say with the Apostle: "Jerusalem the mother of us all," and so forth.

Caution: For one sermon let one correction, one exemplification, one exhortation, one definition, one question suffice.

Faults[52] of character and skill: the preacher's ignorance—an intolerable vice; lack of fluency—a natural vice; excessive pointing of the fingers; tossing of the head; closing of the eyes; defective application.

Summary of the whole art: [a] composition, exhibiting itself as form; [b] authorization, as proof; [c] method, as coherence; [d] application, as expansion; [e] accessory function: the execution.

Supplementary books of the present art: *Concordance of Authorities from the Bible*,[53] *The Authority of the Decree*,[54] *The Light of the Soul*,[55] in alphabetical order; *The Book of Similitudes*,[56] *The Compendium of Theological Truth*,[57] the *Summae* of St. Thomas [Aquinas].[58]

The end happily is here.

[52] Cf. Aquinas-tract [p. 58].

[53] The first Concordance of the Bible was completed in 1230 by the first Dominican cardinal, Hugh of St. Cher, aided, it is said, by 500 Dominicans. Supplying merely an index, by book and chapter, to passages where a word is found, this work formed the basis for revisions made at the Monastery of St. Jacques in Paris: The *Concordantiae S. Jacobi* or *Concordantiae Breves*, so called because the wording of passages was omitted, and the *Concordantiae Anglicanae*

Majores, or *Maximae,* wrought (about 1250), with full quotations, by three Englishmen, John of Darlington, Richard of Stavenesby, and Hugh of Croyndon. Later, the Franciscan Minister-General, Arlotto of Prato, made improvements, and in 1310 Conrad of Halberstadt very materially amended and abridged Hugh's work, retaining only the essential words of a quotation. Conrad aimed "ad commodum non modicum quidem eorum qui vel in cathedra docent vel in ecclesia sermocinando praedicant." His was the first concordance to be printed (Strassburg, 1470). See J. A. Fabricius, I and II, 381–383; P. C. L. Daunou in *Hist. litt. de la France,* (1838) XIX, 38–49; J. Quétif and J. Echard, *Scriptores Ordinis Praedicatorum* (Paris, 1719), I, 194–209; Cruel, p. 453; Hurter, II, 339 ff. and 410; F. Kaulen, art. "Bibelconcordanzen," in *Kirchenlexikon,* ed. H. J. Wetzer and Benedikt Welte; C. R. Gregory, art. "Concordances," in *The New Schaff-Herzog Encyclopedia of Religious Knowledge;* J. F. Fenlon, art. "Concordances of the Bible," in *Cath. Encyc.*

⁵⁴ The *Tabula Auctoritatum et Sententiarum Bibliae cum Concordantiis Secretorum et Secretalium* of Joannes Calderini, professor of canon law at Bologna (died 1365). The title of a copy in the British Museum (c. 13. b. 2., Cologne, 1470) reads: *Auctoritates decretorum omnem effectum tum textus quam glossarum nuclialiter . . . in se continentes.* The *Tabula* is a concordance of Biblical citations in the *Decretum* of Gratian and the decretals. A goodly number of manuscripts are extant, mostly in Germany, and at least three editions were printed in that land during the fifteenth century. See Fabricius, I and II, 297; Cruel, p. 453; Hurter, II, 659–660; and especially J. F. von Schulte, *Die Geschichte der Quellen und Literatur des Canonischen Rechts* (Stuttgart, 1875–1880), II, 247–253.

⁵⁵ *Liber moralitatum elegantissimus magnarum rerum naturalium lumen anime dictus, cum septem apparitoribus necnon sanctorum doctorum orthodoxe fidei professorum poetarum etiam ac oratorum auctoritatibus per modum pharatre secundum ordinem alphabeti collectis feliciter incipit* (ed. Augsburg, 1479), on the authority of two manuscripts (at Marseilles and Augsburg) regarded by Cruel, p. 460, Linsenmayer, p. 175, n. 1, and J.-Th. Welter, *L'exemplum dans la littérature réligieuse et didactique du moyen âge* (Paris–Toulouse, 1927), pp. 341–344 (which see), as the work of Berengarius of Landora (1262–1330), Master General of the Dominican order (1312–1317) and Archbishop of Compostela (1317–1330). The Prologue in the printed editions I have consulted, Augsburg, 1479 and 1482 (Hain, Nos. 10331 and 10333), shows that the editor, the Carmelite Matthias Farinator of Vienna, was largely responsible for the form in which the work was printed. Hurter, II, 614, assigns the authorship (1332) to a Hermann de Gotschah, otherwise unknown, a Canon of Vorau in Steiermark, Austria, but nowhere gives the evidence for this attribution. One of the most learned books of the Middle Ages, it was compiled, with the preacher's needs in view, from innumerable Greek, Latin, Arabic, and Jewish sources that were investigated in many parts of Europe; and with the aid of three translators from Greek and Latin works in natural science. It took the author twenty-nine years to complete (it was begun in 1293 and finished in 1323). It is a mine of all things conceivably of interest to the Middle Ages, used as subjects for moralistic comparison; and was especially popular in Germany, as many manuscripts, several incunabula, and a German translation of the fifteenth century attest.

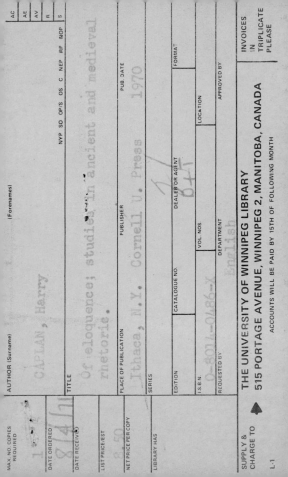

For the life of Berengarius—these do not mention the *Lumen Animae* among his works—see Quétif and Echard, I, 514–517; C. Douais, *Les frères prêcheurs en Gascogne au xiiime et au xivme siècle* (Paris–Auch, 1885), 373–374; Ulysse Chevalier, *Répertoire des sources historiques du moyen âge (Bio-Bibliographie)* (Paris, 1905–1907), *s.* Bérenger de Landorre; *Enciclopedia universal illustrada,* *s.* Landora, Fray Berenguer de; B. M. Reichert, *Monumenta Ordinis Fratrum Praedicatorum Historica (Cronica Ordinis Praedicatorum,* Rome-Stuttgart, 1897), II, 1, 107 ff. For Farinator (fl. third quarter of fifteenth century), see Chevalier, *s. v.*

⁵⁶ Most certainly the *Summa de Exemplis et Rerum Similitudinibus Libris Decem Constans,* by all now attributed to the celebrated Dominican preacher, Joannes Gorinus (di Coppo) of San Gimignano. This small encyclopedia of the natural sciences, composed about the year 1300 for the use of preachers (*Incipit summa insignis ac perutilis praedicatoribus de quacumque materia dicturis*), was extremely popular in the Middle Ages (especially in Germany) and thereafter well into the seventeenth century. It is a carefully arranged treatise, each book containing a prologue, and alphabetical rubrics divided into paragraphs which present the materials for moralistic comparison; it deals with such diverse subjects as the sky, the elements, metals, stones, vegetables, plants, terrestrial animals, man and his members, dreams, civil and canonical law, arts and crafts, manners of man, and the like. See Cruel, p. 460; Quétif and Echard, I, 528; T. F. Crane, *The Exempla of Jacques de Vitry* (London, 1890), p. xciv; Hurter, II, 491; and especially Welter, pp. 310–311. Conrad of Halberstadt later compiled an inferior and abridged *Liber Similitudinum Naturalium,* but there is no evidence that this work exerted much influence.

⁵⁷ Now generally considered the work (completed not long before 1281) of the Dominican Hugh Ripelin, Prior of Strassburg. See Félix Lajard, in *Hist. litt. de la France,* (1847) XXI, 155–163; Quétif and Echard, I, 470; Cruel, p. 455; Joseph Schroeder, art. "Hugh of Strasburg," in *Cath. Encyc.;* Hurter, II, 383–384; especially Luzian Pfleger, "Der Dominikaner Hugo von Strassburg und das *Compendium theologicae veritatis,*" in *Zeitschr. für kath. Theologie,* XXVIII (1904), 429–440; Martin Grabmann, "Studien über Ulrich von Strassburg," *ibid.,* XXIX (1905), 321–330; and Grabmann, *Die Geschichte der scholastischen Methode* (Freiburg im Breisgau, 1909–1911), II, 370–371. This work, called the "classic school text of the Middle Ages," was later often printed, and several times translated into German, and had a continuous influence for several centuries. It comprises seven books dealing with the nature of Deity, Creation, the Fall, the Incarnation, the Sanctification through Grace, the Sacraments, and the punishment of the wicked and rewards of the blessed when the world shall come to an end. Ulrich Surgant includes this work, the *Concordantiae Majores,* the *Liber Similitudinum,* and the *Lumen Animae* among supplementary books for study by preachers in his influential *Manuale Curatorum,* Book I, *Consideratio* 25, fol. 67ʳ, ed. Basel, 1507–1508.

⁵⁸ The *Summa Theologica* and the *Summa contra Gentiles.* Cruel, p. 460, quoting this passage, mentions only one *Summa S. Thomae,* but fails to give any information concerning the copy of the Henry-tract that he used. That the *Summa contra Gentiles* was used by preachers is perhaps evinced by the quotation from it, on demons instilling false opinion, in the *Lumen Animae,* Titulus 37 T.

VIII

The Decay of Eloquence at
Rome in the First Century[*]

I

WITH the death of the Roman republic "a hush fell upon eloquence."[1] Political oratory was restricted virtually to the emperor, who wielded absolute authority, and when he addressed the Senate his aim was rather to impose his will than to persuade. The Emperor himself presided over the Senate, and its duties were largely administrative. Speech there was not really free, and especially not when Caligula, Nero, and Domitian occupied the throne. The popular assemblies, certainly by the time of Tiberius, lost their importance altogether. Forensic oratory was confined largely to the Centumviral courts, which were charged with civil cases such as arose out of rules of inheritance, and with like cases of no great import. Secundus in Tacitus' *Dialogue on Orators* ruefully observes that the lawyers are reduced to trying cases of theft, or winning an interdict for a client (37). *Causes célèbres* carrying political implications, such as Tacitus and Pliny did indeed handle against provincial governors, are rare. Jurisprudence, to be sure, is making great strides, but advocacy, in so far as it followed the rules of rhetoric, seems not to have had a great effect upon the theory of juristic interpretation; so at any rate

---

[*] Reprinted from *Studies in Speech and Drama in Honor of Alexander M. Drummond*, ed. Herbert A. Wichelns (Ithaca, N.Y., 1944), pp. 295–325.

[1] Secundus in Tacitus, *Dialogus de Oratoribus*, chap. 38.

most modern students of Roman law contend. Epideictic speaking, in the form of the funeral oration and especially the panegyric, continued, and enjoyed a history of progressive degradation for several centuries. For oratory the first century is a time of decadence.

Yet eloquence was still the most popular and most conspicuous of the arts. It had lost its power, but not its prestige.[2] If the issues were not great, there were yet brilliant speakers. The younger Pliny thinks Tacitus the best orator of his day, and ventures the hope that he himself occupies the second place (*Epist.* 7. 20). Fragments of speeches from several other orators have been collected;[3] many speeches were too strictly legal for preservation. We know a good deal about Pliny's career at the bar, and especially how carefully he revised his speeches after delivery, tried them on his friends, and recited them before large audiences he had invited to hear him. From him and others we learn that the public was deeply interested in the speeches delivered in court. Quintilian thinks that the law-courts of his day can boast a glorious wealth of talent, the best speakers being serious rivals of the ancient great (10. 1. 122). Several of the emperors were accomplished speakers. That Seneca was on occasion "ghost-writer" for Nero was a scandal; after listening to Nero's panegyric on Claudius "the older men in the audience remarked that he was the first emperor to be in need of borrowed eloquence" (Tacitus, *Ann.* 13. 3). There *were* brilliant speakers, and, unfortunately, among the most effective of these were the public informers.[4]

---

[2] See Gaston Boissier, *Tacitus*, tr. W. G. Hutchison (New York, 1906), pp. 180 ff.

[3] Heinrich Meyer, *Oratorum Romanorum Fragmenta* (2d ed.; Zürich, 1842); ed. H. Malcovati (Paravia, 1930).

[4] See Victor Cucheval, *Histoire de l'éloquence romaine depuis la mort de Cicéron jusqu'à l'avènement de l'empereur Hadrien* (Paris, 1893), chap. 13.

Of Eloquence

But in greatest part the activity was shunted off and confined to the schools of rhetoric. The lecture-halls were often crowded to the doors by the public come to hear distinguished professors. Many a Roman and many an inhabitant of the provinces (Gaul especially was later a lively centre of rhetorical studies) continued rhetorical exercises long after their school-days were over. Juvenal, for one, practiced exercises until he was forty.

The type of oratory that predominated in the schools, and was there pursued with consummate ardor, was *declamatio*.[5] Introduced probably from Rhodes soon after the beginning of the first century B.C. or earlier (and it is fair to remember that declamation was inherited from the time of the republic), it underwent a change in nature. Early rhetorical fare was comprised of narratives, eulogies of famous men, commonplaces such as invectives against some vice, general *theses* (for example, Is the lawyer's life preferable to the warrior's?), deliberative questions (Should one marry?), or specific *causae* resembling actual cases at law. In each the reference to real life was close. But now we have the *suasoriae* and the *controversiae*. Several of the rhetors published collections of their declamations, and works such as those of the elder Seneca and of Ps.-Quintilian give us a clear picture of what these declamations were like.

Seneca's third *suasoria* is typical: Agamemnon deliberates

[5] See Cucheval, I, 217–293; Henri Bornecque, *Les déclamations et les déclamateurs d'après Sénèque le Père* (Lille, 1902); Boissier, pp. 163–194; Bornecque, *Sénèque le rhéteur, controverses et suasoires,* 2 vols. (Paris, no date); W. A. Edward, *The Suasoriae of Seneca the Elder* (Cambridge, 1928); J. Wight Duff, *A Literary History of Rome in the Silver Age* (New York, 1927), pp. 1–64; Caplan, "The Latin Panegyrics of the Empire" [pp. 26–39 of this volume]; Wilhelm Kroll, art. "Rhetorik" in Pauly-Wissowa, *Real Encyc. der class. Altertumswissens.*, Suppl. VII, sect. 38; Werner Hofrichter, "Studien zur Entwicklungsgeschichte der Deklamation von der griechischen Sophistik bis zur römischen Kaiserzeit" (diss., Breslau, 1935).

whether to sacrifice Iphigenia. Here the source is Greek legend, but Greek or Roman history might supply the subject. The *controversiae*, harder to treat, belonged to the judicial type, but the situations were almost invariably subtle, complicated, unreal, and sensational, and the "laws" involved were often vague, imaginary, or borrowed from the Greeks. Seneca, *Contr.* 9. 4, will serve to illustrate a less extreme type: The "law" reads, "He who has beaten his father shall have his hands cut off." A tyrant has summoned to his citadel a father and his two sons. He orders the sons to beat their father. One son throws himself down from the height. The other beats his father, and when he is thereafter accepted as a friend by the tyrant, kills him. The penalty—that he have his hands cut off—is demanded of him. His father defends him. We may select Musa to represent for us the twelve declaimers who speak in the father's rôle, and one *sententia* to represent Musa's style. "Cut off the hands of the tyrannicide," he exclaims, "when the tyrant in his tomb possesses all his limbs!"

Tyrants, pirates (there had been none in the Mediterranean since the time of Pompey), disinherited children, poisonings, adultery, seduction—these comprised much of the little-varied diet fed the youngster at school. Variety was sought rather by introducing novel, striking, and intricate complications. Emphasis was placed on ingenuity, not solid argument, and on abundance, bizarre extravagance, mannerism, dazzling ornament in *sententia* and *color*. The imagination had free rein, and historical truth was often distorted and falsified—a privilege which, as Atticus in Cicero's *Brutus* (42) smilingly admits, is accorded to rhetoricians when they wish to achieve "point" (*dicere argutius*). Pollio says that declamation is not persuasion but playing with words (Seneca, *Suas.* 2. 10), and Montanus that its aim is not victory but entertainment (Seneca, *Contr.* 9, *Praef.* 1). In Seneca, *Contr.* 9. 6. 10, Montanus laughs at those rhetors who treat as though she were a baby the girl accused of poisoning her half-brother, and especially at Cestius who represents the mother as saying to her daughter: "Give your brother poison," and receiving the reply: "Mother, what is poison?" Triarius, outdoing Cestius, has the daughter say: "Give me some, too." Cestius at least admitted the ineptitude of his dialogue, but maintained in extenuation that many of the things he said were intended to please his audience. Again, it was a fiction preserved in the schools that a certain Popillius was the murderer of Cicero, and that once when charged with parricide, he had been successfully defended by the great orator. Inevitably one of the rhetors (Sabidius Paulus, Seneca, *Contr.* 7. 2. 14), describing the moment when Popillius is about to behead Cicero, makes the orator recite to his slayer the very speech he had given during the trial.

The elder Seneca himself of course has a high opinion of declamatory eloquence. To his son Mela he says: "It equips also those whom it does not train for its own purposes" (*Contr.* 2, *Praef.* 3). But always a man of sense and of excellent judgment, he can be critical of it too (e.g., Montanus in *Contr.* 9, *Praef.* 1). In *Contr.* 3, *Praef.* 12–13, he quotes Cassius Severus on the bad side of this discipline: "In the school-exercises what is not superfluous, since they are themselves super-fluous?" "Declaimers are like hot-house plants that cannot stand up in the open air."

The schools, then, were sealed, as it were, from public life and had no contact with reality. The younger Seneca cries: "We educate ourselves for the class-room, not for life" (*Epist.* 106. 12). Latro, in the first rank of *ex tempore* declaimers, yet funked appearance in the forum when called upon to plead a case (Quintilian, 10. 5. 18).

The declaimers occasionally gave utterance to ideals of political liberty. Albucius dared in Milan to invoke Marcus

Brutus, whose statue was in sight, as "the founder and de-
fender of our laws and our liberty," and for that "narrowly
escaped punishment" (Suetonius, *De Rhet.* 6). In the two
Senecan *suasoriae* dealing with Cicero (6 and 7), the attacks
on Antony and on the proscriptions by which Cicero lost his
life may have borne implications that Octavian shared in the
responsibility as a member of the triumvirate. Julius Caesar is
never eulogized in the declamations. But most of the rhetors
did not touch on politics. It is precisely because Seneca's son
Mela finds civic duties and ambition repugnant to his spirit
that he is urged by his father to indulge his sole passion—
declamation (*Contr.* 2, *Praef.* 3). Furthermore, since the declaimers were trained to take either side of a question, we
must in the case of some who expressed republican sentiments
beware of exaggerating their sincerity, just as we must not
overrate the influence they wielded in the realm of political
action. For example, Haterius could say to Cicero (in retrospect, of course): "I would urge you to hold your life dear, if
liberty still had its abode in our State, and eloquence its
abode in liberty," and could utter noble words on Cato
(Seneca, *Suas.* 7 and 6), yet Tacitus paints an abject picture
of him in his relations with Tiberius (*Ann.* 1. 13).

The contentions of modern apologists for *declamatio* must
have a hearing. Certain benefits did indeed accrue from it: it
often showed respect for things of the spirit, provided an outlet
for some criticism of society, satisfied the desire for "romance,"
insured the students facility and stylistic finish. It is likewise
only just to remind ourselves that some of the contemporary
critics who attacked declamation (when is education not a
target for criticism?) themselves practiced it; that the declaimers preserved eloquence when otherwise it would virtually have died; and, finally, that most of the great writers
of the Silver Age underwent this training. Indeed it is astonish-

ing that at a time when oratory itself was in such sore straits, rhetoric was making inroads into all the fields of literary activity, of prose and of poetry, and especially history and the epic, exercising a potent influence upon them, and in a sense taking them over as her own. And we must further agree that it was not education which corrupted the national taste, but rather that this training was itself a reflection and manifestation of the decline in taste.

As will soon be clear, *declamatio* was almost universally criticized; yet its popularity continued. As it differed from the oratory of the forum in subject matter, kind of audience, and even language, so it was a very different system of education from the *tirocinium fori* of republican times. Then the young speaker had been under the patronage of a leading statesman. He would attend at his patron's home where current topics were discussed, assist in the trying of cases, exchange opinions on the speeches delivered by other orators. He learned to fight, as Messalla in Tacitus' *Dialogue* says (34), on the firing-line, and won experience, self-possession, and sound judgment. But oratory now, during the Empire, is deprived of the inspiration that comes from reality, since the forum is no longer the centre of public life.

II

The elder Seneca, who died *c.* A.D. 37, reproduces for us the *declamatio* of the earlier period, its brilliant products as well as inept. That the themes continued unreal and melodramatic, and the style pompous and grandiloquent, all the witnesses[6] of the first century agree, expressing their dislike and disgust in varying tones—the humorous satirist Petronius, the philosopher Seneca, the historian-critic Tacitus, the lawyer-epistolographer Pliny, the bitter castigator of Roman society

---

[6] The texts in this paper are for reasons of space often presented with omissions.

Juvenal. In the time of Nero, Petronius (*Satyricon* 1–2) thus condemns the schools:

I believe that our young men become utter simpletons in the schools, because they neither hear nor see anything of actual life there. It is rather pirates standing on the shore with chains in hand, tyrants writing edicts which order sons to cut off their fathers' heads, oracles in time of pestilence calling for the sacrifice of three virgins or more, rounded phrases, honey-sweet, every word and act be-sprinkled as it were with poppy-seed and sesame. Persons who are nourished on this diet can no more be intelligent than persons who live in the kitchen can be sweet-scented. With your good leave I must tell you that it is primarily you teachers who have ruined eloquence. Your light and empty tones produce absurd effects, and as a result the *substance* of your speech withers and fades. In the days when Sophocles or Euripides found the indispensable word to use, young men were not yet confined to declamations. When Pindar and the nine lyric poets humbly refrained from using Homer's lines, no pedant in his study had yet ruined the talents of the young. I certainly do not find that either Plato or Demosthenes resorted to training of this kind. Great style, and that is also, if I may say it, modest style, is neither spotty nor swollen, but rises up by virtue of its natural beauty. Your puffed-up and extravagant verbosity is a recent immigrant to Athens from Asia. Like a pestilential planet it paralyzed the minds of young men who aspired to great achieve-ments, and when the old standards were once corrupted, eloquence came to a standstill and lost the power of speech.

A letter (108. 6–7) of the younger Seneca (his letters were written in A.D. 63–65, during the reign of Nero) describes and censures the levity of the students, their apathy towards ideas, and their passion for the sound of empty words:

To a large part of the listeners the philosopher's class-room is a retreat for their leisure. Their purpose is not to receive a rule of life there, but to enjoy thoroughly the pleasures of the ear. Some appear even with writing-tablets, not to take down the matter, but only the words, that they may repeat them to another, providing him with no more advantage than they themselves received in hearing them. The right kind of hearer is rapt and stirred by the beauty of the subject-matter, not by the thunder of hollow words.

If we accept the argument of some scholars that Tacitus' *Dialogue on Orators* was composed probably in A.D. 80/81, then Messalla's words in that book speak for the time of Titus. They express a judgment no different from that of Petronius above:

The exercises in which the schools engage largely run counter to their own purposes. Ye gods! what stuff the *controversiae* are made of, and how unnaturally they are contrived! And furthermore, in addition to the matter that is so at variance with real life, there is the declamatory style in which it is delivered. And so it comes that themes like "the reward for the tyrannicide," or "the options left to the ravished maidens," or "a remedy for the plague," or "the unchaste matron," and all the other topics that are daily treated in the school, but seldom or never in the forum, they set forth in grandiose style (35).

At the end of the century, Pliny the Younger in a letter (2. 14) to a friend describes in painful detail how the declamatory method has invaded and come to dominate the ancient tribunal of the *Centumviri:*

Your supposition is correct: I am kept busy by cases in the Centumviral court, and they bring me more toil than pleasure. They are generally paltry and meagre, and it is very seldom that one of significance comes up. Furthermore, there are very few counsel with whom I care to plead; the rest are a bold lot, and the majority in fact obscure youngsters who have come over from the schools to practice declamation, and do so without reverence or consideration. In the old days young men, even of the best families, were not admitted to the bar unless introduced by some person of consular rank; so great was the respect with which our ancestors honored this noblest of professions. But now that everything is opened wide to everybody, the young men are not introduced; rather they break their way in.

The hearers are worthy of such pleaders, having been hired and bought; the dole is paid out to them in the middle of the court-house as openly as if it were a dining-room, and for the like fee they go from one court to another! Just yesterday two of my nomenclators, scarcely old enough to wear the toga, were bribed to applaud at the price of three denarii [about thirty-six cents] each—that is how much it costs if you wish a reputation as "The Most Eloquent." At this price we fill crowded benches, and at this price endless shouts are raised when the chorus-leader gives the signal. Indeed these claqueurs need a signal, for they understand nothing of what is said, and do not even listen to it. If at any time you should pass by the court-house, and should like to find out how well any of the speakers is doing, you can be sure that the speaker who receives the loudest praise is the worst.

I am ashamed to tell you with what a mincing utterance they deliver their speeches; this sing-song oratory lacks only hand-clapping, or rather cymbals and drums.

Up to now, only the interests of my friends and the consideration of my youth have kept me in this court; but I attend less often than I used to, and so am preparing a gradual retirement.

Finally Juvenal, writing perhaps in A.D. 118, after observing Roman life for many years, bears satiric witness to the persistence of theme and method in the schools:

O Vettius, of iron must your bowels be when your mob of pupils butchers the cruel tyrant in a chorus. The cabbage, so served up repeatedly, is death to the unhappy teacher! "It is made out to be the teacher's fault that the dull Arcadian youngster feels no flutter in his left breast when dinning my unhappy ears on every sixth day of the week with his 'Hannibal the dire,' whatever be the question which he is deliberating." If the teacher of rhetoric takes my advice, he will give himself a gladiator's discharge, and enter upon some other walk of life (*Sat.* 7.150 ff.).

The actual tyrant on the Palatine did not always ignore the "academic" habit, inherited from the Greeks, of inveighing against tyranny; Caligula banished Carrinas Secundus, and Domitian put a certain Maternus out of the way, for delivering such speeches as rhetorical exercises.[7]

These Roman critics make amply plain what the nature and inspiration of public discourse in their times were. The final expression of the spirit of *declamatio*, however, we find in a Greek satirist of the next century. The following excerpts from Lucian's dialogue, "The Professor of Public Speaking," show that the meretricious methods employed by the teachers in the first century persisted in the next, despite the fact that Quintilian's *Training of an Orator*, which represented a return to the rhetoric of Cicero, was published before the second century opened. But the influence of this great work, strong for a time, was thereafter impeded by Fronto and the arch-aizers. I should remind the reader that Lucian was himself a rhetorician, and that he pleaded in court, but enjoyed much more his wide travels in many countries as a lecturer before educated audiences; further, that the aim of his satire was amusement. Lucian makes the same points as his Roman predecessors: the successful speaker needs none of the old type of training, no study of good authors, no command of fact and logic, no wealth of ideas, but only a loud and assertive manner, and a style of purple patches all compact. The young man ambitious to become a public speaker is encouraged to join the great company of nonentities who by the power of speech have gained a reputation for respectability, wealth, and even gentle birth. To the summit where sits Rhetoric, attended by Wealth, Fame, and Might, two roads lead. The narrow, steep, and thorny track must be avoided, for it promises thirst and sweat, and the poet who said that the Good is got by toil was wrong. The guide of this rough road must not be heeded. Pointing out the footprints of Demosthenes and Plato, "this

[7] Dio Cassius, *Roman History* 59. 20; 67. 12.

quack and old fossil will expect you to unearth long-buried speeches as if they were a treasure, forgetting that we are now at peace, with no aggressor Philip to make the speeches of a sword-maker's son [Demosthenes] perhaps seem useful." But the young man is to take, at a leisurely pace, the other road, which, pleasant and short, leads through flowery meadows. At this road he will meet a man of honeyed voice who will modestly speak as follows:

My good man, surely not Apollo sent you to me? Ah, you will find that my voice overcomes all others, as the trumpet the flute, as the cicada the bee, as the choir the master who gives the key-note of the tune. You could not learn to be a speaker with so much ease from anyone but me. Have no scruples and be not disturbed that you have not passed through all the weary rites of initiation which the ordinary system of preparatory teaching sets in the path of silly fools. Sail right in, even if—a by no means uncommon thing—you do not know how to write. Speaking is something else again! I will first list all the equipment for your journey, then add some advice, and, before sunset, I shall make you known as a better speaker than all the others, as good indeed as myself, without doubt the first, middle-most, and last of all the speaker-profession.

Bring then, first of all, ignorance, and then self-assurance, effrontery, and shamelessness. Modesty, fairness, moderation, and shame? Leave them at home; they are useless and cumbrous. Then too, a very loud voice, and an impudent sing-song delivery. Further, have a company of attendants, and always a book in your hand.

You must take special care of your appearance. Next, pick out from some source or other fifteen old Attic words—or twenty at the outside; exercise yourself in their use carefully and have them at the tip of your tongue; for example: *sundry, upon which, surely not, in some wise, Good my Sir;* these are the seasoning which you will apply in every speech, and you are not to concern yourself about any dissimilarity, incompatibility, or discord between them and the rest. Go after esoteric, unfamiliar words only rarely used by the ancients, and have ready an accumulation of them to discharge at your hearers. Thereby you will draw the attention of all the crowd, and they will consider you marvelous, if, for example, you do not say "earnest"-

[171]

but "caution"-money. You may also now and then create monstrous neologisms of your own, and ordain, for example, that a "sage" shall be called a "sapient."

If you commit a solecism or barbarism, let your one remedy be boldness: be ready to cite as your authority the name of some poet or historian who does not now exist and never did exist. As for reading the ancient classics, that is not for you to do—whether that silly Isocrates, that insipid Demosthenes, or that spiritless Plato. Study rather the speeches of the last generation, and the exercises which they call declamations; these will supply you with a store of provisions on which you can draw at need.

When the time comes for you to speak and the hearers have proposed themes and starting-points for discussion, find fault with all the difficult ones; disparage them as offering no challenge, any of them, to a he-man. Do not hesitate, but say whatever comes into your head. Have no care that the first thing shall be said first because it actually is first, or that your second and third shall be in the proper order. Just say first what comes first to you. But press on, keep going, and only do not stop. For all occasions have Marathon in readiness; you cannot do without it. And always have a fleet crossing Mount Athos in ships, and an army the Hellespont on foot, the sun eclipsed by the arrows of the Medes, Xerxes in flight, and Leonidas receiving acclaim. And in everything let those few words of your selection, your seasoning-condiment, abound and flourish—apply *sundry* and *doubtless* constantly, even if you do not need them; they are lovely words, even when used haphazardly. Exclaim "Ah, woe unto me" often, smite your thigh, bellow, punctuate what you say with clearings of the throat, and sway your hips as you pace about.

That they may admire the copiousness of your speeches start with the Trojan war, and bring your narrative down to today. Perspicacious people are rare; any comment they may make will be laid to jealousy. Never write anything out, nor think a subject through before you come forward to speak; that will certainly give you away.

Be sure to have a chorus of your own, one that sings in unison, and as you go home afterwards, analyzing what you have said, let them attend you as a bodyguard. And if you meet anyone on the way, talk vaingloriously about yourself. Ask him: "Who is Demosthenes compared to me?"

But the most important and most cogent means of winning repute

I had almost left out: ridicule all the other speakers. If one of them speaks well, the charms he displays are borrowed; if mild exception is taken to his speech, all of it is censurable. In general smile faintly; make it clear that you do not accept what is being said.

Learn these instructions thoroughly, my boy, and I confidently promise that you shall very soon become a first-rate speaker, like myself. And now I have given you my advice, so help you the Goddess of Venery.

III

For the effects which the changed political conditions brought about in the position held by public utterance in the Roman State, we must turn to Tacitus in his capacity of historian. In the *Annals* 1. 2 (about A.D. 115) he describes the effect upon character wrought by the change from Republic to Empire, and in the *Histories* 1. 1 (A.D. 104–9) the effect upon the writing of history:

> There was no opposition, since the most courageous had fallen on the fields of battle or by proscription; while the rest of the nobility found that the readiness to accept servitude brought them elevation to wealth and office, and having flourished on revolution, they preferred now the new order with its security to the old with its perils.
>
> Many historians, so long as they were treating of the Roman republic, wrote with equal eloquence and freedom. But after the battle of Actium [31 B.C.], when in the interests of peace all power was placed in the hands of one man, historians of like great talent passed out of existence. And at the same time the truth was falsified in many ways: first, because historians were ignorant of politics as though politics were not their business, later because of their inordinate desire to flatter; or again, because of their hatred of their rulers. If my life lasts long enough, I have saved for my old age the history of the deified Nerva's reign and of Trajan's rule, a richer and safer subject, thanks to the rare good fortune of an era in which you may feel what you wish and may say what you feel.

The prosecutions for seditious utterance under Domitian moved Tacitus, breathing the freer air of a more enlightened reign, to write some of his most eloquent lines (*Agricola* 2–3; A.D. 98):

> The records tell us that when Arulenus Rusticus praised Thrasea Paetus, and when Herennius Senecio praised Helvidius Priscus,[8] their praise constituted a capital crime, so that vengeance was wreaked not only on the authors themselves but also on their books; to the public hangman[9] was delegated the task of burning in the Comitium and Forum the memorials of these noblest of characters.
>
> No doubt they believed that in those flames were being effaced the voice of the Roman people, the liberty of the Senate, the conscience of mankind; especially when in addition the professors of philosophy were expelled, and thereby all worthy accomplishments banished, in order that nowhere might anything that is honorable occur.
>
> Surely we have given abundant proof of our tameness of spirit; and just as men of former times saw the extremes of liberty, so have we seen the extremes of slavery, the public informers having robbed us even of the intercourse of conversation. We should have lost memory itself as well as voice, if only we had found it as easy to forget as to be silent.
>
> Now at last spirit is returning to us; from the very beginning of the dawn of this happiest of eras Nerva has joined two things formerly irreconcilable, monarchy and liberty; and Trajan is daily increasing the happiness of our times.
>
> During a period of fifteen years [the reign of Domitian, A.D. 81–96], a large space in human life, many of us have died from natural causes; the most courageous have perished by the Emperor's cruelty; while the few of us who survive have survived not only our friends but also, so to speak, ourselves; since from the prime of life have been effaced fifteen years, during which those of us who were young reached old age, and those who were old reached the very limits of a completed life, and all in enforced silence.

---

[8] Thrasea was an outspoken opponent of Nero; his son-in-law Helvidius opposed Vespasian. Rusticus Arulenus in his biography of Thrasea spoke of him and of Helvidius as *sanctissimi viri*. Rusticus Arulenus was executed in A.D. 94, Herennius Senecio in A.D. 93.

[9] *Triumviri capitales*. These minor officials superintended the prisons. The insult was greater in that the burning of books was usually performed by the aediles.

When in the *Annals* (4. 34) Tacitus dealt with the famous prosecution of Cremutius Cordus, he seized the opportunity to present his own views on freedom of speech:

During the consulship of Cornelius Cossus and Asinius Agrippa [A.D. 25] there took place the prosecution of Cremutius Cordus, upon the novel and up to then unheard-of charge that in a history which he had published he had eulogized Brutus, and termed Cassius the last of the Romans. That the accusers were dependents of Sejanus was of fatal consequence to Cordus, and so also was the grim countenance of Tiberius as he listened to the defence. Cremutius began the defence as follows: "It is my words, Conscript Fathers, that are under accusation—so true is it that I am guiltless of deeds. Nor are they even words directed against the emperor or his parent, the only persons embraced by the law of treason. I am said to have praised Brutus and Cassius, whose exploits ever so many writers have recorded, and none has mentioned except with respect. Livy [who eulogized Pompey without forfeiting Augustus' friendship] nowhere refers to Brutus and Cassius by the now popular appellations of brigand and parricide, but again and again as distinguished men. Cicero's book lauded Cato [of Utica] to the skies, and how did the dictator Caesar reply to it? Only in the form of a written speech,[10] as though he were presenting his case before jurors. The letters of Antony, the speeches of Brutus, the poems of Bibaculus and Catullus contain invectives and insults against the Caesars, yet the deified Julius and the deified Augustus tolerated these works and left them alone—whether with the motive of forbearance or of wisdom it would not be easy to say. For the things you spurn soon pass from memory, while your anger is taken as an admission that they are true.

I do not mention the Greeks. Among them not only liberty but even license went unpunished; or if a man paid heed, he avenged words by means of words. But especially free from punishment and immune from detraction was the publishing of opinions on those whom death had removed beyond the bounds of hate or of partiality. Are Brutus and Cassius now upon the plains of Philippi, armed for battle, and am I upon the hustings, inflaming the people to civil war?

[10] Caesar replied to Cicero's *Laus Catonis* with *Anticatones*, in two books.

Of Eloquence

If my condemnation is upon me, there will not be lacking those who will remember not only Brutus and Cassius, but me as well!

Cordus then left the Senate, and ended his life by starvation. The fathers ordered that his books be burned by the aediles; but there remained hidden copies, which were later published—and that fact disposes me the more to deride the senselessness of those who believe that by the use of power in the present there can be blotted out also the memory of a subsequent age. On the contrary, if genius is punished, it grows in influence; nor have alien kings or such men as have adopted their cruel practices thereby begotten anything but ignominy for themselves and glory for their victims.

IV

A number of authors in the first century were deeply conscious of the decadence in oratory and the other arts, and were interested in its causes. I shall let them in most part speak for themselves, and by way of preface shall merely call attention to two considerations. The reader of these passages must make allowance for what "Longinus" (44. 6) calls the human tendency to find fault with one's own era, realizing also that an age which produces great satirists and other writers who are alive to the faults of their civilization is on that very account itself praiseworthy. We can doubtless find in every period of history, whether it be of a high or a low state of culture, some reputable observer who looks upon his day as one of decline. Aper in Tacitus' *Dialogue* says: "You must lay it to the fault of human malignity that the old is always held in high esteem. the modern in scorn" (18).[11] And especially in the first century it was a pious convention among Romans to glorify the good old times. Secondly, the question of the decline of eloquence has been treated by some scholars as one which arose only at this special time, a burning literary question of the day, com-

[11] On the popularity of the commonplace see Alfred Gudeman's edition (Boston, 1894), pp. 201–202.

parable, for example, to the Battle of the Books in the time of Bentley and Swift.[12] Such issues, it is maintained, are always hotly fought for a time, and at the end neither side wins the victory. "'Tis best to dismiss the question, and to let things go as they please," says Orestes in Euripides' *Electra* (379), and these words are used by "Longinus" as an epilogue to his discussion of decay. In any event, the attitude to be observed at this period is obviously different from that of Cicero's *Brutus*, in which, as Rand has said, the course of oratory is onward and upward, "with a precious little autobiography at the end."[13] Yet in *Tusc. Disp.* (2. 1. 5) Cicero wrote: "And in oratory the renown of Rome has from a humble beginning reached its acme, so that now, as is the law of nature in virtually everything, it is in its decline and seems destined soon to come to nothing," and these words should be borne in mind when we read Velleius below.

It was possible to be conscious of a decline, and to find the causes in the private morality of the citizens, rather than in the shaping influence of political institutions. Thus Livy in the Preface to his history of Rome, which was begun about 27 B.C., looks upon his own time as one of debased morality "when we can endure neither our vices nor their cure," and yet this ethical critic of history sees in the establishment and enlargement of the Empire the realization of the qualities he hoped to instill by means of his history. He was aristocratic and republican in sympathy, but under Augustus a sentimental regard for the brave days of old (*prisca illa*) was not incompatible with loyalty to the emperor, whose respect for tradition and whose moral reforms Livy must have warmly approved, and whose intimate friendship he enjoyed. Augustus could overlook the *licentia* of Livy's question whether the birth

---

[12] See Gudeman, pp. xxxii ff.

[13] E. K. Rand, *The Building of Eternal Rome* (Cambridge, 1943), p. 160.

of Julius Caesar had brought more harm or good to the State (Seneca, *Nat. Quaest.* 5. 18. 4), even as when, instead of punishing his nephew for reading a book by Cicero, he said of the orator: "A learned man, my child, a learned man, and a great patriot" (Plutarch, *Cicero* 49. 3). Livy attributes the cause of decline to wealth, bringing avarice in its train, and to the physical pleasures, bringing licentiousness and through it personal and universal ruin. Eumolpus in Petronius' *Satyricon* (88), discoursing on the fine arts, likewise traces the decline to the root of all evil:

> Love of money brought these changes about. For in former ages, when virtue was still loved for herself alone, the liberal arts flourished. But we, immersed in wine and women, attack the past, and teach and learn nothing but vices. Where is dialectic now, or astronomy? Who has ever come to a temple and made an offering in the hope of attaining to eloquence? They do not even ask for good sense or good health, but one promises an offering if he may bury his rich neighbor, another if he may dig up a treasure, another if he may make thirty millions in safety. So do not wonder that painting is decadent, when all the gods and men think a mass of gold more beautiful than anything ever done by those crazy Greeklings, Apelles and Phidias.

Pliny the Elder, in a digression from a study of viticulture (*Nat. Hist.* 14. 1; about A.D. 77), offers some scholarly comments in explanation of the "accidie" of his day. He essentially concurs with Petronius, but goes beyond the satirist in tracing the cause of moral decadence to the complexity of the Empire:

> Who would not admit that now, when the sovereignty of the Roman Empire has united all the world, civilization has advanced, through the exchange of goods and the common fellowship in the joys of peace? Yet the ancient writers have handed down to us much which, I swear, no one now knows. So much more fruitful was their research, or so much more fortunate their industry. We of today must inquire not only into the discoveries of modern times, but also into

those of the ancients, discoveries which our slothfulness has let fall
into utter oblivion. The causes of this lethargy—shall we not find
them to be the same as those which operate generally throughout
the world? New fashions, no doubt, have now sprung up; new interests engage the minds of men; and the only arts that are now
cultivated are those of avarice.

In former times, when the sway of nations was circumscribed by
their own narrow limits, and consequently so also circumscribed was
the genius of their people, what I may call the niggardliness of fortune forced them to exercise the faculties of the intellect. Innumerable kings received the homage of the arts, and when displaying their
resources gave special prominence to these arts, believing that
through them immortality would be secured. Hence rewards as well
as the works of civilization multiplied. To succeeding ages an expanded world and the grandeur of our Empire have been injurious.
Ever since senators began to be chosen according to their wealth,
judges appointed according to their wealth, and it became usual to
think that nothing confers greater honor upon magistrates and gen-
erals than their wealth, ever since legacy-hunting became the most
remunerative of occupations, and it became usual to think that
there are no pleasures except those of possession; ever since that
time, all the rewards of life have gone to ruin, and all those arts which
we call liberal, from liberty, that greatest good, now deserve the
opposite name, and indeed only servility is profitable. And so, I
swear, pleasure has begun to live, and life itself is now no more.

Compare with Pliny, and with each other, two authors of the
next century: Appian extols with high praise the spread of the
Roman Empire and the unification of the world (*Roman History*, Preface 7); the philosopher Epictetus minifies the achievement, wishing to indicate the limitations of the Caesar's
power to provide peace as against the power of philosophy to
do so in a more vital sense (Arrian's *Disc.*, 3. 13. 9 ff.).

At the end of the first century Quintilian wrote a treatise,
now lost, on the Causes of the Decline of Eloquence; evidence indicates that the point of view was purely technical.
He wrote his great work, *The Training of an Orator* (before

A.D. 96), because he thought the time ripe for a rebirth of eloquence. When we talk about decay in this century, we must yet always be mindful that this great work belongs to the period. More than once Quintilian refers to the decline of eloquence, but again his observations are technical and not historical. The teachers are to blame for the extravagance and ignorance of our declaimers, and therefore for the decline in oratory (2. 10. 3 ff.). He is aware of the unreality of declamation and its extravagance in the choice of words (8. 3. 23). But Quintilian is a constructive teacher. He thinks eloquence an accomplishment transcending even success in navigation and astronomy (12. 11. 10). The idea of declamation is basically sound. Only choose subjects modeled on the pleadings for which it is devised as training. Have the young man write out speeches of his own dealing with cases which he has actually heard pleaded, and argue them from both sides. Make utility again the aim of eloquence. Choose cases that are longer to deliver and more complicated, use more humor, use words drawn from the speech of every day. Go back to the old practice of declaiming commonplaces. *Occasional* magnificence, *occasional* unreality are not too harmful, if these are limited to the exercises in the schools and do not appear in actual practice. The danger of engaging the young too long in false semblances of reality is that they will shrink with terror from the real perils of public life, like men dazzled by unfamiliar sunlight. Seek virility of style instead of the effeminate quality now popular. Emphasize careful preparation; some declaimers are led by a perverse ambition to speak the moment the theme has been given them, and even ask for a word with which to start—an affectation which is in the worst and most theatrical taste.[14] It is significant of the times that

---

[14] See 2. 1. 9; 5. 12. 17 ff.; 10. 5. 17 ff.; 10. 7. 21.

Quintilian bases his treatment of deliberative oratory almost entirely on the *suasoriae*.

Velleius Paterculus (*Roman History* 1. 16 ff.), writing in A.D. 30, does not explain the phenomenon of decline by defective education or by the growth of luxury and avarice, however stimulated, but by a natural "law" of reaction:

I cannot refrain from making note of a subject which I have often revolved in my mind, but have never clearly reasoned through. Who can wonder enough that the most eminent geniuses in each art come together within the same narrow space of time? A single epoch gave lustre to tragedy through three men of divine inspiration—Aeschylus, Sophocles, and Euripides; a single epoch to the old and new Comedy. The philosopher-geniuses, too, inspired by Socrates, how long did they flourish after the death of Plato and of Aristotle? And as in Greece, so in Rome. Oratory burgeoned forth under Cicero, so that there are very few before his time who can give you pleasure, and none whom you can admire unless he had seen Cicero or had been seen by Cicero.

Though I often search for the reasons why men of like genius are confined to certain periods, I can never find any of whose truth I am sure. Yet I do find some reasons which are perhaps plausible, and among them the following: Genius is nourished by emulation, and it is sometimes envy, sometimes esteem which enkindles imitation; and it is natural that that which is cultivated with greatest zeal rises to the highest point of perfection. Yet to stay at the point of perfection is difficult, and naturally that which cannot go forward recedes. When we have given up hope of being able to surpass or equal those whom we regard as our superiors, our zeal declines with our hope; it ceases to follow what it cannot catch up with, and abandoning the subject as though it were in another's possession, it seeks a new one. The greatest obstacle to perfection in any work is our fickle habit of deserting to something else.

Seneca the Elder (*Contr.* 1, *Praef.* 6 ff.), writing in A.D. 37, finds a possible explanation in the same "law" of nature, and applies the "law" in the same way as Velleius:

Of Eloquence

Whatever quality Roman eloquence has which can vie with or surpass insolent Greece flourished about the time of Cicero. All the talents which gave lustre to our studies were born then. Since his day the art has daily deteriorated, whether through the luxury of our time (for nothing is so deadly to talent as luxury); or whether, when the reward accorded to this most beautiful art vanished, all efforts were turned toward base practices abounding in glory or profit; or whether by some fate whose spiteful and constant law in all things decrees that what has risen to the greatest heights slips back again to the lowest depth, and more quickly than it ascended.

To this same "law," it must be noted, Blass[15] has recourse in his endeavor to explain the decay of eloquence in Greece after Alexander, and Cucheval[16] makes it the primary factor in the decay at Rome. True, thinks Cucheval, liberty was lost. True that the education was defective. But the most important consideration in his eyes is the validity of Velleius' "law": decay would have come in any event. So far as Velleius himself is concerned, one cannot help remembering at this juncture that he was not ordinarily of a philosophical bent and in practice was unable to discern the great movements in history.

In wistful retrospect Pliny the Younger describes (*Epist.* 8. 14) the sounder method on which in other days the training for public life was based, and from the security of Trajan's reign he looks back with repugnance upon the dark days of Domitian, in whose insolent and repressive tyranny he finds the true causes of the decline. This letter, published about A.D. 109, in special gives a picture of the wretched degradation into which the Senate had sunk:

Our subjection under a former reign covered with a blanket of oblivion and ignorance all the arts of culture; for who is so tame-spirited as to desire to learn an art which he will be unable to put

---

[15] Friedrich Blass, *Die griechische Beredsamkeit in dem Zeitraum von Alexander bis auf Augustus* (Berlin, 1865), pp. 12–13.

[16] II, 369.

in practice? And so liberty when restored on Nerva's accession [in A.D. 96] found us wanting in skill and experience.

It was our rule in the olden days that we should learn from our elders both by precept and example the principles which we ourselves should one day put in practice, and in our turn hand down to the younger generation. So when our elders became candidates for office, they used to stand at the doors of the Senate-house, and were spectators before they were colleagues in this body. Thus they were taught by the most unfailing method of instruction, example, all the Senatorial practice.

[During Domitian's reign] I paid a visit to the Senate, but a Senate that was frightened and speechless; since it was dangerous if you said what you felt, and detestable if you said what you did not feel. What could be learned, what pleasure was there in learning, when the Senate was convened either for utter idleness or for business of utter sinfulness, was kept in session either for ridiculous or grievous ends, and passed resolutions that were never serious, but often saddening? On becoming a Senator, and hence a sharer in these evils, I witnessed and suffered them for many years, and as a result my spirits were dulled, broken, and crushed even for a time thereafter.

And in an earlier letter (3. 18; A.D. 101), in which Pliny reports that his panegyric of Trajan was listened to for three days, he states briefly but emphatically the main prerequisite for a healthy epideictic: "The reason is not that we write with more eloquence, but with more freedom than formerly, and as a result with greater enjoyment. It will redound to the further glory of our present Emperor [Trajan] that discourses of this kind, once as detested as they were false, are now as pleasing as they are sincere."

A word about the recluse Persius (A.D. 34–62) and the realist Juvenal[17] (A.D. ?60–?138). Both satirists seem unconscious of the main cause of the decline, and their silence under the despotisms of their day is of course understandable. Persius ex-

---

[17] For this section see G. G. Ramsay, ed. and tr., *Juvenal and Persius* (Loeb Classical Library, 1920), Introduction.

plains the weakness of poetry and oratory by the decay of morality, which he does not connect with the loss of freedom. But even when you think that he may really discuss the qualifications of the Statesman in Satire 4, or when he discourses on human freedom in Satire 5, you find no recognition of the state of political subjection in which the Romans now found themselves. The discourse on freedom is a typical Stoic treatment of the subject—How can one master one's own soul?; political considerations are entirely absent. Juvenal had lived through the terrible latter years of Nero's reign and through Domitian's. He believes deeply in the virtues of the past, admires the heroes of the republican time, and cites them as models; he criticizes Roman life caustically, but Roman *private* life. The degeneracy which he brilliantly describes he relates but seldom to the despotic character of the government. Only a few verses emerge from his silence: "But Rome was free when she called Cicero parent and father of his country" (*Sat.* 8. 243–244, and see also 1. 151 ff.). Contrast with Persius and Juvenal the words of Lucan (A.D. 39–65) on Pharsalus (*Civil War* 7. 639 ff.):

More was lost there than mere life and safety; we were overthrown for all the future ages of the world; all the generations, which shall ever live in slavery, were conquered by those swords. For what crime of their own commission were the sons and grandsons of those who fought at Pharsalus born to servitude? If to us born after that battle, thou, Fortune, gavest a master, thou shouldst have given us also the chance of fighting for our freedom.

But Lucan's revolutionary enthusiasm and audacious championship, during Nero's reign, of the defenders of the ancient republican system are subjects that cannot be enlarged upon here. Nor, on the other hand, may I discuss the contradiction offered us by his oily flattery of Nero (1. 33–66); all the horrors of the Civil War were not too high a price to pay if the Fates could not otherwise have willed the coming of Nero: "When your watch on this earth has come to an end, and you seek the stars at last, the sky will rejoice. But to me you are already a god." For Lucan believed that Fate had ordained the monarchy.[18]

"Longinus" and Tacitus I have saved for the last, because more specifically than all the other observers they see that the main issue is between political freedom and autocracy. The one permits an insight into the truth to show through his protective coloration; the other comes perhaps as closely to grips with the question as was in the conditions of his time possible. We must of course read both in the light of these conditions.

In the last chapter of his essay *On the Sublime*, "Longinus" brings up a question "lately raised by a certain philosopher," who speaks as follows:

I wonder, as no doubt do many others, too, how it is that in the present age there are men who are gifted with the powers of persuasion and statesmanship in the highest degree, and are keen and versatile, and especially expert in the charms of style, yet truly lofty and sublime natures are no longer produced, or only quite exceptionally. So great and universal is the dearth of eloquence that has its hold upon our age! Must we really believe that oft-repeated observation that democracy is the kind foster-mother of greatness, and that literary excellence may be said to flourish only with democracy, and with democracy to die? For freedom, it is said, has power to nourish the imagination of the high-minded and to kindle hope, and where it prevails there spreads abroad the zeal of mutual rivalry and the ambitious struggle for preëminence. Moreover by reason of the rewards which are open to all in free states, the mental powers of the speaker are continually sharpened by exercise, and as it were rubbed to brightness, and shine forth, as is natural, with the same freedom as animates the State. But today we seem to be trained to righteous servitude in our childhood, being all but swathed in its customs and practices when our minds are still tender, and never tasting of that

18 See, e.g., 3. 393.

most lovely and most abundant fountain of eloquence, I mean liberty. And so we turn out to be nothing but sublime flatterers. One has aptly represented all servitude, even if it be most righteous, as the cage of the soul and a public dungeon.

"Longinus'" formal answer to the question posed by the philosopher is far from satisfactory. What enslaves us, he says, is rather love of money and pleasure: "No, for such as we are it is perhaps better to be held in subjection than to be free, since our appetites, if let loose altogether upon our neighbors like beasts from a den, would set the civilized world on fire with evil deeds." Gibbon comments: "Longinus was forced to enervate [his noble ideas on liberty] not only by the term 'most righteous,' which he takes care to apply twice to the present despotism, but by employing the stale pretence of putting his own thoughts into the mouth of a nameless philosopher."[19]

In Tacitus' distinguished little book of criticism, *The Dialogue on Orators*, Maternus bids Messalla to discuss the decline of eloquence and in doing so to avail himself of the old-fashioned freedom of speech "from which we have degenerated even more than we have from eloquence" (27). Maternus had said: "The mercenary eloquence of the present day is a recent innovation, born of a degenerate state of society" (12). Messalla discusses the laxity of the training at home, the carelessness of parents, the ignorance of teachers, the decline in old-fashioned virtue, and especially the vices characteristic of the city Rome—the passion for play-actors and the interest in the contests of gladiators and of horses. The past is not solidly learned, nor as in Cicero's day is universal knowledge sought, but now the essential thing is declamation, the training of tongue and voice in imaginary debates which have no relation

[19] *Journal*, Oct. 25, 1762; W. Rhys Roberts, *Longinus On the Sublime* (Cambridge, 1907), p. 13, n. 2; and cf. Ulrich von Wilamowitz-Moellendorf, *Der Glaube der Hellenen* (Berlin, 1932), II, 547.

with real life. He prefers the rough home-spun of Gracchus and Crassus, and bewails the practice of some speakers of his day, who boast that their speeches can be sung and danced to (25–26, 28–32).

But of special significance are the utterances of another interlocutor in the *Dialogue*, Secundus, and of Maternus himself. Secundus argues that the unsettled political conditions which prevailed during the republic, the dissensions and feuds of those days of unrest and unrestraint, when there was no single ruler to apply a strong hand, and freedom of speech was untrammeled, tore the State apart. But it is in such an environment that eloquence thrives. "Great oratory, like a flame, needs fuel to sustain it, movement to excite it, and it brightens in the burning." Eloquence was, then, an indispensable passport to success in public life, and great issues and trials brought it immense rewards. Cicero's reputation would never have been great if there were no Catiline, no Milo, no Verres, no Antony (36 ff.).

Maternus admits that the turbulent days of the republic encouraged greater oratory, but insists that the blessings of peace and the tranquillity of the present more than compensate for the superior oratory of the past:

The art we are discussing is not a quiet and peaceable art. Truly great and distinguished oratory is rather a foster-child of license, which foolish men call liberty,[20] an associate of sedition, a goad for the unbridled multitude; and it does not grow in a well-regulated civic order. Do we hear of the existence of any oratory at Sparta or in Crete, States whose constitution and laws were the most rigorous ever recorded? Eloquence was unknown in Macedonia certainly, and in Persia [all these States were either militaristic or autocratic], and

[20] Cf. Plato, *Rep.*, Bk. 9, 572E, on the democratic man turned into the tyrannical: "complete lawlessness, called by his seducers 'perfect freedom'"; Ps.-Plutarch, "On Listening to Lectures" *Moralia* 37 C–D): "unconstraint, which some of the young, lacking education, think to be freedom."

in fact in all States that were content with an undisputed government. There were some orators at Rhodes, at Athens a great many; in both States the populace could do everything, the ignorant multitude could do everything, everybody, so to speak, could do everything. Likewise in our own State, so long as it swayed hither and thither, so long as it spent itself in partisan struggles and dissensions and disagreements, so long as there was no peace in the forum, no harmony in the Senate, no self-control on the part of the speakers in the law-courts, no obedience to authority, no sense of restraint on the part of the magistrates, such turbulent times produced an eloquence that was no doubt more vigorous. But the eloquence of the Gracchi was not so beneficial to the country that it should endure their laws as well, and ingloriously did Cicero pay for his fame in oratory by such a death. . . . Just as the art of medicine is least needed and is consequently of least advantage amongst peoples who enjoy great good health and sound constitutions, so oratory has less value and repute where people are well-behaved and ready to obey their sovereign. What need is there of long arguments in the Senate, when gentlemen agree so quickly? What need of a long succession of speeches before the public assembly, when it is not the ignorant multitude that deliberates upon the common welfare, but *one man*, and he the all-wisest? (40–41).

I refrain from putting any of the emperors of the first century to the test of the appraisal in this last sentence, even as I omit to draw modern analogies.

It may seem that Maternus is bluntly taking issue with Cicero, who in a number of places[21] expresses himself to the following effect: "The ambition to speak does not arise among men who are shackled and bound fast by the tyranny of kings. Eloquence is an associate of peace and an ally of tranquillity and is, so to speak, a foster-child of a well-regulated civic order." "This one art has constantly flourished above all others in every free nation, and especially in those States

[21] *Brutus* 12. 45; *De Oratore* 1. 8. 30. See also *De Oratore* 1. 4. 14; 2. 8. 33; *Orator* 41. 141; and cf. *De Inv.* 1. 1 and *De Oratore* 1. 9. 38.

which have acquired peace and tranquillity." But Cicero's thought is not necessarily in conflict with that of Tacitus' interlocutor. Cicero is thinking of freedom from foreign wars, and his "well-regulated civic order" is opposed not to a State torn by dissensions, but to one whose institutions have not yet been firmly established. Quintilian, on the other hand, stresses the part played by oratory in the establishing of stable governments: Denouncers of eloquence say that it "stirs up not only sedition and popular tumult, but wars that can never be expiated." Yet "never, I believe, would the founders of cities have brought it about that the nomadic multitudes should join into communities if these had not been persuaded by learned utterance; nor without the consummate power of oratory would the great law-givers have prevailed upon humankind to yield to the servitude of Law" (2. 16. 1 ff.). More directly opposed to Maternus would be J. A. Symonds, discoursing on an art allied to eloquence. A comparison of the drama of different peoples proves to him that one of the two conditions necessary for the creation of great drama is that a nation must be free: "It requires a *free* and *active* race, in which young and turbulent blood is flowing, to produce a drama."[22]

V

It is likely that some of the authors I have cited avoided for reasons of prudence a discussion of political causes. "Longinus," for example, may indeed have written with timidity. We are not even sure that the treatises by "Longinus" and Tacitus were intended for other than private circulation.[23] From passages in different works of Tacitus we are led to assume that he realized the past could not be recalled; he felt that the inevi-

[22] *The Greek Poets* (New York, 1882), II, 11.
[23] See Roberts, p. 15.

table must be accepted, and that even under the Empire prudence and moderation could assure one honor and dignity.[24] In the *Dialogue* Maternus says: "Let everyone enjoy the advantages of his own era without disparaging any other age" (41). Seneca the Elder acquiesced in the new order (e.g., *Contr.* 2. 4. 13). Velleius accepted it with enthusiasm—its peace, stability, public works, the generosity of its princes— and we read his rhapsodical eulogies of the emperor Tiberius (e.g., *Roman History*, 2. 104, 111, 119–120). Yet he said of Cicero that when he "was beheaded by the crime of Antony, the voice of the people was cut off" (2. 66). Quintilian held a chair of rhetoric under the Caesars, and wrote fulsomely of Domitian—"a prince pre-eminent in eloquence as in all other virtues" (4, *Praef.* 3, and see also 10. 1. 91–92).

Eloquence is, of course, traditionally connected with democracy. According to Aristotle[25] it was democracy which first gave birth to rhetoric in the revolutions of Sicily. When the Sicilian tyrants were expelled in 465 B.C., democracies came into being, and numerous lawsuits were instituted to recover the property which the tyrants had illegally confiscated. Corax wished to influence the people by speech and to that end wrote an art of rhetoric. The Greeks considered that the only kind of agreement desirable among rational men is that got from free discussion, and *parrhesia*, the right of the citizen to speak his mind, was staunchly prized. And if we wish to find a clear outline of the rôle discussion plays in a democracy we had better go, as for so many other touchstones, to the funeral speech Thucydides puts into the mouth of Pericles: "Those of our countrymen who are occupied chiefly with business yet do not lack a knowledge of public affairs. For we alone regard a man who takes no part in these public duties not as one who only

---

[24] For pertinent passages see *Annals* 1. 9; 1. 74; 4. 33; 14. 12; *Agricola* 42; *Hist.* 1. 1; 1. 16; 4. 5; Gudeman, p. xxxvii.

[25] In Cicero, *Brutus* 12. 46; see art. "Korax" in Pauly-Wissowa.

minds his own business, but as a useless person; and we at least decide for ourselves, or reflect rightly upon, public questions, believing that it is not discussion that is a stumbling-block to action, but rather not to be instructed by discussion before entering upon action" (2. 40. 2). Rhetoric was forbidden in militaristic and bureaucratic Sparta.

Political bias is bound to affect our criticism of eloquence. Consider the varied fate of Demosthenes in recent times. If you believe in democratic principles, you are likely to read Demosthenes sympathetically, as the spokesman of democracy against Macedonian autocracy. But if your ideal is the empire of the Caesars, you will feel only contempt for the mean little State that had to yield to efficient Macedon, and feel only scorn for her provincial lawyer-spokesman who swam against the current without realizing that it was the wave of the future. It was in this spirit that, in 1916, the scholar Drerup made an appeal to banish the Greek orator from the schools of Germany.[26]

Want of space forbids us to compare the decline of eloquence in Greece after Alexander. Hellenistic scholars may have discussed the question. And at the beginning of chapter 36 in Tacitus' *Dialogue* we read: "In our State, *too*, the eloquence of our fathers was promoted by the same conditions." A lacuna is properly thought to belong here, representing a discussion of Attic oratory, in which the same political-historical causes which brought about a high state of eloquence in Rome were set forth as bringing about like results in democratic Athens. Blass[27] thinks that the main cause of decay at Athens was the loss of free speech, and the resultant debasement of the character of the people. Thus we have the servile spectacle of the Athenians erecting 300 statues to one governor, Demetrius of Phalerum, and giving divine honors to his successor who over-

---

[26] Engelbert Drerup, *Aus einer alten Advokatenrepublik* (Paderborn, 1916).
[27] P. 12.

threw him. Jebb[28] accepts the political explanation for the decay of deliberative and forensic oratory, but for the decline of epideictic speaking, a fine art, he assigns another cause. The decay of citizen-life of the Greek republics brought about a change in the nature of Greek art. That art had been popular, fixing its attention on the essential and typical, and suppressing the accidental, trivial, and transient. When the moral unity of the city-state was broken, and men lived life apart from the city, the artist worked for a few, and caste and coterie make capricious judges. "In this sense, it may justly be said that nothing is so democratic as taste." If, by the way, we use this criterion for a comparison of Cicero and Pliny, we are forced to place Pliny in an age of decadence. Cicero repeatedly says that the opinion of a real ordinary Roman audience supplies the best test of good speaking;[29] whereas Pliny shows disdain for an audience other than intellectual.

In contrast to the situation in Greece, in the Roman Empire epideictic flourished, so far as popularity is concerned, for centuries. It became more and more debased. Compare Cicero's eulogy of Pompey (66 B.C.), Pliny's panegyric of the emperor Trajan (A.D. 100), and the panegyrics of the third and fourth centuries. Cicero's speech contains overmuch adulation, but is after all a *free* man's speech. Pliny's, except for a few passages, shows decency in the relations of orator and imperial patron. But "Mamertinus'" oration addressed to Maximian in A.D. 289 represents the extreme of unhealthy servility: "When our enemies would have invaded our provinces, O Emperor, what need was there of a multitude, since you in person contended?" "Yes, you were so carried away through all the battle as a mighty stream, enhanced by winter snows and showers, is wont to invade the field on every side." "He who would enumerate your exploits, Emperor, must hope to have in-

[28] R. C. Jebb, *Attic Orators from Antiphon to Isaeos* (London, 1876), II, 433 ff.
[29] E.g., *Brutus* 49. 184.

numerable years, aye, centuries—indeed a life as long as *you* deserve."[30] Seyss-Inquart in Vienna on March 15, 1938: "My Fuehrer, wherever the way may lead we follow. Hail, my Fuehrer."

While we are in this general way considering the relation between the democratic civic order and eloquence, let us briefly glance back at an earlier day in our own democracy, and review the essay by Edward T. Channing, entitled "The Orator and His Times."[31] It was first published in 1819 and was reprinted by him in 1852. I report in condensed form, yet mostly in his own words, certain points of his argument:

Public Speaking cannot have now the importance and power it had in Greece and Rome. The ancients had a false estimate of national grandeur; the spirit of their governments was utterly war-like, their love of freedom was another name for ferocious lawless-ness, and their love of country cloaked a boundless ambition for power. Society seemed to be a combination for extending power rather than for setting up a prosperous security. The population was ignorant and inflammable, and in the courts of justice the speaker was allowed to go beyond the law. Today [1819, 1852] we have a stable foundation and the ample protection of government. In free countries we are now disposed to make the security of indi-viduals and of the State rest on laws and institutions, and not on the popular caprice, or on the power of any one man. That helps to explain what is reproachfully called the *temperate* and *inefficient* character of modern eloquence. [Recall that Channing's contem-poraries included Clay, Calhoun, Webster, and Wendell Phillips!] In Greece and Rome individuals seem to create great changes; but we think it one of the happiest, and we trust most permanent, dis-tinctions that today we do not need the great man to take the place of our laws and institutions. The great man's sole power is restrained; he is perpetually taught that we can do without him. The orator is fortunately less able to do harm, and less needed to do good. The diffusion of knowledge helps us to help ourselves and to do without

---

[30] See "Latin Panegyrics" [p. 34 of this volume].
[31] *Lectures* (Boston, 1856), pp. 1–25.

the orator's instruction. The orator in ancient times controlled his audience; today the audience controls him. Modern eloquence aims at making men think patiently and earnestly; it has only to secure a lodgment for truth in the mind, and then by and by the truth will quietly prevail. It seems as if the effect of our increased knowledge has been to make men more contemplative, and it is indeed true that the imagination and passions do not predominate—they are not our turbulent masters. It is the general effect of our improved society to give an influence to purity, firmness, and stability.

One might wish to defend the ancients against some of the accusations made by Channing, but would find it even more tempting to study how far the conditions which he describes for his time hold today.

Hume in his essay "Of Eloquence" also thinks the modern world inferior to the ancient in eloquence. "It would be easy to find a Philip in modern times, but where shall we find a Demosthenes?" And De Quincey in his essay "Rhetoric" believes that the complexity of modern business will ever prevent the resurrection of rhetors.

The causes then, direct or contributory, to which the decay in the first century is assigned by our ancient theorists are the complexity of the Empire, degraded morality, debased education, general factors of cultural development (a natural "law" of reaction), and the loss of political liberty. The truth may well be that all these causes operated in a complex, but certainly the loss of political liberty is the major and ultimate consideration. The subject deserves profounder study than it has had. "Maturism," for example, is a favorite theory in the observation of human institutions—that they finish growing, become ripe and ready to fall after passing, as do individuals, through a process of youth and flowering.[32] Livy's figure is

[32] The cyclical view of history is very prevalent today; cf., e.g., the plan of A. J. Toynbee's *A Study of History* (London, 1934, 1939), which includes a treatment of the Genesis, Growth, Breakdown, and Disintegration of Civilizations.

akin; he likens the downward plunge of morals in Roman life to a falling edifice (*Praef.* 9). De Quincey, deeply impressed by Velleius' reflections on the tendency of intellectual power to gather in clusters, endeavors to show that the observation founded by the Roman author's review of two literatures "we may now countersign by an experience of eight or nine"; his illustrations of the phenomenon in Greek and English literature in the essay on Style (Part III) must be known to all my readers. Further, symptom must be distinguished from cause. The education of the period cannot be divorced from the society of which it was a manifestation and accompaniment. The younger Seneca in *Epist.* 114 takes the position that the style of speaking reproduces the general character of the time. He thus replies to the question set him by Lucilius, "why during certain periods a corrupt style of speech comes to the fore, and how it happens that men's natural capacities have declined into certain vices." And Persius in *Sat.* 1 takes a comparable stand. The schools, as modern critics say, were not responsible for the decadence. Nor can the character of the times and of the people be separated from the political conditions of which they were largely the result. I have here not attempted such a study as I think to be needed, nor even emphasized the part played by Stoic thought in this period— in particular by Stoic opposition to the worship of the Caesars, and adherence to the tradition of *Cosmopolis* and the brotherhood of man. I have not in detail discussed the decline of the arts in their broadest form or of civilization in general, nor the philosophy of history maintained by the historians, nor the attitude to Fate held by the poets. My aim has been simply to review what observers in the first century said on the decline of oratory in particular, and we learn that some of these clearly realized that eloquence flourishes best on soil dedicated to free institutions.

IX
Memoria: Treasure-House of Eloquence[*]

MEMORY was important in many realms of Greek and Roman life and thought, religion, poetry, and education. It was already a subject of inquiry in the early theories of psychology. Alcmaeon of Croton[1] (early fifth century B.C.), founder of empirical psychology, placed the seat of sensation in the brain, which combines the sensations, stores up the perceptions, and so gives us memory; Parmenides[2] explained memory and forgetfulness as depending on the kind of mixture of the cold and warm manifestations of nature; and Diogenes of Apollonia[3] (latter half fifth century), Ionian physicist, attributed memory to the motions of air in the body.

You are familiar with the part Memory played in the mysteries—in the Orphic cult as reflected in the verses inscribed on the Petelia Tablet[4]—the two streams, of which one is to be avoided by the soul of the departed, but if his soul has

---

[*] Presidential address delivered in Chicago before the American Philological Association on December 28, 1955. Footnotes to the address have been added by the author for publication in this volume.

[1] Diels-Kranz, *Die Fragmente der Vorsokratiker* (10th ed.; Berlin, 1961), 1. 213 (Alcmaeon A 11); Plato, *Phaedo* 96 AB.

[2] Diels-Kranz, *Fragmente* 1. 226, ll. 5 ff. (Parmenides A 46); Theophrastus, *De Sensu* 1. 3–4.

[3] Diels-Kranz, *Fragmente* 2. 56, ll. 23 ff. (Diogenes A 19); Theophrastus, *De Sensu* 45. See J. I. Beare, *Greek Theories of Elementary Cognition* (Oxford, 1906), pp. 258–260.

[4] Fourth-third century B.C. Diels-Kranz, *Fragmente* 1. 15 (Orpheus B 17).

drunk from the refreshing stream on the right, which flows from the Lake of Memory, he will rule among the other heroes; the two fountains sacred to the oracular god Trophonius in Boeotia, one bringing oblivion of the past and the other memory, so that the applicant may remember what he sees when he goes down into the cave to receive revelations;[5] and Plato's account of the soul's catharsis as a process of forgetting and remembering[6]—of forgetting the evils of the flesh and in the end remembering forever universal truth and virtue. Only the mind of the philosopher has wings, and with all his power he engages himself in memory upon those things by the contemplation of which Deity is divine; by his right use of these memories he is ever being initiated into perfect mysteries and alone becomes truly perfect.[7]

The Socratic doctrine is that all learning is reminiscence, and the memory is the guardian of the highest spiritual values.[8] In Plato's *Republic* the true philosopher, to whom the State is to be entrusted, must, among other noble qualities, have a good natural memory.[9]

In the *Phaedrus* when Theuth boasted that his invention of writing would be an aid to memory, Thamus replied that the more likely result would be to weaken the memory by disuse.[10] If Plato deplored the enfeebling of memory that came with the invention of writing, Emerson[11] thought that as much or more

[5] Pausanias, *Descript. Greece* 9. 39. 8; see W. K. C. Guthrie, *Orpheus and Greek Religion* (2d ed.; London, 1952), pp. 177–178.

[6] *Republic* 10. 620 D ff. (Myth of Er); see J. A. Stewart, *Myths of Plato* (London, 1905), pp. 155 ff., on the connections with Virgil, *Aeneid* 6. 703 ff. (Lethe) and with Dante, *Purg.* 28 (Eunoe and Lethe).

[7] *Phaedrus* 249 C.

[8] *Phaedo* 72 E ff.

[9] 6. 486–487, 490, 494 B, 503; 7. 535 C.

[10] 247 E f.

[11] "Memory," in *Complete Works*, ed. E. W. Emerson (Boston and New York, 1903–4), 12. 99.

could be said of printing, and Aldous Huxley is in accord: "We read so much that we have lost the art of remembering."[12] The same exalted view of the value of memory in the oral tradition is apparent in Julius Caesar's account of the Celtic Druids: they are said to learn in school a great number of verses, and some of the learners stay there for twenty years. They think it unlawful to commit their lore to writing, and fear that in relying on their writing the learners would relax their zeal for learning and their memory.[13]

To the Neo-Platonist Plotinus memory is of things that are no more, and relates to our life in time; when the soul enters upon the eternal life of contemplation, the memory of things of earth will have no place there.[14]

Pythagoras used to say—so Heraclides Ponticus (fourth century B.C.) tells us—that in an earlier incarnation he was held to be the god Hermes' son, and when Hermes told him that he could choose any gift he wished except immortality, he asked to preserve throughout his life and throughout his death a memory of his experiences. Hence he remembered everything that happened through the several migrations of his soul.[15] The exercises which Cato in Cicero's *De Senectute*[16] says he practiced in order to improve his memory—the recalling each evening of all the events of the day—had with the Pythagoreans a moral and religious meaning, as an examination of conscience and a way of getting to know oneself.[17] Add that

[12] Paul Shorey, *What Plato Said* (3d impression; Chicago, 1957), p. 555 (on Plato, *Phaedrus* 275 A).

[13] *Bellum Gallicum* 6. 14.

[14] *Enneads* 4. 41 ff.; see W. R. Inge, *The Philosophy of Plotinus* (2d ed.; London, 1923), I. 226–228.

[15] Diogenes Laertius 8. 1 (Pythagoras) 4. 4–5; Diels-Kranz, *Fragmente* I. 467–468 (Iamblichus, *Vita Pythag.* 164–166).

[16] 11. 38.

[17] See Pierre-Maxime Schuhl, *Essai sur la formation de la pensée grecque* (2d ed.; Paris, 1949), p. 251; Diogenes Laertius 8. 1 (Pythagoras) 19. 22.

Philolaüs (contemporary of Socrates) of this school in his mystical love of numbers calls the perfect number, 10, Memory;[18] and that, according to Porphyry (third Christian century), Pythagoras called the harmony of the spheres "Mnemosyne."[19]

Memoria figures in the ethical thought of a variety of schools. The first philosophic theologian, Xenophanes of Colophon (sixth century B.C.), lauds the ancient institution of the Symposium, which keeps alive the memory of true *arete:* "Praise that man who even in his cups can show forth goodly thoughts, according as memory serves him and his zeal for virtue is at full stretch."[20] The Stoic Antipater of Tarsus (second century B.C.), believing that every gift of a kindly Fortune invited deep gratitude, kept it to the end of his life in his memory—than which there is no more secure storehouse (ταμιεῖον) of blessings for a man.[21] In *De Finibus*[22] Cicero contests the Epicurean principle that it is the recollection of pleasures enjoyed that gives happiness, and that the wise man ought to forget past evils: the recollection of past misfortunes can be pleasant. In his *De Anima* Cassiodorus lists seven virtues which aid in attaining the qualities of the good Christian life—the four cardinal virtues, Justice, Fortitude, Wisdom, Self-Command, and also Contemplation, Judgment, and Memory;[23] and Augustine in *De Trinitate*[24] finds the image of the

---

[18] Diels-Kranz, *Fragmente* 1. 401, l. 1; 402, ll. 14–15 (Philolaüs A 13); *Theologoumena Arithmeticae*, ed. Vittorio de Falco (Leipzig, 1922), pp. 81–82.

[19] *Vita Pythagorae*, XXXI, ed. Augustus Nauck (Leipzig, 1886), p. 34: τὴν δὲ πασῶν ἅμα σύγκρισιν καὶ συμφωνίαν καὶ ὡσανεὶ σύνδεσμον, ἧσπερ ὡς αἰδίου τε καὶ ἀγενήτου μέρος ἑκάστη καὶ ἀπόρροια, Μνημοσύνην ὠνόμαζεν.

[20] Athenaeus, xi. 462 f.; tr. C. B. Gulick (Loeb Classical Library, London and New York, 1933), v. 17.

[21] Plutarch, *Lives (Marius)* 46. 2 (433).

[22] 2. 32. 104 ff.

[23] Chap. 7; ed. J. W. Halporn, in *Traditio*, XVI (1960), 82–83.

[24] Book 10, chaps. 11–12; Migne, *Pat. Lat.*, XLIV, 982–984. Cf. St. Thomas Aquinas, *Summa Theologica* 1, Quest. 79, art. 6 f.

Trinity in man's three powers of the soul: *intellectus, memoria,* and *voluntas.*

Mnemosyne, in Hesiod daughter of Earth and Heaven, and mother of the Muses,[25] who "call to the mind" of the poet they inspire the story he has to tell, is, as Friedrich Solmsen has written, "the first divine incarnation of a spiritual power as such".[26] In the Homeric *Hymn to Hermes,* the son of Maia honors Mnemosyne in his song first among the gods; for she had won him to her following.[27] Before Pierus established nine Muses, the Boeotian town of Askra honored Μνήμη as one of three, together with Practice (Μελέτη) and Song ('Αοιδή).[28] It is much later, in Afranius[29] (second Christian century), that she appears, as the mother of Wisdom to be sure, but now also as the wife of Experience. And Philostratus[30] (third Christian century) will not argue with the poets as to whether Memory should be called the mother or daughter of Time. The Homer-relief of Archelaüs of Priene (*c.* 130 B.C.) represents the four attributes of a poet like Homer: Mneme appears with Arete, Pistis, and Sophia.[31] J. A. Notopoulos has discussed the great importance of memory among oral peoples, and richly explained the creative role she played as a living instructor in oral literature;[32] and W. C. Greene[33] has built for us a broad picture of this rôle—embracing not only the architectonic power of the poet in ordering his remembered material,[34] but

[25] *Theogony* 53 ff., 75 ff., 135, 915–917.
[26] *Hesiod and Aeschylus* (Ithaca, 1949), p. 70.
[27] Vv. 429–430.
[28] Pausanias, *Descript. Greece* 9. 29. 2–3.
[29] In his *Sella;* Gellius 13. 8. 1–3.
[30] *Lives of the Sophists* 1. 523.
[31] Carl Watzinger, *Das Relief des Archelaos von Priene* (63d *Programm zum Winckelmannfeste;* Berlin, 1903), p. 17 and Plate I.
[32] "Mnemosyne in Oral Literature," *Trans. Amer. Philol. Assoc.,* LXIX (1938), 465–493.
[33] "The Spoken and the Written Word," *Harvard Studies in Class. Philology,* LX (1951), 23–59.
[34] *Ibid.,* p. 29.

the memory of the race that he preserves in his poem—of its "myths and traditions and proverbs, heroic legends and characters, religious rites and folkways."[35] Fundamental in the purpose of the heroic poems is that they assure the memory of the κλέα ἀνδρῶν,[36] of the heroes of old and their glorious deeds.

The writer of history has a like end in view. Herodotus: "Here are published the results of the historical researches of Herodotus, in order that the exploits of men may not be obliterated by lapse of time."[37] Or Diodorus (first century B.C.): "The deeds of those whose virtue has won them fame are evermore remembered, for being proclaimed by the divine voice of History."[38] Or Livy: "Writing . . . the only faithful guardian of the memory of past events."[39] Or Catulus in Cicero, *De Oratore:* "History, which gives life to memory."[40] The "modern Quintilian," Vives (1492–1540), speaks like an ancient historian: "Our own experiences come to us in the course of time and through the events of circumstances; what others have experienced we get to know from the memory of the past, which is called History."[41] We inevitably think of Francis Bacon's division of human learning into the realms of philosophy, guided by the faculty of reason; poetry, ruled by the imagination; and history, presided over by the memory.[42]

---

[35] *Ibid.*, p. 28.

[36] Homer, *Iliad* 9. 524; Hesiod, *Theogony* 100: κλέεα προτέρων ἀνθρώπων; see Notopoulos, "Mnemosyne," p. 468.

[37] Book 1, Pref. See also 2. 77: The Egyptians living in the cultivated parts of the country were, of all the nations he knew, the best historians because of their care to preserve the memory of the past.

[38] 1. 2. 3.

[39] 6. 1. 2.

[40] 2. 9. 36.

[41] *De Tradendis Disciplinis*, Book V; *Io. Lodovici Vivis Valentini Opera* (Basel, 1555), 1. 505.

[42] *Advancement of Learning*, 2.1, in Spedding, Ellis, and Heath, eds., *Works of Francis Bacon* (Boston, 1863), 6. 182 ff. The four intellectual arts: Inquiry or Invention, Examination or Judgment, Custody or Memory, Elocution or Tradition; 5. 1 ff., *Works* 6. 260 ff.

History is, of course, more than memory; the past "requires historical investigation where it is not, and cannot be remembered"—and I would recommend R. G. Collingwood's interesting criticism of Bacon in *The Idea of History*.[43] But it is safe to say that to the ancients the reënactment of the past in present thought is not unlike the operation of memory.

The best ancient thought on the psychology of memory[44] is contained in several pages of Aristotle, especially in the treatise *De Memoria et Recollectione*, and in *De Anima*. Here is the theory in brief.

The states of knowledge in the development of mind are sense-perception, memory, experience, art, and science. Out of the synthesizing of sense perceptions comes memory; out of repeated memories of the same objects experience develops; from experience come the artisan's skill and the knowledge of the man of science.[45]

Memory, an active principle, involves an awareness of the lapse of time. The experience of memory is a sort of picture stamped upon the sense-organ by the act of perceiving—like the impression which a seal makes on wax—and this impression is a copy, an image, of the event in the past.[46]

[43] (Oxford, 1948), pp. 58, 69, 234 ff., 238, 252–253, 257, 293–295, 307.

[44] See Léon Robin, *Greek Thought* (New York, 1928), p. 301: "All that was best in orthodox psychology down to the end of the nineteenth century is contained, in sum, in a few pages of Aristotle."

[45] Aristotle, *Post. Analyt.* 2. 19 (99b–100a); *Metaphysics* I. 1 (980a ff.). See also, anent the Hippocratic corpus, Precept 1, P. H. and E. A. DeLacy, *Philodemus: On Methods of Inference* (Philadelphia, 1941), p. 123: "By combining many perceptions through memory, the physician can establish reason (λόγος), and hence make systematic [and certain] inferences from appearances." See Plato, *Phaedo* 96 B, for a dissenting view; and on the importance of memory for acquiring true knowledge, see *Theaet.* 191 D f.

[46] *De Mem. et Recollect.* 449b–451a. In contrast, see Thomas Reid, *Essays on the Intellectual Powers of Man*, ed. A. D. Woozley (London, 1941), pp. xxvi, 216 ff., 219, 233, 251; criticizing Hume, and Locke, Reid denies both that there are images (as the word is popularly used) in memory, and that the analogy between memory and a repository is valid.

There is a unifying, central function of sense inherent in all the special senses. This "common sense"[47] perceives the common sensibles—number, shape, size, motion and rest, unity, and time—and discriminates and compares the data of the special senses; to it belongs the consciousness that we perceive; and to it are assigned memory and imagination. Memory, then, belongs to the same faculty as imagination. The seat of the common sense is in the heart, and ultimately that is why, perhaps, we say "learning by heart."[48]

Awareness in actual memory may be continuous since the past event, but in *recollection* must not have been continuous. We can remember without recollection if the image has not been lost, but in recollection we recover what has disappeared from consciousness—yet without going through the business of learning afresh. Recollection implies a process of reasoning.[49] An event in consciousness necessarily, or usually, brings another in its train, and we eventually reach the item we wish to remember if in our reasoning we are guided by the laws of sequence in the order of our ideas—the so-called laws of association.[50] One experience suggests another on the basis of similarity, contrast, or contiguity. Things having a necessary connection are easily remembered; things contingently related less so. The more frequent the repetition of the particular

[47] *De Mem. et Recollect.* 450a, *De Anima* 418a 17–18, 425a 6, 428 b. See G. R. T. Ross, ed. and tr., *Aristotle, De Sensu et de Memoria* (Cambridge, 1906), pp. 14–15, and n. 7; J. I. Beare, *Greek Theories*, Part III, pp. 250–336; Sir David Ross, ed., *Aristotle, De Anima* (Oxford, 1961), pp. 33 ff., esp. p. 39. Cf. Plato, *Theaet.* 184B ff. Time is included in *De Mem. et Recollect.* 451a 17; Edwin Wallace, *Aristotle's Psychology* (Cambridge, 1882), Introduction, pp. lxxv ff., esp. p. lxxix.

[48] *De Iuventute* 496ab; *De Generat. Animal.* 743b; *De Partit. Animal.* 656b. See in Plato, *Theaet.* 194, the section dealing with the likeness of the soul to wax, the play on κῆρ-κηρός in Homer (cf. *Iliad* 2. 851, 16. 554); Wallace, *Aristotle's Psychology*, pp. lxxxiii ff.

[49] *De Mem. et Recollect.* 453a.

[50] *De Mem. et. Recollect.* 451b, *De Sensu* 442b; see G. R. T. Ross, *De Sensu*, p. 39; Wallace, *Aristotle's Psychology*, pp. xciv ff.

sense of connections by which an idea is reinstated in recollection, the more readily can it be recalled. These "laws of association" did duty not only in the later history of mnemonics, but also in the theory of style, in relation to simile, metaphor, and contrast. And I observe that in a recent, and influential, book, Sir Frederic C. Bartlett's *Remembering*,[51] the author's experimental method considers the principles of associationism. He finds that they are useful in describing the characteristics of associated details, "when they are associated," but explain nothing of "the activity of the conditions by which" the details "are brought together."[52]

Memory and recollection are different from learning, too. In the first acquirement of learning, there is no recovery or acquisition of memory. We must keep this in mind when we think of the process of "committing to memory."

So Aristotle. When the rhetoricians treated the subject, though they used the analogy of the seal's impression on wax, and saw the uses of association, they did not offer a systematic psychological theory, but made it a practical and applied art. They were interested in how they could best put memory to use in public speaking.

Memorization seems to have held a primary place in Greek and Roman education, both theory and practice. I need not emphasize the point to this audience, who, despite our "habits of reading and writing," do not fail to comprehend "the speaking and listening ancient world,"[53] the intensity of the grammatical and rhetorical training, the unwieldiness of the scrolls, the lack of indices.[54] As Lord Brougham put it, the

[51] (Cambridge, 1954), pp. 304 ff.

[52] P. 308. See also Henri Bergson, *Matter and Memory*, tr. N. M. Paul and W. S. Palmer (London, 1912), pp. 272 ff.; E. J. Swift, *Psychology and the Day's Work* (New York, 1923), pp. 239 ff.

[53] C. S. Baldwin, *Ancient Rhetoric and Poetic* (New York, 1924), p. 82, n. 20.

[54] See Wilhelm Kroll, art. "Rhetorik" in Pauly-Wissowa, *Real-Encyc. der class. Altertumswissens.*, col. 1098.

orator was the Parliamentary debater, the speaker at public meetings, the preacher, the newspaper, the published sermon, the pamphlet, the volume, all in one.[55] One finds many instances, in both literatures, Greek and Latin, of tasks set for memorization. Nicias (fifth century B.C.), eager to make of his son Niceratus a good man, had him get by heart all of Homer, and Niceratus boasts that this mastery never left him.[56] Isocrates is said to have had his pupils report (repeat? ἀναφέρειν τὰ εἰρημένα) to him the speeches they heard at the public assemblies;[57] Cicero had to learn the Laws of the Twelve Tables in his boyhood;[58] Orbilius dictated verses of Livius Andronicus for the future poet Horace to memorize;[59] Quintilian[60] wishes boys to learn as much by heart as feasible at the earliest stage, when they cannot as yet produce anything of themselves and while their memory is retentive—passages to be selected carefully from the poets, orators, and historians. They will thus without awareness reproduce the style of these models, and gain a rich and choice vocabulary, a command of artistic composition, and a supply of figures; and Ps.-Plutarch, *On the Education of Children*,[61] urges above all the training and exercise of the memory—when in mythology they made Memory the mother of the Muses, they meant that nothing can compare with Memory for creating and educating. Train not only those children who have a good natural memory, thus adding strength to the advantage supplied by

[55] Henry, Lord Brougham, "Eloquence of the Ancients," *Works* (Edinburgh, 1872) 7. 4: "Nor is it enough to say that the rostrum . . . monopolized in itself all the functions of the press, the senate, the school, and the pulpit, in our days. It was a rival to the stage also."

[56] Xenophon, *Symposium* 3. 5.

[57] Ps.-Plutarch, *Lives of the Ten Orators* 838 F.

[58] *De Legibus* 2. 23. 59.

[59] Horace, *Epist.* 2. 1. 69–71.

[60] 2. 7. 1 ff.; 11. 2. 41; 1. 1. 19; 1. 1. 36; 1. 3. 1; 1. 10. 29.

[61] 9 E. Cf. Vives, *De Vita et Moribus Eruditi, Opera*, 1. 518: the four constituents of learning are *ingenium, iudicium, memoria, studium.*

Nature, but also those who are forgetful, so that they may surpass their former selves. Nor should parents forget that the branches of learning which involve memory contribute in no small measure not merely to education, but also to the practical activities of life; for the memory of past activities forms a model of good counsel for the future.

I come now to the field of rhetoric. The law required that each citizen must plead his own case, and several of the canon of Greek orators—Antiphon, Isaeus, Hypereides, Isocrates (for about ten years), Demosthenes, Dinarchus, and especially Lysias—were *logographoi*, professionals who wrote speeches to be recited (sometimes doubtless from memory)[62] by their clients. Early rhetorical theory, like that of Isocrates,[63] rated memory among the qualities necessary to a speaker. But memory was already of great interest to the Sophists for its importance in their highly esteemed art of improvisation, in which Protagoras, Gorgias, and especially Hippias were expert. They prepared commonplaces which their students memorized—dissertations so broad and general as to be adaptable each to many occasions.[64] These were on subjects that might present themselves, and were introduced when appropriate into the speech.[65] Socrates says to Menexenus:

[62] See Greene, "The Spoken and Written Word," p. 41; J. H. Lipsius, M. H. E. Meier, and G. F. Schömann, *Das Attische Recht und Rechtsverfahren* (Leipzig, 1915), 3. 906; Marius Lavency, "Lecture et récitation dans les plaidoyers logographiques," *Les études classiques*, XXVI, No. 3 (July, 1958), 225–234. In Cicero, *De Oratore* 1. 54. 231, Socrates was to learn by heart, if he thought it best to do so (*quam, si ei videretur, edisceret*), the speech which Lysias was supposed to have written for him to use in his defense at his trial.

[63] *Antidosis* 189.

[64] Cicero, *Brutus* 11. 46; Quintilian, 3. 1. 12.

[65] See Hazel L. Brown, *Extemporary Speech in Antiquity* (Menasha, Wis., 1914), pp. 95 ff. Aristotle, *Topica* 8. 14 (163b ff.), advises learning by heart arguments on questions of most common occurrence, and primary propositions; see the comments on this section by Friedrich Solmsen, *Die Entwicklung der aristotel. Logik und Rhetorik*, in *Neue Philolog. Untersuch.*, IV (Berlin, 1929), 170–175.

"Every rhetorician has speeches ready-made—nor is it hard to improvise that kind of stuff."[66] The *Introductions* and *Conclusions* produced by Antiphon,[67] and the *Characters* (παρασκευαί)— of poverty and riches, youth and old age—published by Lysias[68] are of a piece with these κοινοὶ τόποι. Gorgias' boast[69] that he was ready to speak on any subject was based on commonplaces elaborated beforehand, and in the *Sophistici Elenchi*,[70] Aristotle censures Gorgias' method of handing out finished portions of speeches to be learned by heart, on the ground that though the method was rapid, it was ἄτεχνος—not scientific—that it imparted not *art*, but the *products* of art.

Several centuries later Quintilian[71] adds his voice in opposition to this method still followed by some rhetoricians in his day: he regards as an admission of great weakness the writing out of passages dealing with common topics—like whether we should rely on presumptive proof (*argumenta*, circumstantial evidence), or always believe a witness—and the memorizing of these passages and keeping them ready for immediate use should opportunity offer. This is no way, he says, to learn to meet new situations. Furthermore, there is no single commonplace so "common" that it can fit harmoniously any actual pleading. And finally, the commonplace will appear to have been affixed as a tag to the speech, not fused into its texture. Speakers who do this must feel shame in displaying their

---

[66] Plato, *Menexenus* 235 D: εἰσὶν ἑκάστοις τούτων λόγοι παρασκευασμένοι, καὶ ἅμα οὐδὲ αὐτοσχεδιάζειν τά γε τοιαῦτα χαλεπόν.

[67] See Ludwig Radermacher, *Artium Scriptores* (Vienna, 1951), p. 80 (Nos. 13-15); Friedrich Solmsen, *Antiphonstudien*, in *Neue Philolog. Untersuch.*, VIII (Berlin, 1931), 64 ff.

[68] Radermacher, *Artium Scriptores*, p. 149 (Nos. 13, 14); Marcellinus on the στάσεις of Hermogenes, in Christian Walz, *Rhetores Graeci* (Stuttgart, 1833), 4. 352; Friedrich Blass, *Attische Beredsamkeit* (Leipzig, 1868), 1. 372 and n. 3.

[69] Plato, *Gorgias* 447 C.

[70] Chap. 34 (183b–184a).

[71] 2. 4. 27 ff.

miserable and worn-out furniture to an audience whose memory must have recognized it so often already.

Involved also is the habit common among several even of the best orators—of borrowing, sometimes verbatim, passages from one another's speeches, and from one's own former speeches. Isocrates boasts that he never appropriated matter from others, but admits repeating himself. "When I see that others use my writings, why should I alone refrain from employing what I have previously said? I have preferred not to labor at striving to express differently what I have already well expressed."[72] Lucian's *Pseudologistes* glibly recited what he had learned by heart; like Aesop's jack-daw, his speech was patched together out of motley feathers from others,[73] and his hearers, with great laughter, tested their memory of the borrowed expressions. In a letter to Atticus,[74] Cicero reports a like experience with respect to a speech of Crassus: "Crassus wove in quite impressively that whole patch which I so often like to paint in varied colors in my speeches—the one on 'Fire and Sword'. But you know that kind of fustian."

It was of Antonius that Cicero[75] said his speeches were in appearance unpremeditated, and yet in reality were prepared with consummate skill. Ancient rhetoricians repeat the observation[76] that the judge suspects the advocate who has planned hard to outwit him, and that this suspicion may be disarmed and good will secured by seeming to speak without preparation. This almost universal prejudice extended to delivery that failed to conceal art and to a speech that was obviously memorized.

[72] *Antidosis* 74; see also *Epist.* 6. 7, and *Philippus* 93–94. On Demosthenes' practice, see Werner Jaeger, *Demosthenes* (Berlin, 1939), pp. 64–65, 103, 142, 217, n.36; 237, n.43.

[73] See *Rhetorica ad Herennium* (Loeb Classical Library, London and Cambridge, Mass., 1954), p. 236, note b.

[74] I. XIV. 3.

[75] *Brutus* 37. 139.

[76] Cf. *Rhet. ad Herennium*, pp. 250–251, note a.

In modern times we too suspect the memorized speech, conceal verbal premeditation, and affect the semblance of impromptu speaking, wishing to be considered "Nature's elect." When Samuel Rogers had been criticized in the *Quarterly Review* by John William Ward, Earl of Dudley, he took his revenge in the form of the well-known epigram:

> Ward has no heart, they say, but I deny it.
> Ward has a heart—and gets his speeches by it.[77]

The like point is made in the retort courteous of the playwright and statesman Richard Brinsley Sheridan to Mr. Dundas in the House of Commons: "The Right Honourable Gentleman is indebted to his *memory* for his *jests*, and to his *imagination* for his *facts*"—a felicitous bit of wit which Sheridan had, however, long worked to condense and point, and had patiently treasured up "till he at length found an opportunity of turning it to account," bringing it forth "with the most extemporaneous air."[78]

Indeed published collections of Introductions and Perorations of several of the great orators were available throughout the ancient period, and were not uncommonly pillaged by other speakers.[79]

Lucian satirized the custom in his "Zeus Tragōidos."[80] Zeus, having to make a speech to the assembled gods, appeals to Hermes, patron of public speakers: "Either because of the magnitude of the impending calamities, my lad, or the great number of those attending, I am confused in my thinking, and all atremble, and I seem to be tongue-tied; and most unseasonable thing of all, I have forgotten my prepared Introduction." Hermes: "You've ruined everything, Zeus. They are

---

[77] *Dict. Nat. Biogr.* 20. 783.

[78] Anon., *Sheridaniana* (London, 1826), pp. 252–253.

[79] See Eduard Stemplinger, *Das Plagiat in der griechischen Literatur* (Leipzig and Berlin, 1912), pp. 225 ff.

[80] Chaps. 14–15.

suspicious of your silence." "Well, then, do you want me to begin chanting to them that famous Homeric Introduction of mine?" "Which one do you mean?" "Hark to me, all ye gods, and all ye goddesses, too."[81] "Come, come, Zeus, stop that tedious versifying. Engraft one of Demosthenes' speeches against Philip—any one at all, making only a few changes. As a matter of fact, that is how most people practice oratory these days." "Good advice! A short cut, and this easy way is a very present help to any one who is at a loss what to say." Then Zeus parodies the beginning of Demosthenes' First Olynthiac: "Men of Heaven, it is fitting and proper that you give me your close attention. The present crisis, gods, well nigh breaks out in speech, telling us that we must confront manfully the issues of the day, which it is obvious we are totally neglecting. But at this point, for my Demosthenes is in fact running dry, I'd like to explain to you why I called this meeting."

Now the traditional divisions of classical rhetoric—also called functions, elements, faculties, or kinds of competence— are five: the Invention of ideas, their Arrangement in the speech, Style, Memory, and Delivery. The pre-Aristotelian theory treated only the first three. Aristotle would add Delivery, and his pupil Theophrastus did so. When precisely in the Hellenistic period Memory was added as a fifth division, by the Rhodian or Pergamene School, we do not know. The author of the treatise addressed to Herennius, belonging to the second decade of the first century B.C., which supplies us with our oldest extant treatment of memory, refers to previous writers—Greek—on the subject of memory, but gives us no names.[82]

The quinquepartite scheme is the most common. But the number of divisions used by the various rhetoricians actually

[81] *Iliad* 8. 5.
[82] 3. XXIII. 38.

varies from two to seven. When memory and delivery are excluded, the reason advanced is that these two faculties are the gifts of nature, and are not acquired by art.[83] A curious feature of Quintilian's book is that though he adheres in his theory to the fivefold system, in the ordering of his books he treats Memory and Delivery under the head of Style.[84]

But Memory in rhetoric is not confined to special treatment as one of the five major divisions. It serves as one of the three parts of wisdom (*prudentia*)—the course which wisdom should take is an important consideration in both deliberative and epideictic speaking;[85] *memoria* recalls what was, while *intellegentia* perceives what is, and *providentia* foresees what is to be.[86] In Aristotle's *Rhetoric*[87] memory shares in the analysis of things pleasant, which we must study if we are to understand the part voluntary actions play in wrong-doing, when such a problem arises in a forensic case. Remembered things are pleasant—both those that were pleasant when they happened, and some that were unpleasant at the time but had a good or honorable consequence. Memory is also listed among the faculties productive of what is good—the good and the expedient are the object of deliberative speaking.[88] Again, in the sketch of the stages of life which Aristotle drew for the ends of the speaker we are reminded that the elderly live in memory, and are forever talking of the past, with enjoyment in the recollection.[89] Duty requires me to add also Quintilian's warning that if we use fictions in the Statement of Facts, we should

[83] E.g., Quintilian, 3. 3. 4; 11. 2. 1.
[84] See Book 1, Pref. 22; 3. 3. 1 ff.
[85] *Rhet. ad Herennium* 3. II. 3–3. III. 4; 3. VI. 10.
[86] Cicero, *De Inventione* 2. 53. 160; on the use of this concept made by Albertus Magnus and St. Thomas Aquinas, see Frances A. Yates, "The Ciceronian Art of Memory," *Medioevo e Rinascimento: Studi in onore di Bruno Nardi* (Florence, 1955), pp. 882 ff.
[87] I. 11 (1370 ab).
[88] *Rhet.* I. 6 (1362 b).
[89] *Rhet.* II. 13 (1390 a).

in the rest of our speech not forget the truth of the saying that *liars* ought to have a good memory.[90] In the field of style, the periodic structure is easily retained in memory because it is measurable, and that is why we remember verse more easily than prose.[91]

Nor, of course, is the memory of the hearer neglected. An anonymous scholiast on Hermogenes divides receptiveness (εὐμάθεια) into speed (ὀξύτης) of thought, penetration (ἀγχίνοια), and memory.[92] In Proof, since what is said last is easily remembered, it is useful, says the *auctor ad Herennium*, to leave some strong argument fresh in the hearer's mind.[93] And in the Conclusion of the speech, the summing up recalls the points we have made—so as to refresh the memory. We shall reproduce all the points in the order in which they have been presented, so that the hearer, if he has committed them to memory, is brought back to what he remembers. Yet we are not to carry the summary back to the Introduction or Statement of Facts, for then the speech will appear to have been fabricated and devised with elaborate pains so as to demonstrate the speaker's skill, advertise his wit, and display his memory.[94]

But indeed to Aristotle only two parts of the discourse are essential—the Statement of Facts and the Proof—the Introduction and Conclusion being merely aids to memory.[95]

Memory is often compared to writing on a wax tablet or the imprint of a seal-ring, the simile first used by Socrates in Plato's *Theaetetus*,[96] and borrowed by Aristotle in his treatise

[90] 4. 2. 91.

[91] Aristotle, *Rhet.* III. 9 (1409 b).

[92] Walz, *Rhetores Graeci*, 7. 696; "ἀγχίνοια searches out, from what one has learned, what one has not learned."

[93] 3. X. 18.

[94] 2. XXX. 47.

[95] *Rhet.* III. 13 (1414 ab).

[96] 191 D ff. Emerson, "Memory" (*Works* 12. 97–98), uses also the simile of an impression made on sand. Antonius in Cicero, *De Oratore* 2. 86. 354, treating Simonides, and in *Part. Orat.* 7. 26, employs the analogy with wax tablets, but

On Memory and Recollection;[97] although we must think also of Memory the recorder within us which seems to Socrates in Plato's *Philebus*[98] to write down words in the soul. Recall, in Proverbs (3:3): "Write them upon the table of thy heart" (*'al lūªḥ libbékhā*); in Aeschylus: "The unforgetting tablets of thy mind";[99] "the table of my memory" in Shakespeare's

---

'M' in *Tusc. Disp.* 1. 25. 61, following Chrysippus' refutation of Cleanthes, rejects the analogy—and also that of the vessel (*vas*). Cf. Sextus Empiricus, *Adv. Math.* 1. 228, on the Stoic φαντασία καταληκτική and its "roominess" (*capacitas*).

[97] 450 a. Cf. *De Anima* 424 a 17 ff., where the simile is used to illustrate sense-perception.

[98] 38 E ff.

[99] *Prometheus* 789 (μνήμοσιν δέλτοις φρενῶν); *Choeph.* 450: ἐν φρεσὶν γράφου; *Eumenides* 275: δελτογράφῳ φρενί (see Friedrich Solmsen, "The Tablets of Zeus," *Class. Quarterly*, XXXVIII, Nos. 1 and 2 [1944], 27–30); *Suppl.* 179; Pindar, *Olymp.* 10. 2–3; Sophocles, *Philoct.* 1325: γράφου φρενῶν ἔσω; *Trach.* 683; *Fragm.* 597 (Jebb-Pearson 2. 244). See also Simia in Plautus, *Pseud.* 940 ff.: *Memorem immemorem facit qui monet quod memor meminit. Teneo omnia: in pectore condita sunt;* Seneca Rhetor, *Contr.* 1, Pref. 18: [Porcius Latro] *aiebat se in animo scribere;* Cicero, *Acad.* 2. 1: *ille* [Lucullus] *in animo res insculptas habebat;* II *Cor.* 3:3: ἐν πλαξὶ καρδίας; Cassiodorus, *Institutiones,* ed. R. A. B. Mynors (Oxford, 1937), 1. 5. 2: *bibliotheca;* Owen Feltham: "library" (Carroll Camden, "Memory, the Warder of the Brain," *Philol. Quarterly,* XVIII, No. 1 [1939], 52); Vives, *De Tradit. Disciplinis,* Book 4, chap. 3, in *Opera,* 1. 492: *imprimant et insculpant;* Shakespeare, *Hamlet,* Act 1, Sc. 5. line 103: "the book and volume of my brain"; Julia in *Two Gentlemen of Verona,* Act 2, Sc. 7. l. 3: "table wherein all my thoughts Are visibly character'd and engrav'd"; Beaumont and Fletcher, *Philaster,* Act 1, Sc. 2: "the dear love writ in my heart"; Peter de la Primaudaye, *The French Academie* (London, 1586, tr. T. B.), chap. 8, p. 88: "Mind is as a white paper wherein a man writeth his cogitations and thoughts"; Anthony Shorly, Robert Fulke, Pierre Charron (Camden, "Memory," p. 52, and n. 7): "table" or "register"; John Huarte (Camden, "Memory," p. 53): "paper"; Samuel Johnson, *Rambler* 41: "signature impressed upon the mind"; Emerson, "Memory," (*Works* 12. 93): "There is no book like the memory, none with such a good index"; Tennyson, "Isabel" II: "the blanched tablets of her heart."

The Jewish New Year, anniversary of the first day of Creation, is termed the Day of Remembrance; the Lord remembers the everlasting covenant (Ezek. 16:60), the worshipper remembers his obligations before the Lord, and prays to be inscribed for a happy life; the record of every person is set before the Lord. See P. A. H. De Boer, *Gedenken und Gedächtnis in der Welt des Alten Testaments* (Stuttgart, 1962); B. S. Childs, *Memory and Tradition in Israel* (London, 1962); Willy Schottroff, '*Gedenken*' *im Alten Orient und im Alten Testament* (Neukirchen-Vluyn, 1964).

Of Eloquence

Hamlet,[100] and the "leaves of memory" in Longfellow.[101] Longinus' simile of the furrows made in the street by the repeated passage of wagons is not unrelated.[102] Or memory is the guardian of the matter and the language thought out and reflected upon,[103] or of all the parts of rhetoric; recall Shakespeare's "warder of the brain" in *Macbeth*,[104] and Francis Bacon's Memory as the intellectual art of Custody.[105] Pindar[106] tells us that in only one way can we hold a mirror up to noble deeds—when by grace of Memory a hero wins the reward of his toils in renowned strains of verse; recall that Emerson,[107] too, sees memory as a kind of looking-glass. Most common is the metaphor best phrased by Quintilian[108]—Memory, treasure-house (*thesaurus*) of eloquence—storehouse of the ideas supplied by invention,[109] or chest,[110] mine,[111] magazine,[112]

[100] Act 1, Sc. 5. l. 98.

[101] "The Fires of Driftwood," stanza 7.

[102] Spengel-Hammer, *Rhetores Graeci* 1, Pars II (Leipzig, 1894), 201: ὡς γὰρ τὰ τρίμματα τῶν ἀμαξιτῶν κοιλαίνεται.

[103] Cicero, *De Oratore* 1. 5. 18; *Rhet. ad Herennium* 3. XVI. 28; cf. *Part. Orat.* 1. 3. (guardian of all the constituent parts of delivery); Martianus Capella 5. 443: *firma rerum verborumque custodia;* Anon. on Hermogenes, in Walz, *Rhetores Graeci* 7. 696 (the τήρησις of what one has learned); John of Salisbury, *Metalogicon* 1. 11 (839a): *memoria quasi mentis archa et fidelis custodia perceptorum.*

[104] Act 1, Sc. 7. l. 65; see Camden, "Memory," pp. 52–72.

[105] Book II, *Works* 6. 280 ff.

[106] *Nem.* 7. 20–22.

[107] "Goethe, or The Writer" (*Works* 4. 262), and "Memory" (*Works* 12. 93). Cf. Samuel Rogers, "The Pleasures of Memory," Part I: "What soften'd views thy magic glass reveals"; M. F. Tupper, *Proverbial Philosophy*, first series, "Memory": "some grand globe . . . partial telescope of memory."

[108] 11. 2. 1; Cicero, *De Oratore* 1. 5. 18: *thesaurus rerum omnium;* Longinus, *Ars Rhet.*, Spengel-Hammer, *Rhet. Graeci* 1, Pars II, 200: σωτηρία φαντασιῶν, and σ. τῶν τόπων; Ps.-Plutarch, *De Liberis Educ.* 9 E (ταμιεῖον); so also Antipater of Tarsus (note 21 above); Sextus Empiricus 7. 373: θησαυρισμὸς φαντασιῶν; St. Augustine, *Conf.* 10. 8: *thesauri;* Cassiodorus, *De Anima*, chap. 7: *thesaurarium;* Thomas Wilson, *Arte of Rhetorique* (1560), ed. G. H. Mair (Oxford, 1909), p. 209: "treasure of the mind"; John Locke, *An Essay Concerning Human Understanding*, ed. A. C. Fraser (Oxford, 1814), p. 210: "storehouse," "repository"; Tupper, "Memory": "storehouse"; Thomas Fuller, *The Holy State*, Book III, chap. 10, ed. M. G. Walten (New York, 1938), 2. 174, "Of Memory": "treasure-house."

vessel,[113] cask;[114] Thomas Fuller's comparison of memory to a
purse[115] belongs in this class. St. Augustine,[116] St. Ambrose,[117]
and others in the Middle Ages call memory *venter animi* (or

[109] *Rhet. ad Herennium* 3. XVI. 28.

[110] E.g., *archa;* see n. 103 above (John of Salisbury); St. Augustine, *Conf.* 10. 8:
abstrusiora receptacula; Cassiodorus, *De Anima,* chap. 7: *conceptaculum;* St. Thomas
Aquinas, "Epistola . . . de Modo Acquirendi Scientiam sive Humanam sive
Divinam" (Helga Hajdu, *Das mnemotechnische Schrifttum des Mittelalters* [Vienna,
Amsterdam, and Leipzig, 1936], p. 65, n. 13): *in armariolo mentis;* Guglielmo
Grataroli: "chest" (see Camden, "Memory," p. 52); Wilson, *Arte,* ed. Mair,
p. 209: "chest"; Montaigne, "De la présomption," 2. 17: *réceptacle et l'estuy de la
science;* Samuel Johnson, *Rambler* 41: "great deposit of his Creator"; I. M. L.
Hunter, *Memory: Facts and Fallacies* (London, 1957), p. 159: ". . . our learning
capacities are like a suitcase. The size of the case may be limited, but we can
pack more by packing more systematically."

[111] Samuel Rogers, "The Pleasures of Memory," Part II, Conclusion: "Hail,
Memory, Hail, in thine exhaustless mine"; Fuller, "Of Memory," ed. Walten,
2. 174: " . . . it seems the mine of Memory lies there [in the rere of the head],
because there naturally men dig for it, scratching it when they are at a losse."

[112] Montaigne, *Essays* 1. 9 ("Des menteurs"): *magasin;* Samuel Johnson,
Idler 44: "magazines of memory."

[113] E.g., Seneca the Younger, *De Beneficiis* 28.2: *vas fragile;* St. Thomas Aquinas,
Letter cited in note 110 above: *vas.*

[114] Ammianus Marcellinus 16. 5. 8: *dolium.*

[115] "Of Memory," ed. Walten, 2. 175. Cf. Stephen Hawes, *Pastime of Pleasure,*
ed. W. E. Mead (London, 1928), p. 52: "wallet," discussed by W. S. Howell,
Logic and Rhetoric in England, 1500–1700 (Princeton, 1956), p. 86; St. Augustine,
Conf. 10. 8: *secreti et ineffabiles sinus;* Cassiodorus, *Inst.,* Praefatio 2, and *Regensburger
Briefe* (see note 117 below), p. 274: *sinus;* Emerson, "Memory" (*Works* 12. 92):
"Memory is not a pocket but a living instructor"; Augustine, *Conf.* 10. 8: *grandis
recessus,* and *penetrale amplum et infinitum;* John of Salisbury, *Metalogicon* 1. 23
(853a): *in archanis memoriae;* Cassiodorus, *De Anima,* chap. 7: *in penetralibus animi;*
Augustine, *Conf.* 10. 9: *mirae cellae;* Bacon, *Works,* II (6. 202): "cells, domiciles,
or offices of the mind"; Augustine, *Conf.* 10. 17: *antra, cavernae,* 10. 10: *cavi
abditiores;* T. H. Bayley, "Teach Me to Forget": "caverns pure and deep";
Tupper, "Memory": "small cavern"; Emerson, "Method of Nature" (*Works*
1. 205): "cave." Cf. also Samuel Rogers, "The Pleasures of Memory," Part I:
"countless chambers of the brain"; Tupper, "Memory": "thine airy chambers";
Emerson, "Intellect" (*Works* 2. 334): "dark chamber"; Beaumont and Fletcher,
The Bloody Brother, Act 1, Sc. 1: "room"; Emily Dickinson, *The Complete Poems,* ed.
T. H. Johnson (Boston and Toronto, 1960), No. 1273: "sacred closet."

Of broader scope: Augustine, *Conf.* 10. 8: *in aula ingenti;* Tupper, "Memory":
"some common hall of intellect," and "spacious market-place for thought";
William Fullwood's rendering of Grataroli's *De Memoria* as *The Castel of Memory*

mentis), "belly of the mind"; recall Shakespeare's "ventricle of memory" in *Love's Labour's Lost*.[118]

The stories of prodigious memories are numerous and varied—of Cyrus the Great, Simonides,[119] Themistocles, Hippias,[120] Theodectes[121] (fourth century B.C.), Cineas (died *c.* 276 B.C.), Charmadas (fl. *c.* 107 B.C.), Metrodorus (fl. *c.* 100 B.C.),[122] Lucius Lucullus,[123] Hortensius, and many of the

---

(Camden, "Memory," p. 67); Augustine, *Conf.* 10. 17: *campi*, 10. 8: *campi et lata praetoria*. See in Ulrich Surgant, *Manuale Curatorum* (Basel, 1507–8), Book I, *Consideratio* 20, fol. 48[r and v], the various *mansiones*, listed *per ordinem alphabeti*, which he suggests for use in the mnemonic system treated here below: e.g., *apotheca, bibliotheca, capella, dormitorium*, and the like.

[116] *Conf.* 10. 14.

[117] *Explanatio Psalmi* 39. 22 (= 40, 18), in *Corp. Script. Ecclesiast. Lat.* 64. 227. See also Carl Erdmann and Norbert Fickermann, *Briefsammlungen der Zeit Heinrichs IV* [eleventh and twelfth centuries], in *Mon. Germ. Hist.*, V (Weimar, 1950), "Die Regensburger rhetorischen Briefe," Nos. 5, 7, 9, 12, 22, pp. 294, 313, 331, 348; and for the metaphor in other mediaeval writings, note p. 294. Camden, "Memory," p. 55, discusses the figure as used by Elizabethan writers on the subject of memory.

[118] Act 4, Sc. 2. l. 69 (Holofernes). *Animi anima* appears in "Die Regensburger rhetorischen Briefe" (see note 117), No. 30, p. 363; cf. Wilson, *Arte*, ed. Mair, p. 209: "The same is memory to the mind that life is to the bodie."

Other metaphors: Wordsworth, *Excursion*, Book 8, line 28: "silent shores of memory"; James Montgomery, "Night": "Night is the time . . . to wet with unseen tears those graves of memory, where sleep the joys of other years"; Emerson, Preface to "Demonology" (*Works* 9. 295): "Night dreams trace on Memory's wall Shadows of the Thoughts of day," "Love" (*Works* 2. 175): "the amber of memory," "Perpetual Forces" (*Works* 10. 78): "the diving-bell of memory," "Society and Solitude" (*Works* 7. 13): "Memory, base mendicant with his leathern badge"; Carlyle, "Characteristics": "Moonlight of memory."

[119] Cicero, *Tusc. Disp.* 1. 24. 59; Aelian, *De Nat. Animal.* 6. 10(2).

[120] Plato, *Hipp. Major* 285 E; Aelian, *loc. cit.;* Philostratus, *Lives of the Sophists* 1. 11. 495 (even in old age Hippias could repeat fifty names from memory, after hearing them but once—and recite them in the order in which he heard them).

[121] Cicero, *Tusc. Disp., loc. cit.;* Quintilian, 11. 2. 51; Julius Pollux, *Onomast.* 6. 108; Aelian, *loc. cit.*

[122] Cicero, *De Oratore* 2. 88. 360, 3. 20. 75, *Tusc. Disp., loc. cit.;* Quintilian, 10. 6. 4, 11. 2. 22, 26; Pliny, *Nat. Hist.* 7. 24. 89.

[123] Cicero, *Acad.* 2. 1. 2; Cicero's friend (died 56 B.C.), distinguished for a memory both natural and trained.

period of declamation and the Second Sophistic. Cyrus made it a special duty, for the sake of *esprit de corps*, to call all his officers by name,[124] and was believed to have retained the name of every soldier in his army; Mithridates knew well each of the languages of the twenty-five nations he held under his sway;[125] Cineas, sent as ambassador to Rome by Pyrrhus, greeted each senator and member of the plebs by name the day after his arrival;[126] Charmadas could recite the contents of any volume he was asked to quote, as if he were reading the book;[127] Hortensius could without being prompted recall not only his own words (whether thought out or written), but also everything that was said by his adversaries, and at a sale remembered everything sold during the whole day, its price, each buyer, and the order in which each article was sold;[128] Lucius Scipio knew the names of all the inhabitants of Rome,[129] even as Themistocles was said to know the names of all the citizens of Athens.[130] Seneca the elder (*c.* 55 B.C. to *c.* A.D. 40), writes of himself: "That my memory was excellent in my day, and even miraculous, I do not deny; for I could repeat two thousand names in the order in which they were dictated . . . and, in reverse order, more than two hundred verses, one by

[124] Xenophon, *Cyropaedia* 5. 3. 46–51; Quintilian, 11. 2. 50; Pliny, *Nat. Hist.* 7. 24. 88.

[125] Gellius, 17. 17; Pliny, *Nat. Hist., loc. cit.*, and Quintilian, 11. 2. 50 (twenty-two languages).

[126] 280 B.C. Seneca Rhetor, *Controv.* 1, Pref. 19; Cicero, *Tusc. Disp., loc. cit.;* Pliny, *Nat. Hist., loc. cit.* (*equites* rather than *plebs*).

[127] Pliny the Elder, *Nat. Hist.* 7. 24. 89; Cicero, *De Oratore* 2. 88. 360; *Tusc. Disp., loc. cit.;* Quintilian, 11. 2. 26.

[128] Seneca Rhetor, *Controv.* 1, Pref. 19; Quintilian, 11. 2. 24; Cicero, *Brutus* 88. 301. See also Cicero, *De Oratore* 3. 61. 230, *Acad.* 2. 1. 2, *Tusc. Disp., loc. cit.;* Quintilian, 10. 6. 4.

[129] Pliny, *Nat. Hist.* 7. 24. 88. Although some have thought that this reference is to Scipio Asiaticus, brother of Scipio Africanus, the identification is uncertain; see Münzer, art. "Cornelius" in Pauly-Wissowa, *Real-Encyc. der class. Altertumswissens.*, col. 337.

[130] Cicero, *De Senectute* 7. 21; Valerius Maximus, 8. 7. 6.

one as recited by my pupils in turn."[131] But then the whole of his extensive *Suasoriae* and *Controversiae* represents a marvelous feat—a reproduction from memory in old age of the sayings and arguments of contemporaries in his youth. It is regrettable that he does not fulfil his promise[132] to explain to his sons the method he practiced.

The Younger Pliny urges Nepos to come hear the declaimer Isaeus. "His memory is incredible; he repeats what he has previously spoken extempore, nor does he miss a single word."[133] Apollonius of Tyana (first Christian century) at the age of 100 *still* surpassed Simonides in power of memory, says Philostratus,[134] and used to chant a hymn addressed to Memory. When enemies of the Christian Sophist of the fourth century, Prohaeresius, proposed a difficult theme to him, he extemporized in well-rounded periods, and with an avalanche of words, and then declaimed the very same speech a second time. Some of his audience, so his faithful pupil Eunapius tells us,[135] kissed his feet or hands, and others declared him to be the very model of Hermes Logios—while his opponents lay in the dust, consumed with jealousy. But Philagrus of Cilicia, two centuries earlier, enjoyed no such success. Since Philagrus had once in Asia declaimed on a certain subject and published his discourse, the pupils of Herodes Atticus set a trap for him. They proposed the same theme, and when he pretended to be improvising, they read the published declamation aloud. Great shouting and laughter then spread among the audience in the theater of Agrippa.[136]

[131] *Controv.* 1, Pref. 2.
[132] *Controv.* 1, Pref. 19.
[133] *Epist.* 2. 3. 3. ff.
[134] *Life of Apollonius* 1. 14; in *The Lives of the Sophists* 21. 604 Philostratus makes the same claim for Proclus of Naucratis at age 90.
[135] *Lives of the Philosophers and Sophists* 488 ff.
[136] Philostratus, *Lives* 2. 579–2. 580.

I like Quintilian's pious comment on such tales of extraordinary memory: "We must yet well have faith in such
virtuosity, so that he who believes may also hope to accomplish
the like!"[137]

Of special meaning for us is that in many of these instances
art and exercise, and not alone nature, were involved; Pliny
attributes Isaeus' control to study and practice: "For night
and day he does nothing else, hears nothing else, talks nothing
else";[138] and some, like Charmadas and Metrodorus, used the
topical system of mnemonics[139] that we know from the
rhetoricians. Apparently a number of philosophical schools
were affected.

The relative benefits of thoroughly prepared and extempore
speaking were argued by the ancients as they are by us

[137] 11. 2. 51. Hippodromus the Thessalian "learned more by heart than any
of the Greeks," and Alexander the Cappadocian had an even better memory
(Philostratus, *Lives* 2. 7. 618); Apsines of Gadara excelled in this faculty (Philostratus, *Lives* 2. 33. 628); Tiberius Victor Minervius remembered what he had
read or heard once, and could recount every throw of the dice made by either
side (Ausonius, *Commemoratio Professorum Burdigal.* 1. 21 ff.); Nepotianus surpassed Cineas in memory, knew the works of the grammarians Scaurus and
Probus by heart (Ausonius, *Commemoratio* 15. 12 ff.); St. Augustine's friend
Simplicius could recite all of Virgil's verses forward and backward (Augustine,
De Anima et Eius Origine 4. 7, Migne, *Pat. Lat.*, XLIV, 529); Vespasiano da
Bisticci records that the famous lawyer Benedetto d'Arezzo (1415–1466) surpassed all others of his time in the power of his memory (*The Vespasiano Memoirs*,
tr. W. G. and Emily Waters [London, 1926], pp. 370–372). Cf. Fuller, "Of
Memory," ed. Walten, 2. 175: Theodore Beza, when over eighty, "could say by
heart any Greek Chapter in S. Paul's Epistles, or anything else that he had
learnt long before, but forgot whatsoever was newly told him; his memory like
an inne retaining old guests, but having no room to entertain new"; concerning
Fuller's own famous memory, consult the Walten ed., 1. 174–179; and see
Hunter, *Memory: Facts and Fallacies*, pp. 158–159, on the mnemonic power of
Lord Macaulay and "Memory" Woodfall. Contrast the young lawyer of Boston:
he addressed a lady who had, like himself, attended Ralph Waldo Emerson's
lecture on Memory the previous day: "I can't remember a thing he said, can
you?" "Yes," replied the lady; "He said: 'Shallow brains have short memories' "
(Emerson, *Works* 12. 445–446, editor's note).

[138] *Epist.* 2. 3. 4.

[139] Quintilian, 11. 2. 26.

today.[140] If the speech was written, it was either read—a rarer practice, but adopted for example, by the Emperor Augustus[141] ("though he had the faculty of speaking impromptu")—or delivered from memory, while yet some speakers wrote their speeches, but without learning and delivering them *memoriter*. Extemporizing involves premeditation of the ideas and arrangement, but, in general, not the memorizing of the words. True impromptu speaking—speaking on the spur of the moment without specific preparation—had often to be resorted to by most orators in practical situations. The artistic school of all periods maintains that the best oratory has been written and memorized[142]—in the spirit of Goldwin Smith's dictum that nobody can speak *literature* extempore.[143] Writing assures exactitude, coherence, proportion, graceful ornamentation, and subtle transitions; and the time taken in it helps the ideas to adhere in memory. Memorized delivery is superior to reading in that it provides more opportunity for action. The ancient advocates of extempore speaking were willing to surrender some of the virtues of memorized delivery and to run the risk of rash utterance in favor of self-possession, naturalness, and liveliness of delivery, and without the dangers of a laboring memory and of putting manner and artifice on display. Alcidamas (fourth century B.C.) strikes the note for this school: to learn and keep in mind written speeches is a hard and laborious task, and to forget a speech in the course of a trial is a shameful experience. Lapse of memory is followed

[140] See Paul Shorey, "What Teachers of Speech May Learn From the Theory and Practice of the Greeks," *Quarterly Journal of Speech Education*, VIII, No. 2 (1922); W. S. Howell, *Fénelon's Dialogues on Eloquence* (Princeton, 1951), pp. 105–111, 140.

[141] Suetonius, *Lives of the Caesars* 2. 84.

[142] See Shorey, "Teachers of Speech," p. 124.

[143] See his *Reminiscences*, ed. by Arnold Haultain (New York, 1911), p. 238 (on John Bright).

inevitably by distress, wandering of the mind, a search for the omitted or altered detail, and often not only by loss of time, but also by abrupt silence, and unhappy, ridiculous, and hopeless uncertainty.[144]

Apparently partisan opinion on this kind of question could reveal itself in the actual speech. If your adversary should reproach you with writing and reading your speech or with practicing it beforehand, the *Rhetorica ad Alexandrum* (before 300 B.C.) advises you to retort that the law does not any more prohibit you from reading a written speech than it prohibits your opponent from speaking without a written text; or if he should charge you with studying and practicing public speaking, admit the fact, and argue that it would be better for the citizens if he, too, learned to be an orator.[145]

It was Cicero's regular practice to write out only the most essential portions of his speech, especially the Introduction, to prepare what else he could by premeditation, and then to meet emergencies with improvisation.[146] The fifty-six Introductions we have under the name of Demosthenes[147] seem to indicate a like method on his part. According to Plutarch,[148] Demosthenes, self-styled the most laborious of all orators, who regarded consummate care as a mark of deference to occasion and audience, and early learned to attend to the disposition of the words, reported that his speeches were neither entirely

[144] "On the Sophists"; see La Rue Van Hook, "Alcidamas vs. Isocrates; the Spoken vs. the Written Word," *Classical Weekly*, XII, No. 12 (1919), 89–94, esp. sections 12, 18, and 21, pp. 92–93.

[145] Chap. 36 (1444a). The Ithaca, N.Y., *Journal* of October 1, 1965 reports that a writer in the *Liberal News* (London) has criticized Queen Elizabeth II for reading and not memorizing her public speeches.

[146] Quintilian, 10. 7. 30.

[147] See Albert Rupprecht, "Die demosthenische Prooimiensammlung," *Philologus*, LXXXII (1926–1927), 365–432; on published Introductions, Stemplinger, *Das Plagiat*, pp. 224 ff.

[148] *Lives* (*Demosthenes*) 8. 4.

unwritten nor on the other hand fully written out. And we learn from the studies of A. P. Dorjahn[149] that Demosthenes extemporized a great deal more than some of us thought he did. Plutarch reports[150] that those orations which Demosthenes spoke impromptu had more courage and spirit than those which he wrote out.

Quintilian makes three observations of special import in connection with extempore speaking: first, that premeditation not only secures the arrangement of the matter, but also arrays in order the words, and brings the whole texture of the speech into connection—which clearly implies some verbal memorization;[151] secondly, that writing is never more necessary than when we must speak extempore, for the solidity it preserves, the depth to which it brings verbal facility, and the precision it supplies—and we should not write out what we do not intend to deliver from memory;[152] and thirdly, that even extempore speaking depends on no mental activity so much as on memory—while we are giving utterance to one thought, we must consider what we are going to say next, and the memory transmits to the delivery that which it has received from the imagination.[153]

I now turn to the beginnings of mnemonics.

The lyric poet, Simonides of Ceos, who died in 468 or 465 B.C. at an advanced age, once wrote an ode to celebrate the achievement of a victorious boxer. In writing the poem he had contracted for a certain sum, but part of this was refused him on the ground that, following the custom of poets, he had introduced a digression in praise of Castor and Pollux, patron

---

[149] *Trans. Amer. Philol. Assoc.*, LXXVIII (1947), 69–76; LXXXI (1950), 9–15; LXXXIII (1952), 164–171.
[150] *Lives (Demosthenes)* 9. 4.
[151] 10. 6. 2.
[152] 10. 7. 28, 32.
[153] 11. 2. 3.

gods of pugilism. He was told that for this reason he had better demand from these two gods, whose deeds he had celebrated, the remainder of the sum due.

Castor and Pollux discharged their debt. At a great banquet honoring the boxer's victory, Simonides was called away from the company by a message announcing that two young men were at the door and eagerly desired to see him. He did not find them, but what followed made the gods' gratitude evident. No sooner had he crossed the threshold on the way out, when the banqueting-hall collapsed upon the guests and wrought such confusion that the relatives who came to look for the bodies in order to bury them were unable to identify by any mark either the faces or the limbs of the dead. Then Simonides, by remembering the *order* in which the guests had been seated, was able to restore to each his own dead. He thus discovered the principle that the best aid to clearness of memory consists in orderly arrangement.

Quintilian tells this story,[154] following the tradition, which we find also in the inscription on the Marmor Parium (third century B.C.)[155] and in Cicero,[156] that Simonides was the inventor of the art of memory. In any case the invention is assigned to the early fifth century. Cicero several times tells us[157] that when a certain professor (in one place Cicero says "when Simonides or someone else"[158]) offered to teach Themistocles the art of mnemonics *which was then being introduced for the first time*, Themistocles asked what exactly could that art achieve, and when told that it would enable him to

[154] 11. 2. 11 ff., with reservations on the historicity of the part that concerns Castor and Pollux.

[155] Felix Jacoby, *Das Marmor Parium* (Berlin, 1904), pp. 16 and 180 (for the years 477–476 B.C.).

[156] *De Oratore* 2. 86. 351 ff.

[157] *De Oratore* 2. 74. 299; 2. 86. 351; *Acad.* 2. 1. 21; *De Finibus* 2. 32. 104.

[158] *De Finibus, loc. cit.*

remember everything, Themistocles replied that it would be a greater kindness if the professor taught him to forget, "for I remember even things I do not wish to remember, and I cannot forget things I wish to forget."[159]

The distinction of having been the first to apply the art to oratory is often assigned to Hippias of Elis. In Plato's Dialogue *Hippias Minor*[160] Socrates pokes fun at him. He compliments Hippias upon his extraordinary versatility—his impressive showing at the Olympic games, his skill in many arts, in engraving gems and making clothes and shoes and fine fabrics, and in writing a great variety of poetry and prose. "And indeed, it appears that I forgot to include your art of memory, in which you regard yourself as specially brilliant, and I dare say I have forgotten a great many other things as well." And when Hippias cannot recall the illustration of a point he is making, Socrates says: "Oh, you are now perhaps not making use of your art of memory. . . . But I will remind you of what you said." The earliest allusion to a specific system is indeed to that of Hippias. In Xenophon's *Symposium*[161] Socrates points out the effect upon Callias of learning the memory-system he got from Hippias: "Callias has now become more amorous than ever—he cannot forget any beauty he sees."

[159] Cf. Publilius Syrus, ed. R. A. H. Bickford-Smith (London, 1895), p. 11: *Etiam oblivisci ⟨quod scis⟩ interdum expedit;* St. Augustine, *De Civitate Dei* 7. 3: "For no one who is bad has a good mind; some of the wicked, on the other hand, have a marvelous memory yet are all the worse in the degree that they cannot forget the evil they conceive"; the epigram by Macedonius the Consul, *Greek Anthology* 10. 65: "Warm welcome, Memory and Forgetfulness! Memory where blessings are concerned, Forgetfulness where sorrows"; Alexander Pope, "Eloisa to Abelard," lines 189–190: "Of all affliction taught a lover yet, 'Tis sure the hardest science to forget."

[160] 368 D ff.

[161] 4. 62. Other references to *memoria technica*: Aristotle, *De Somniis* 458b 17 ff.; Claudius Ptolemaeus, περὶ κριτηρίου καὶ ἡγεμονικοῦ, sec. 16, ed. Friedrich Hanow (Leipzig, 1870), p. xi.

We have an early sample of Sophistic instruction in the fragmentary art of memory set forth in the *Twofold Debates*,[162] which belongs to the late fifth or early fourth century B.C.: "Memory is the greatest and finest discovery, useful for wisdom and for life." The rules: First, give close attention—and here come to mind Samuel Johnson's definition: "The true art of memory is the art of attention";[163] John Locke's observation: "When the ideas that offer themselves . . . are taken notice of, and, as it were, registered in the memory, it is attention";[164] and Martin Tupper's verse in *Proverbial Philosophy:*[165] "Memory, daughter of attention, is the teeming mother of wisdom." Secondly, listen and repeat often what you hear. Thirdly, associate the new with the known; to remember the name Chrysippus, think of χρυσός and ἵππος. And as for activities, associate these with their exemplars—acts of courage with Ares and Achilles, smith's work with Hephaestos. It is believed that this may have been the method of Hippias.[166] Evenus of Paros, Sophist and elegiac poet, and contemporary of Socrates, was the first known to write mnemonic verses; it was said that he wrote his Art of Indirect Censures in verse so as to aid the memory.[167]

Some of the ancients doubted that there can be an art of memory, but how far back this skepticism goes we do not know. The *auctor ad Herennium* gives the impression that the subject was debated in his time, and promises to explain elsewhere the grounds of his belief in the efficacy of art and

---

[162] Diels-Kranz, *Fragmente* 2. 416, ll. 13 ff. (chap. 9).

[163] *Idler*, No. 74.

[164] *Human Understanding* 2. 19 (1. 298); see also 2. 10 (1. 194).

[165] First Series, "Of Thinking," line 13.

[166] E.g., Kathleen Freeman, *The Pre-Socratic Philosophers* (3d ed.; Oxford, 1953), p. 417.

[167] Plato, *Phaedrus* 267A.

method.[168] An anonymous commentary on Hermogenes[169] dismisses memory and delivery from the number of functions as being advantages of nature and not acquirable by training —the borrowed source of the statement may belong to an early period. The younger Seneca felt that the memory is more to be depended upon when it has no support outside *itself*.[170] Aelian (early third Christian century) seems to take delight in pointing out that animals remember what they have experienced, and do not need the art of Simonides, Theodectes, and Hippias.[171] A passage in Philostratus[172] reveals both his own firm opinion on this matter as well as the belief on the part of some in the influence of magic upon the acquisition of a good memory. Discussing Dionysius of Miletus (a rhetorician of the time of Hadrian), who was alleged to train his pupils in mnemonics by the aid of Chaldaean magic, Philostratus says: "There are no arts of memory, nor could there be, for though memory gives us arts, it cannot itself be taught nor be acquired by any method, since it is a natural advantage or a part of the immortal soul."[173] A teacher "would be foolishly thoughtless of his reputation" to practice sorcery on his young pupils. How then did these pupils of Dionysius win the name of μνημονικοί? It was merely that his declamations gave his pupils such delight that he was compelled to repeat them often, and the quick learners, by diligent practice, carved

[168] 3. XVI. 28.

[169] Hugo Rabe, *Prolegomenon Sylloge* (Leipzig, 1931), p. 202, ll. 5 ff.; cf. the like contention of Albutius (Augustan period) and others in Quintilian, 3. 3. 4. Alexinus the Megarian philosopher (fourth–third century B.C.) finds fault with the rhetorical sophists for their many useless researches into subjects like diction and memory; Siegfried Sudhaus, *Philodemi Rhetorica* (Leipzig, 1892), 1. 79. 23 ff.; H. M. Hubbell, *The Rhetorica of Philodemus* (New Haven, 1920), p. 278.

[170] *Epist. ad Lucilium*, Book 13, 88. 32: *nescio an certior memoria sit quae nullum extra se subsidium habet.*

[171] *De Nat. Animal.* 4. 35, 44; 6. 10 (2), 48; 7. 23, 48; 8. 3; 10. 48; 11. 14.

[172] *Lives* 22. 523.

[173] Cf. Plato, *Meno* 81 C D.

these declamations on their minds. If we can trust Ammianus Marcellinus, various writers thought that Cyrus, Simonides, and Hippias got their strong memories by drinking certain potions.[174] Poor Curio (fl. 76 B.C.), notorious for his bad memory, in a private suit of major importance suddenly forgot his whole case, and could only offer the lame excuse that the opposing lady-client's potions and incantations were the cause of the lapse.[175] At this juncture one thinks of the education of Gargantua,[176] of how the physician Theodore purged him with hellebore, to cleanse the "perverse habitude" of his brain, and make him forget all he had learned under his former teachers; of Peter of Ravenna,[177] mnemonician of the late fifteenth century, believed to be a necromancer; and of Lamprecht Schenkel's mnemonic work,[178] at the end of the sixteenth, denounced by the University of Louvain as the work of the devil. The superstition current in ancient times, that those who read epitaphs lose their memory, we meet of course in Cicero's *De Senectute*.[179] And medical recipes for the improvement of the memory have been common at virtually all periods.[180]

There were, as I have said, works on memory among the

[174] 16. 5. 8.

[175] Cicero, *Brutus* 60. 217; C. Scribonius Curio (died 53 B.C.). The elder Pliny, *Nat. Hist.* 7. 24. 90, discusses the amnesia resulting from injury and disease. The orator Valerius Messalla Corvinus (64 B.C.–A.D. 8) forgot his own name. In Erasmus, *Moriae Encomium*, Folly has no peroration to offer, for she cannot recall anything she has said.

[176] François Rabelais, *Gargantua et Pantagruel* 1. 23.

[177] Pietro Tommai, *Artificiosa Memoria seu Foenix* (Venice, 1491); Howell, *Logic and Rhetoric*, pp. 95–98.

[178] Lamprecht Thomas Schenkel, *Gazophylacium Artis Memoriae.*

[179] 7. 21.

[180] On the connections also with magic, see, e.g., Lynn Thorndike, *A History of Magic and Experimental Science* (New York, 1923), 5. 560, 577, 606–607; 6. 429; 7. 302, 328, 465, 605; 8. 63, 85, 262, 405, 535, 575; Hajdu, *Das mnemotechn. Schrifttum des Mittelalters*, pp. 71 ff; for the Elizabethan period, see Camden, "Memory," pp. 57–61; Wilson, *Arte*, ed. Mair, p. 212.

Greeks, but only the section in Longinus' *techne*,[181] of the third Christian century, is extant. It provides a general discussion of the subject, a brief consideration of the system of backgrounds and images—which I shall in a moment discuss—and hints for memorization according to the parts of the discourse. I shall now give you a short summary of the fuller treatment of mnemonics in the Latin *Rhetorica ad Herennium*.[182] The unknown author, who is heir to the Rhodian school of rhetoric, composed his book between 86 and 82 B.C. If the doctrine at first appears odd, or if like myself you approach the subject of mnemotechny with suspicion, I ask you to withhold final appraisal of it until you have compared it with other methods, until you have seen that in its visual principle it underlies most of subsequent mnemonic theory, and until I have reminded you that it appears in an excellent, very influential, and highly esteemed treatise.[183]

There is the natural memory and there is the memory which is the product of art. The latter involves the use of backgrounds and images. A background is a scene set off on a moderate scale, complete and conspicuous—a house, inter-columnar space, a recess, arch, or the like. An image is a figure, mark, or portrait of the object we wish to remember, and is set in this background. Backgrounds should be arranged in a series, and each fifth may be marked; that is, a golden hand may be set in the fifth background, in the tenth someone named Decimus, and so on. The images chosen should be such as will adhere long in the memory—striking

---

[181] Spengel-Hammer, *Rhet. Graeci* I, Pars II, pp. 197–206. For references to mnemotechny in Aristotle, see *Topica* 814 (163b): Just as the system of τόποι is useful in mnemonics, so in reasoning one is made readier by having committed to memory premises of most frequent occurrence and general application; n. 65 above; also *De Anima* 427b 19, *De Mem. et Recollect.* 451a.

[182] 3. XVI. 28 ff.

[183] E.g., see Spengel's appraisal, p. 24 above.

images, doing something, of exceptional beauty or ugliness, dressed distinctively, or stained with blood, or soiled with mud, or smeared with red paint, or even comic in character. The backgrounds are like wax tablets or papyrus, the images like the letters, the arrangement of the images is like the script, and the delivery like reading the script. When you wish to revive the memory of the facts, demand the deposits in turn from the custodians, proceeding in either direction from any background you please.

The aim in rhetoric was *copia rerum et verborum* and so the mnemonic theory sought the acquisition of both. Memory embraces everything which enters into the composition of a speech; and that includes both the products of invention and committing to memory the *words* we propose to use.

We form a likeness of a *matter* when we enlist images that present a general view of the matter with which we are dealing. If, for example, we wish to remember the prosecutor's first charge, that the defendant killed a man by poison and the motive for the crime was an inheritance, in the first background picture the man in question as lying ill in bed, and the defendant at the bedside, holding in his right hand a cup, and in his left, tablets. In this way you record the man poisoned, the poisoner, the poisoning, and the inheritance. Likenesses of words are established when the record of each single noun or appellative is kept by an image.

The *auctor* regards as ridiculous the listing of the images of a *great many* words,[184] here having in mind perhaps the method discussed later by Quintilian[185]—a ship to be symbolized by an anchor, a battle by a spear, the name Fabius by Cunctator, or the names Aper, Ursus, Naso, and Crispus to be recalled by their etymology. Training the memory of *words* is, however,

[184] 3. XXIII. 38.
[185] 11. 2. 29–31.

useful as an exercise whereby to strengthen the more important memory of matter.

To illustrate the likenesses of words:[186] we wish to remember the verse

> Iam domum itionem reges Atridae parant.

> Now their home-coming the kings, the sons of Atreus,
> are making ready.

In the first background put someone named Domitius raising his hands to heaven as he is being lashed by members of the family of Marcius Rex. That will represent *Iam domum itionem reges.* In the second background place the actors Aesopus and Cimber being dressed as for the rôles of Agamemnon and Menelaüs in the play *Iphigenia;* that will represent *Atridae parant.*

L. A. Post has written an interesting account[187] of his successful use of this system, and to it appended the following observation: "Primitive man possessed and organized vivid pictorial powers, and early writing arose naturally from the graphic representation of the pictures by which a series of events or a poem was remembered. . . . Primitive pictures are a transfer of memory images. The same may well be true of the earliest form of writing. Painting stayed representational, while writing is now entirely symbolic." That the scheme is an extension of the topical theory of invention is clear to all who are conversant with ancient rhetoric. The τόπος is a place in the mind, a vein, a haunt, a mine, where arguments, general and special, are to be found.[188] What

---

[186] 3. XXI. 34.

[187] "Ancient Memory Systems," *Class. Weekly*, XXV, No. 14 (1932), 105–110.

[188] The spatial nature of the scheme is not unlike that of the so-called "number forms" which Galton and others discuss in connection with imagery. To some individuals, whenever numerals are thought of, a "form" appears in the mental field, each numeral having its own definite place. "This form may consist of a

strikes the critic in the section on the memory of words is that the basis is a pun utilizing the *form* of the word and not its *meaning*. And note that the adverb *iam* is not treated. A competent critic would probably regard the underlying principle of the scheme as being sounder than the illustrations are apt.

From the *auctor ad Herennium* we pass to Cicero's treatment of memory, which is found in *De Oratore*,[189] the product of mature reflection on rhetoric and wide experience in oratory. I shall reproduce for you the substance of Antonius' words on the importance of memory in rhetoric, because his view forms a contrast with the emphasis on verbal memory in the later Roman period. "There is no need for me to observe what an advantage memory is to the orator, how great its usefulness, how great its power. It retains the instructions you have received and the opinions you yourself have formed; it keeps all your thoughts fixed in mind, and all your apparatus of language arranged; it listens attentively to the information supplied by your client, and the speech of your adversary to which you must reply; it knows what, and how much, and in what style you are to speak; what points made by your adversary you have already answered, and what points remain unanswered; it remembers the arguments you have presented in other cases, and many you have heard other speakers present."[190]

Cicero reproduces in briefer form the kind of mnemonics I have just set forth, not wishing, as he says, "to be tedious and dwell at immoderate length upon so well-known and so

---

mere line, of a peculiarly arranged row or rows of figures, or of a shaded place";
see Francis Galton, *Inquiries into Human Faculty and Its Development* (London and New York, 1908), pp. 79 ff., especially pp. 82 and 88.

[189] 2. 86. 351 ff.; 1. 4. 18.

[190] 2. 87. 355; in 1. 5. 18 Cicero would also require of the advocate that he retain in memory the complete history of the past, a store of precedents, a knowledge of the statutory law and of all the binding Roman law.

familiar a subject."[191] But he insists that the proper business of the orator is the memory of facts; the memory of words is less necessary.[192] This is doubtless the result of a belief that words are at the command of a practiced orator. Milton in "An Apology for Smectymnuus" expresses the principle thus: "Whose mind soever is fully possest with a fervent desire to know good things, and with the dearest charity to infuse the knowledge of them into others, when such a man would speak, his words (by what I can express), like so many nimble and airy servitors, trip about him at command, and in well-order'd files, as he would wish, fall aptly into their own places."[193] But the idea underlying Cato's *Rem tene; verba sequentur*[194] was a commonplace in Roman rhetoric and literary criticism. What we miss, rather, is some comment from Cicero revealing that in his own practice he followed the mnemonics he taught, especially since, in several passages, he complains of extreme nervousness.[195]

Yet, in spite of his reservations with respect to verbal memory, the Ciceronian Antonius believes we must invent symbols for the many words that, like joints, connect the sentence-members. He says: "Nor is that true which is said by people who have not cultivated this art, that the memory is oppressed

[191] *De Oratore* 2. 87. 358.

[192] *De Oratore* 2. 88. 359. So also Martianus Capella 5. 5. 38–39. Cicero, *Acad.* 2. 1. 2.: Though Hortensius had a better *memoria verborum* than Lucius Lucullus, the latter had a *divina memoria rerum*, which was the more valuable; see above, notes 123 and 128.

[193] *The Works of John Milton* (New York, 1931), III, Part I, 362; cf. Hugh Blair, *Lectures on Rhetoric and Belles-Lettres* (New York, 1829), lecture 10, p. 102: "Style is nothing else than that sort of expression which our thoughts most readily assume."

[194] C. Julius Victor, *Ars. Rhet.* 1, in Carolus Halm, *Rhet. Lat. Minores* (Leipzig, 1863), p. 374; see H. L. Brown, *Extemporary Speech in Antiquity*, p. 35, n. 131.

[195] *De Oratore* 1. 26. 121; *Div. in Caec.* 13. 41; *Pro Cluentio* 18. 51; *Pro Rege Deiotaro* 1. 1; *Acad.* 2. 20. 64. See A. S. Wilkins, ed. *Cicero, De Oratore* (Oxford, 1892), p. 136, n. 18, on Cicero's reproducing his own feelings under the character of Crassus. See also Quintilian, 11. 1. 44; Plutarch, *Lives (Cicero)* 35. 3 ff.

by the weight of these images, and that even that is obscured which unassisted nature might have retained; for I have myself seen men of consummate ability and an almost super-human faculty of memory . . . who used to say that as they inscribed letters on wax, so they wrote down with symbols whatever they wished to recall, in backgrounds they had formed in the imagination.[196] This faculty of artificial memory we gain by practice, and by selecting similar words, converted or altered in cases, or transferred from species to genus, and through representing a whole idea by the image of a single word."[197]

I come next to Quintilian.[198] Quintilian believes in the memorized speech during the young speaker's training. It is important to train him to acquire precision; so do not let him look at his manuscript, and do not prompt him. Given a sure memory, and enough time, I should wish not a single syllable to escape me.[199] If the speech is well-memorized it will seem to be impromptu.[200] To be sure, if we have dull memories, it is safer to grasp the facts and to speak extempore.[201]

To write out a speech, as against Plato's notion that we cease to guard in memory what we have written, is good prac-tice because the mental effort (*cogitatio*) has engraved it on our memory.[202]

Quintilian, too, recommends the use of localities—a spacious house divided into rooms, or a public building, or a long journey, or the walls of a city, or pictures.[203]

---

[196] *De Oratore* 2. 88. 359 ff.
[197] *De Oratore* 2. 87. 358.
[198] 11. 2. 1–51; 1. 1. 19, 36–37; 1. 3. 1; 2. 7. 1 ff.; 3. 3. 10.
[199] 11. 2. 45.
[200] 11. 2. 46.
[201] 11. 2. 48.
[202] 11. 2. 9–10.
[203] 11. 2. 17 ff., and esp. 21.

But about complex devices:[204] these, he says, are useful for enabling an auctioneer to tell what article he has sold to each buyer, but of less service in learning the various parts of a continuous speech. Such a method cannot grasp a coherent series of words. One cannot, for example, represent a conjunction by a symbol.[205] Even if we have definite symbols for every word, and select an infinite number of localities to recall all the words of a very long speech, the flow of the speech will inevitably be impeded by the double effort forced upon our memory. So let these experts keep their systems for themselves.

The following are Quintilian's precepts.[206] Do not overburden the memory; learn a speech piecemeal, and then unite the parts into a whole. Hard portions you may designate by certain marks. If you are slow to remember your own signs, adapt the symbols to thoughts which are likely to slip from memory. Learn a passage by heart from the same tablets on which you have written it;[207] you will remember pages and lines and will speak as though reading aloud. Memorize out loud—but in a low voice; the mind is stimulated by the sound of the voice (and here we have auditory aid to memory). Artistic structure and correct division are of great value in guiding the memory;[208] it is easier to learn verse than prose, easier to learn well-knit than ill-connected prose.[209] Practice daily; there is nothing that is more strengthened by practice or weakened by neglect. Therefore all who, of whatever age, devote themselves to cultivating the memory, should endure the initial tedium of reading and reading again what they have written or read—of chewing the same cud over again. Learn

[204] II. 2. 23 ff.
[205] Cf. p. 231 above, with regard to the adverb *iam*.
[206] II. 2. 27 ff.
[207] II. 2. 32.
[208] II. 2. 36.
[209] II. 2. 39.

only a little at first, then increase gradually. Begin with poetry, then pass to memorizing speeches.[210] I approve the use of brief memoranda, which may be held in the hand and looked at from time to time.

What I consider especially significant in Quintilian is that as with Cicero and the *auctor ad Herennium* the memory of words was subordinate to *memoria rerum*. Even at this time when declamation and the oratory of display were the rule, and despite his own interest in artistic finish, Quintilian does not urge unmitigated word-for-word memorization. Memory, he says, has raised oratory to its present brilliance through its animating power, that brings before us all the store of precedents, statutes, rulings, and facts which the speaker must possess in abundance and always be ready to produce. He must follow the order of the matter and of the words he has premeditated, but also remember what his adversaries have said, and refute their arguments in the order in which they were presented.[211]

In the high period of Roman rhetoric and oratory *memoria* then transcends verbal memorizing. In C. S. Baldwin's words, "It embraces the speaker's whole command of his material in the order of his constructive plan and in relation to rebuttal, and was most stressed," indeed, "for speeches unwritten."[212] But when we come to the period of the Second Sophistic, and the last centuries of ancient Rome, *memoria rerum* gives way to *memoria verborum*.

The Second Sophistic looked back to the first, and preserved and prized the art of improvisation. Only now the ideal was not intellectual perfection, nor—since oratory was divorced from political life—practical service. Instead rhetoric become

[210] 11. 2. 40–41.
[211] 10.7. 31.
[212] *Ancient Rhetoric and Poetic*, p. 67.

a purely literary activity indulged in for its own sake. With their declamations on historical and fictitious themes, encomia, and emphasis on *decorative expansion*, these Sophists aimed to be artists, and indeed their virtuosity—largely in the field of style—brought to the most successful of them the fame and admiration they sought. Their highly valued training was calculated to produce a good memory.

Their own speeches, their teachers' compositions, and large quantities of the orations of the ancients were learned by heart. When Polemo (time of Hadrian) was asked to suggest a penalty commensurate with the crimes committed by a certain robber, he cried: "Make him learn by heart some old [declamatory] stuff."[213] For Polemo had memorized very many such passages, and thought this the most toilsome of exercises. The declaimer included in his speeches as many commonplaces, stock examples, and quotations as he could remember[214]—not to mention effective phrases and periods—and when asked to repeat his speech he must do so with perfect accuracy. These specialists in extempore speaking were precisely the great memorizers. Lucian's "Professor of Public Speaking" gives his pupils ironic advice: "Don't write anything out, or come forward with a prepared speech, for this is sure to expose you. As for reading the Classics, don't bother with that silly Isocrates, that graceless Demosthenes, or that insipid Plato. Study rather speeches recently delivered and the so-called declamations—these will supply you with a stock of provisions on which you can draw at need!"[215] We see the effects of this preoccupation with *memoria* also in the poems of Ausonius[216]—for a few examples, the verses telling how many days there are

[213] Philostratus, *Lives* 25. 541. See J. W. H. Walden, *The Universities of Ancient Greece* (New York, 1909), pp. 214 ff.

[214] See T. J. Haarhoff, *Schools of Gaul* (Johannesburg, 1958), p. 91.

[215] *Rhet. Didask.* 17 and 20.

[216] See Haarhoff, *Schools of Gaul*, pp. 90–93.

in each month (like "Thirty days has September"), the monostichs on each of the months,[217] and the metrical summaries[218] (composed for his son) of the twelve Caesars whose Lives were written by Suetonius; while the Cento Nuptialis, which he calls "a task for the memory only" (*solae memoriae negotium*[219]) suggests that he must have known Virgil by heart.

Let me now make a few observations on the later career of *memoria* in rhetoric and the arts allied to rhetoric.

St. Augustine, in Book IV of *De Doctrina Christiana*, which applies the principles of rhetoric to Christian eloquence, accepts only two of the traditional divisions—invention and style. But he does not neglect *memoria*, particularly *memoria rerum*. As for *memoria verborum*, he limits himself to advising preachers who cannot devise a sermon to memorize and deliver the wise and eloquent sermons of others.[220] In Eastern Europe in the fourth century, Niceta, Bishop of Remesiana, has his half-Romanized baptismal candidates memorize the creed and the Lord's Prayer.[221] The catechumen is expected to repeat the following week what he has learned this week—a like procedure to that which was followed with his own students in grammar by the famous Bernard of Chartres eight

[217] Book VII, *Eclogues* 9 and 11.

[218] Book XIV, 2–4.

[219] Book XVII, Dedication to Paulus.

[220] See IV. 10. 25 and IV. 29. 62; on St. Augustine's practice (and that of contemporary and near-contemporary preachers), see R. J. Deferrari, "St. Augustine's Method of Composing and Delivering Sermons," *Amer. Journ. Philol.*, XLIII, No. 2 (1922), 97–123, 193–219. Cf. Joseph Addison, *Spectator*, No. 106: "Sir Roger gave [his friend] a present of all the good sermons which have been printed in English and only begged of him that every Sunday he would pronounce one of them in the pulpit. . . . I could only wish that more of our country clergy would follow this example"; Hugh Blair, *Lectures on Rhetoric and Belles-Lettres* (Philadelphia, 1829), lecture 26, p. 283: "With regard to the pulpit, it has certainly been a great disadvantage that the practice of reading sermons, instead of repeating them from memory, has prevailed in England."

[221] See M. L. W. Laistner, *Christianity and Pagan Culture in the Later Roman Empire* (Ithaca, 1951), pp. 29–30, and note.

centuries later.[222] Cassiodorus emphasizes the usefulness of memory to the monk for the study of Holy Writ and the defence of God's word, and observes that it is of common concern also to speakers, dialecticians, poets, and jurists.[223]

In the realm of sacred rhetoric, the art dedicated to the winning of souls to God, the fivefold division does not appear in the treatises. But again memory is not passed by. In the later Middle Ages, the period of thematic preaching based on the intricate inter-weaving of Scriptural passages, Thomas Waleys (1300) would have the preacher, in order to avoid lapses in memory, retain only the ideas of the Scriptural authorities he uses, and commit to memory merely the specially important words therein.[224] The author of the so-called Aquinas-tract bids the preacher memorize the nine ways of expanding a sermon that have been set forth in the manual, and in delivering the sermon beware of looking about too much lest objects disturb the senses, and scatter and confuse the order of memory.[225] By the time of the Renaissance the classical scheme is in full panoply; Surgant, writing in 1502, offers an elaborate treatment of memory, in which appear again the ancient principles of backgrounds and images.[226]

The *Rhetorica Divina* of William of Auvergne, in the thirteenth century, is a rhetoric of prayer, devoted to the per-

---

[222] John of Salisbury, *Metalogicon* 1. 24 (854d, 855c); the student was required to recite daily what he had heard the previous day.

[223] Cassiodorus, *Inst.*, 2. 2. 16; 2. 3. 17. The mnemotechnical treatises of the Middle Ages "were designed for all sorts of classes and people, doctors and lawyers no less than monks and preachers" (Yates, "Ciceronian Art," p. 888).

[224] "De Modo Componendi Sermones," chap. 1, in Th.-M. Charland, *Artes Praedicandi* (Paris and Ottawa, 1936), p. 336.

[225] See pp. 60–71 and 74 above.

[226] *Manuale Curatorum*, Book I, *Consideratio* 20, ed. Basel, 1507–8, fols. 45 ff; Dorothea Roth, *Die mittelalterliche Predigttheorie und das Manuale Curatorum des Johann Ulrich Surgant* (Basel, 1956), pp. 179–180.

suasion of that Highest Judge, God. Even the gestures of prayer are considered in this work, and *memoria* is represented by the service it performs in the recollection of divine blessings.[227]

Mediaeval poetical theory is a merging of poetics and rhetoric. In the early thirteenth century, Geoffrey of Vinsauf devoted a section of his *Poetria Nova*[228] to memory. He who is unwilling to work hard in order to acquire a good memory is like one who wants the fish without fishing for it.[229] Geoffrey knows the ancient doctrine of *loci* and images, but reveals that he himself used *notulae*[230]—and I hope he did so without the excesses suggested by the glosses on a manuscript of a sermon delivered in 1500 by the popular Parisian preacher Olivier Maillard: Here "sit down—stand up—mop yourself—ahem! ahem!—now shriek like a devil!"[231]

In rhetoric proper the minor writers from the fourth century on occasionally followed the tradition with respect to *memoria*, but in sketchy form, Fortunatianus[232] and C. Julius Victor[233] (both fourth Christian century) preserving the doctrine of places and symbols, but not with warm recommendation. Indeed classical rhetoric in its main features has predominated down to our time—certainly in the theory of public address in England and America—although undergoing changes in emphasis and in degree of inclusiveness. Where the fivefold

[227] (Lyons, 1490), chaps. 25 and 50.
[228] Edmond Faral, *Les arts poétiques du XIIe et du XIIIe siècles* (Paris, 1924), pp. 257–259, vv. 1969 ff.
[229] Verse 2029.
[230] Vv. 2009 ff.
[231] Sabine Baring-Gould, *Post-Mediaeval Preachers* (London, Oxford, and Cambridge, 1865), p. 12.
[232] *Ars. Rhet.* 3. 13–14, in Halm, *Rhet. Lat. Minores*, pp. 128–130: learning piecemeal is a better and simpler method.
[233] *Ars. Rhet.*, 23, in Halm, *op. cit.*, p. 440; he doubts the effectiveness of the method.

scheme of functions has been maintained, *memoria* has suffered every possible fate: it may retain the dignity it once enjoyed at Rome, or be treated briefly while yet remaining one of the canon, or be ignored altogether. When it has been pointedly ignored, as occasionally in the nineteenth century, the reason assigned is the same as was occasionally assigned in ancient times—that it does not belong to the *essence* of the rhetorical art.[234] In the sixteenth and seventeenth centuries, Memory had no place in the influential Ramian rhetoric;[235] Peter Ramus and his school had withdrawn Invention and Disposition from rhetoric and transferred them to dialectic—a late victory for dialectic in its battle with rhetoric, begun in the high Middle Ages, for primacy in the trivium. Memory, being involved in Disposition, went along with it. During the flourishing days of Elocution, in the nineteenth century, memory was an adjunct of delivery. In the text-books of today, it is not a major canon, although it receives attention here and there.

Among those who in more recent times have captured the imagination for extraordinary memories have been several classical scholars. J. J. Scaliger said of himself that in his youth he could repeat more than a hundred verses, after reading them once.[236] Richard Porson of Cambridge knew much of Greek, Latin, and English literature by heart; even as a

---

[234] E.g., A.-Ed. Chaignet, *La rhétorique et son histoire* (Paris, 1888), p. 539. On the opposition to mnemotechnical systems among Elizabethan writers, see Camden, "Memory", pp. 68–69. Le P. Mestre, S. J., *Préceptes de rhétorique* (Paris, 1926; 1st ed. 1882), p. 159, thinks that the artificial procedures can be a hindrance.

[235] See W. S. Howell, "Ramus and English Rhetoric: 1574–1681," *Quarterly Journal of Speech*, XXXVII, No. 3 (1951), 301, and *Logic and Rhetoric in England*, pp. 146 ff., 247 ff.; W. J. Ong, S. J., *Ramus and Method, and the Decay of Dialogue* (Cambridge, Mass., 1958), p. 280, and on Ramus' mnemonic system in relation to the ancient, pp. 194–195.

[236] Samuel Johnson, *Idler*, No. 74.

youngster at Eton he construed Horace from memory, when a mischievous boy had thrust some other book in his hand. But there is no question of ingenious devices here: "Sometimes, in order to impress a thing upon my memory, I have read it a dozen times, and transcribed it six."[237]

The topical method of the ancients has persisted to this day, although there have now and then been those like Erasmus[238] and Charles Butler[239] (1629) who thought it rather a hindrance than a help. Thomas Wilson in 1553 treats it, but without full assurance: "Thoughe it seme straunge and folyshe to them that knowe it not, yet the learned haue taken this waye, and doubt not but marvayles maye be done."[240] Francis Bacon sees possibilities in an art of memory, but complains that the art as taught is barren, because not manageable for application to serious affairs; the usual feats of memory are like those of the tumbler or rope-dancer.[241] Although mnemonic aids were a feature of the education of the Middle Ages—with its abecedaria, acrostichs, telestichs, the traditional mood-names of the various syllogisms, and the like[242]—the treatises on rhetoric, as

[237] *Dict. Nat. Biogr.* 16. 155; see also pp. 158, 159, 162.

[238] *De Ratione Studii*, Froben ed. (Basel, 1540), 1. 446; *Ecclesiastes*, Book III (Antwerp, 1539), pp. 309–310: *plus adfert impedimenti quam adiumenti. Nec negligenda memoria lectionis thesaurus. Eam tametsi adiuvari non inficior, tamen tribus rebus potissimum constat optima memoria: intellectu, ordine, cura;* cf. Melanchthon, *Elementa Rhetorices* 1, *Melanthonis Opera*, ed. C. G. Bretschneider (Halle, 1846), 13. 419: *Itaque nos de aliis duabus partibus* [= memoria, pronuntiatio] *nihil praecipiemus, quia memoria parum admodum ab arte adiuvatur.*

[239] See L. S. Hultzén, "Charles Butler on Memory," *Speech Monographs*, VI, No. 1 (1939), 54.

[240] *Arte of Rhetorique*, reprod. R. H. Bowers (Gainesville, 1962), p. 241; Mair ed., p. 215.

[241] Book II (*De Augm.* 55), *Works* 6. 280–282; see also K. R. Wallace, *Francis Bacon on Communication and Rhetoric* (Chapel Hill, 1943), pp. 156–161, 214–215; Fuller, "Of Memory," ed. Walten, 2. 174: "Artificiall memory is rather a trick than an art"; Pierre Charron, *Of Wisdome* (London, 1670), p. 68, belittles the need of a good memory; see Camden, "Memory," pp. 61–2.

[242] See Hugh Tredennick, ed. Aristotle's *Prior Analytics* (Loeb Classical Library, Cambridge, Mass., and London, 1938), p. 197.

I have indicated, dealt with the ancient mnemonic system only occasionally and merely in outline. But with the new lease on life gained by the *Rhetorica ad Herennium* in the twelfth century, the doctrine it taught flourished in Europe in many special treatises and in arts of rhetoric, especially after humanism brought back the ideal of eloquence; although mnemonics served also logic, theology, and the common purposes of life.[243] St. Thomas Aquinas[244] dealt with the topical system; Peter of Ravenna[245] is alleged to have employed 100,000 *loci* and to have been able to recite the whole *corpus juris* by heart.

The German humanist, Conrad Celtes, in 1492, was the first to use letters instead of visual backgrounds.[246] And the chief addition to the ancient method contributed by modern writers has been the figure alphabet—consonants represent certain figures so as to express numbers by words, and these are filled out with vowels. The change to Arabic numerals played a part in this development. For example, the velocity of sound is 1,142 feet a second. One equals *t*, four equals *r*, two equals *n*: 1,142 equals *ttrn*, that is, "tight run." But if you mistakenly recall "hard run," the velocity of sound will be 3,000 feet too great![247]

I have not made a study of the countless systems of modern times, most of which seem to be concerned only with verbal memorizing. But I have examined enough of them to see that sometimes the topical method is combined with the figure alphabet; that quite often it is maintained that Aristotle's "laws of association" form the basis; and that these methods

---

[243] See Hajdu, *Das mnemotechnische Schrifttum des Mittelalters*, esp. pp. 86–87; and note 223 above.

[244] *Ibid.*, pp. 65–69.

[245] *Ibid.*, p. 108.

[246] *Epitoma in utramque Ciceronis Rhetoricam cum Arte Memorativa Nova et Modo Epistolandi Utilissimo* (Ingolstadt, 1492).

[247] See Edward Pick, *Memory and Its Doctors* (New York, 1888), p. 7.

are for the most part complicated, absurd,[248] and stultifying. Take this way of learning the names of the presidents, proposed by Loisette, author of a best-selling system of the nineteenth century. You have learned the names of Washington and Adams, and now wish to remember the name of Jefferson. Begin, then, with Adams: Adams suggests Adam, Adam–the Fall, fall–failure, failure–deficit, deficit–debt, debt–Confederate bonds, Confederate bonds–Jefferson Davis, Jefferson Davis–Thomas Jefferson![249] Or, by W. W. White's method (1888) of "correlations" you wish to remember the principal parts of the Latin verb, *sum: sum*–some, some–plenty, plenty–ease, ease–easy, easy–*esse;* easy–rest, rest–remnant, remnant–few, few–*fui*![250]

I myself can see no educational value in ingeniously artificial methods. The data are to be remembered in indirect relations with a foreign concept, not through the understanding of inner connections—of the order in the links of a chain of facts.[251] The understanding is not called upon to aid the memory. And always present is the danger of equating learning with a dead mass of facts.

Most of these arts antedate experimental work upon memory, and if quackery and pseudo-science are losing ground, it is partly because trained students of the nature and function of memory have begun to indicate a general direction for practical application.[252] I am assured that some people suc-

---

[248] The poet Fuller tells of his encounter with a "memory-mountebank" (Walten ed., 1. 176): "Some ten years since . . . one . . . told me . . . that he in Sidney Colledge had taught me the art of memory. I returned unto him that it was not so, for I could not remember that I had seen his face! Which, I conceive, was a reall refutation."

[249] G. S. Fellows, *"Loisette" Exposed* (New York, 1888), pp. 34 ff.

[250] See Pick, *Memory and Its Doctors*, p. 18.

[251] See Theodor Waitz, *Allgemeine Pädagogik*, ed. Otto Willmann (3d ed.; Braunschweig, 1883), chap. 24, pp. 355–369.

[252] See, e.g., Hunter, *Memory: Facts and Fallacies*, chap. 7, pp. 154–180.

cessfully use mnemonic devices; perhaps some of this audience do. William Dean Howells tells us that when Mark Twain was to make a speech, he set on the dinner table the knife, spoon, salt-cellar, and butter-plate "in a certain succession" that "symbolized a train of ideas." "With a diagram of these printed on the brain, he had full command of the phrases which his excogitation had attached to them, and which embodied the ideas in perfect form."[253] This is not unlike the method of the *Rhetorica ad Herennium*.

As for myself, endowed with a very ordinary memory, I have no devices to proffer, beyond those of attention and repetition; and you see that this paper is being read to you.

In any event we must be impressed by the historical fact that the ancient rhetoricians taught the system I have set forth, that some of the orators doubtless did not disdain to use it, and that it has had a long career.

T. J. Haarhoff, reflecting on the education that prevailed in the schools of Gaul in the fourth century, writes: "In the history of the human race, as in that of the individual, the memorizing stage comes before the development of thought; and the less advanced systems of education all over the world are characterized by their almost exclusive emphasis on learning things by heart"[254]—an observation that brings to mind the scorn which Henry Adams expressed for the experience he underwent in a German gymnasium in 1858: "The arbitrary training given to the memory was stupefying; the strain that the memory endured was a form of torture. No other faculty seemed to be recognized. Least of all was any use made of reason—either analytic, synthetic, or dogmatic."[255] But in

[253] *My Mark Twain* (New York and London, 1910), chap. 5, p. 59.
[254] *Schools of Gaul*, pp. 92–93.
[255] *The Education of Henry Adams*, chap. 5.

present-day American education, I see very few signs of such
an evil over-emphasis; certainly all too few of *my* students
come with a storehouse of good things learned and remembered; and it is not long since John Burnet[256] urged that the
educational system should keep in mind and take advantage
of the fact that "memorizing comes natural to the young," and
that "nothing," for example, "can take the place of the
youngster's instinctive and automatic responsiveness to grammatical forms." "To face a boy who has had no sufficient
drill, with Homer and Virgil, is," he says, "as wicked as to
send an untrained recruit into the firing-line."

In modern psychological research, memory is not treated
as an "independent function entirely distinct from perceiving,
imaging, or even from constructive thinking," but as having
"intimate relations with them all."[257] Where an abstract
separation of memory from understanding is made in education, it is a mistake. To cultivate the intellect we of course need
more than the particulars of knowledge stored in the memory.
As Cardinal Newman phrases it in *The Idea of a University*,[258]
"the end of a liberal education is not mere knowledge, or
knowledge considered in its matter, but intellectual illumina-
tion—thought or reason exercised upon knowledge." Yet
Newman also reminds us "that there is no true culture without
acquirements," and that knowledge stored in the memory
"is the indispensable condition of expansion of mind." Or in
the words of Samuel Johnson: "Memory is, among the faculties of the human mind . . . that of which the agency is
incessant or perpetual . . . the primary and fundamental
power without which there could be no other intellectual

[256] "Ignorance" (Romanes Lecture, 1923), in *Essays and Addresses* (London,
1929), pp. 243 ff.
[257] Bartlett, *Remembering*, p. 13.
[258] Discourse VI (London, 1907), pp. 129, 130, 137, 139.

operation."²⁵⁹ "The necessity of memory to the acquisition of knowledge is inevitably felt and universally allowed, so that scarcely any other of the mental faculties are commonly considered as necessary to a student."²⁶⁰

But now, having discoursed for a long hour, I fear I may have taxed your memory, and so deserve to be chidden for longwindedness, as Protagoras was by Socrates. "I'm a forgetful kind of person," said Socrates, "and if someone makes a long speech to me, I cannot remember what he is talking about."²⁶¹

---

²⁵⁹ *Idler*, No. 44. Cf. Quintilian, 11. 2. 1: *Nam et omnis disciplina memoria constat;* Emerson, "Memory" (*Works* 12. 90): "Memory is a primary and fundamental faculty without which none other can work."

²⁶⁰ *Idler*, No. 74.

²⁶¹ Plato, *Protagoras* 334 C. [To the recent studies of *memoria* referred to in the notes above, the following—which deal with various aspects of the subject—can be added: Eugène d'Eichthal, *Du rôle de la mémoire dans nos conceptions métaphysiques, esthétiques, passionnelles, actives* (Paris, 1920); Beatrice Edgell, *Theories of Memory* (Oxford, 1924); M. P. Sheridan, "Jacopo Ragona and His Rules for Artificial Memory," *Manuscripta*, IV, No. 3 (1960), 131–147; Norman Malcolm, "Three Lectures on Memory" in *Knowledge and Certainty* (Englewood Cliffs, N.J., 1963), pp. 187–240; Richard M. Weaver, *Visions of Order* (Baton Rouge, 1964), pp. 40–54; in *Archiv für Begriffsgeschichte*, sec. 9 (Bonn, 1964), pp. 15–44, articles by Bruno Snell ("Mnemosyne in der frühgriechischen Dichtung"), Harald Weinreich ("Typen der Gedächtnismetaphorik"), Klaus Dockhorn ("Memoria in der Rhetorik"), Herman Schmitz ("Hegels Begriff der Erinnerung"), with the "Bericht" by Hans-Georg Gadamer; F. C. Bartlett, art. "Memory" in *Encyclopedia Britannica*; Frances A. Yates, *Giordano Bruno and the Hermetic Tradition* (Chicago, 1964), pp. 190 ff., and *The Art of Memory* (London, 1966)].

X
A Mediaeval Commentary
on the *Rhetorica ad Herennium**

THE *Rhetorica ad Herennium*, written between 86 and 82 B.C.,
is the oldest Latin Art of Rhetoric preserved entire. It
gives us doctrine of the Hellenistic period; it treats in detail the
five departments of oratory—Invention, Arrangement, Delivery, Memory, and Style—and these for each of the three
kinds of causes—forensic, deliberative, and epideictic. It is a
practical manual, product of the schools, and of the kind
doubtless used by the Roman orators. The fact that it appeared, from Jerome's time on, as a work of Cicero, gave it a
prestige which it enjoyed for over a thousand years. A close tie
binds the treatise to Cicero's incomplete *De Inventione*, which
was near to it in time; some precepts are set forth in virtually
the same language, and some of the illustrations are identical.
But the differences are even greater than the agreements, and
the relationship between the two works has never been clarified
to our complete satisfaction.

The question of the authorship of the *Rhetorica ad Herennium*
has engaged the attention of scholars ever since Lorenzo Valla,
in the middle of the fifteenth century, first doubted that Cicero
could have written it. Today, on several good grounds, all

---

* Delivered at the Fourth International Congress of Classical Studies in
Philadelphia on August 24, 1964. Readers are referred to Essay I in the present
volume.

students reject Ciceronian authorship, and most assign the work to an *auctor incertus*.

The treatise is important for a number of reasons: it stands near the beginnings of Latin prose; it reflects doctrines of virtually all the schools of rhetorical thought; it supplies our oldest surviving theory of delivery and of mnemonics, and our oldest systematic treatment of style in Latin; it has exerted a rich and wide influence in the rhetoric and literatures and literary criticism and education of the Western world; and it enjoys the high esteem of modern students of rhetoric and of composition, and also of the history, and the practice, of law.

Most important for our present discussion is that, together with Cicero's *De Inventione*, this work was the most popular art of rhetoric in the later Middle Ages.[1] The *Fortleben* of *De Inventione* is marvelously continuous, but our treatise, save for references in Jerome, Rufinus, Grillius, Servatus Lupus, and a single mention in Notker of St. Gall, does not really come into its own until the eleventh century. Then a revival of interest becomes clear in Anselm of Besate, Onulf of Speier, Marbod of Rennes, Lanfranc de Bec, the epistolographer Meinhard of Bamberg, the Regensberg Collection of letters, and Aribo the scholastic. And by the twelfth century we find the work frequently listed in library catalogues; we further discover that arts of poetry and *artes dictaminis* are dependent upon it, and also authors as varied as Matthew of Vendôme, Otto of Freising, and the anonymous writer of the Treatise of St. Omer; and finally we have what seem to be the first extensive commentaries that have come down to us. Translations into the vernacular tongues—for example, Italian and French—begin to appear later, in the thirteenth century.

---

[1] See D. E. Grosser, p. 109, n. 14, above; Karl Manitius, "Zur Ueberlieferung des sogennanten *Auctor ad Herennium*," *Philologus* 100 (1956), 62–66.

An anonymous commentary of the early twelfth century is represented by manuscripts at York, Durham, Cologne, Vienna, and Alba-Julia in Roumania, and has been treated by a British scholar, Mrs. M. C. G. Dickey, in a valuable (as yet unpublished) study.[2] She presents reasons to believe that Manegold of Lautenbach (*c.* 1110) wrote a commentary on the *Rhetorica ad Herennium*, and that Thierry of Chartres lectured on the treatise—if these works are extant, they have not been identified. Professor R. W. Hunt[3] has directed our attention to a gloss by Lanfranc (on *Rhet. ad Her.* 2. xxvi. 42) cited in this commentary—indicating that Lanfranc must have lectured on the ancient treatise. And I have collected nine manuscripts of a commentary carrying—in three of the instances—the name of "Alanus" as author; it is this work that I shall discuss. It is a product of the classical revival of the twelfth century, which centered in such cathedral schools as Chartres, Orléans, Paris, and Rheims, where the spirit of a real humanism showed itself in an enthusiastic study of ancient authors. There was a flourishing growth of these schools in northern France; the curriculum was based on the seven arts; and the study of rhetoric in particular nourished the humanism. Giraldus Cambrensis[4] praises the training he received in rhetoric at Paris.

Eight of these copies, three of the fourteenth century and five of the fifteenth, are preserved variously in libraries in London, Florence, Cremona, Perugia, Oxford, Paris, Vienna, and Munich; and not so long ago I was finally able to procure a photostatic copy of a ninth manuscript, written in the thir-

---

[2] "The Teaching of Rhetoric in the Eleventh and Twelfth Centuries, with particular reference to the Schools of Northern France," typewritten copy in the Bodleian Library, Oxford.

[3] "Studies in Priscian in the Eleventh and Twelfth Centuries," *Med. and Ren. Studies*, I (1941–1943), 207.

[4] *De Rebus a se Gestis*, Book I, chap. 2, and Book II, chaps. 1 and 2.

teenth or fourteenth century, from the Bibliotheca Urbica of Breslau, behind the Iron Curtain. Of these manuscripts I have thus far studied only one in detail—the others just far enough to see definite evidence of considerable reworking among them —and so I must advise you that the present paper is a report of only partial progress. The manuscript is Harley 6324, 69 folios, in the British Museum in London, and was written late in the fourteenth century.

An inscription in Greek on the last folio of the manuscript reads: ἡ βίβλος τοῦ Σωζομένου, and another, in Italian, tells us that Sozomenos bought the manuscript on November 24, 1431, for 12 lire and 2 soldi. I have no doubt—and there is a certain fitness in the identification—that this was Sozomenos of Pistoja (dates: 1387–1458), who copied the ninth-century manuscript, found in 1416 by Poggio at St. Gall, of Asconius' commentary on several of Cicero's orations.

Alanus' method is common among mediaeval works of this kind; *lemmata* from the original text are followed by his explanations, sometimes brief, sometimes full—an *explication de texte*, doubtless delivered in lecture form; and there are not many points that he omits to treat, looking with keen eyes at the words before him. He may give more than one explanation when he feels the need to do so, and in the treatment of Book IV, in which the figures of speech are listed, described, and illustrated, he operates almost by a formula, supplying: the Greek name for the figure; a definition in his own words, which often reflects the infiltration—by this time far advanced—of dialectic into rhetoric; remarks on how the figure differs from kindred figures; and suggestions on the kind of issue or argument for which it is useful, and on the place in the discourse and type of style for which it is suitable. Thus the figure of speech, Climax, must not be used in the Statement of Facts; Periphrasis (Circumlocution) is especially suitable for the

Grand Style, Paronomasia is not; Metaphor is appropriate everywhere in the speech except in the Partition.

Alanus' respect for dialectic is apparent in his comment on a passage in which, perhaps under the influence of the Epicurean contempt for that art, the ancient author lashes out against the wordy learning of the dialecticians who think that orators should master all the lore about amphibolies in order to handle skillfully texts involving an ambiguity. Alanus refuses to think that this "school of inarticulateness," as the ancient author calls it, can refer to the dialecticians. "Other interpreters," says Alanus, "are here indicated."

A striking feature at the very outset is that Alanus used a number of manuscripts of the ancient treatise, and that these included representatives of the older group from the ninth and tenth centuries, the *Mutili*, but also of the *Expleti*, which came into existence in the twelfth century. He often says: *Alii libri legunt* or *In quibusdam libris legitur*. He makes his own conjectures; occasionally an emendation of his own; and once or twice suggests that a passage has been interpolated. Sometimes when *Mutili* and *Expleti* differ, he will accept the reading of one; at other times he will express no preference, but explain both. He also had before him other commentaries, which he never specifies: *Alii sic eam exponunt* or *Quidam volunt* or *Alii vero dicunt* or *Alii aliter legunt*. A number of his readings—none, however, of permanent value—are absent from the apparatus supplied in any of the modern editions of the ancient text. And occasionally when he is confronted with a corrupt reading, he is driven to violence in order to make any sense at all. Alanus proves to be an interesting exemplar of the text-critical methods employed by twelfth-century scholars, who play a rôle in the transmission of so many of our ancient texts.

It is easy for us who can benefit from the rich results of the scholarship of several centuries to note Alanus' errors and flights of fancy. Several of these, of course, arise from the errors in his text. But textual errors apart, he confuses *quaesitor* and *quaestor;* calls a dative of indirect object an ablative, further missing the point that the ancient author is in this example using only the Greek cases (the grammatical theory of the ancient Latin author is Greek, and he is adapting a Greek example); and although Alanus knows of the Laws of the Twelve Tables, he fails to identify several of them that appear in the ancient text. That he makes some wrong guesses in placing historical events is not surprising (a *suasoria* referring to the aftermath of Cannae is assigned to the first Punic War), nor that he wrongly assigns a number of the illustrative passages (as in the examples of the Grand and Middle Styles, in Book IV) to Cicero's speeches, which were of course delivered after the time we specify for the *auctor*'s composition of his treatise. Such errors were a natural result of his belief in the Ciceronian authorship of the treatise before him.

Let me now reproduce several characteristic observations concerning the doctrine of rhetoric.

Through grammar we teach how to speak with correctness, through dialectic with credibility, through rhetoric with embellishment and eloquence.

The art of rhetoric has, says Alanus, been much better described, and been transmitted by more writers, than any of the other arts.

The orator handles cases artistically; the rhetor teaches the art; the *sophista* provides practice in speaking for those who wish to pursue it. The source here is the fourth-century commentary on Cicero's *De Inventione* by Marius Victorinus, whom he quotes often. Victorinus, also translator of the *Isagoge* of Porphyry, had a large share in influencing the later commentators to think in dialectical terms.

The elder Cato said that the orator is a good man skilled in speaking. "Good" does not here have reference to religion, says Alanus, but to the knowledge of laws and customs. Eloquence requires wisdom, and because Catiline lacked wisdom, Sallust said he was no orator (*Cat.* 5. 4). I may here remind you that a few centuries later Reuchlin modified Cato's dictum to read: the preacher is a *vir religiosus dicendi peritus*.

We find an interesting comment on the state of epideictic—the oratory of praise and blame—at the time. This kind of cause, says Alanus, used to be employed by the ancients when they wished to choose a consul, king, bishop, or other officer; then speakers would come forward to extol or condemn the candidates. But in our day, he says, when these various matters are handled in an ecclesiastical fashion, that manner of doing business has disappeared. How different from the fifteenth century, "the golden age of speechification," as Symonds called it,[5] when epideictic enjoyed a rich florescence.

In treating the topics on which praise is founded, the physical attribute of manly beauty (*dignitas*) is exemplified by Priam; Plato and Jerome in their lives illustrate the quality of character, *temperantia*.

I add a passage of a political nature. The ancient author wrote: When in an epideictic speech the talk is of virtue, do not indeed, when in critical opposition, propose the abandonment of virtue, but say that virtue consists rather of qualities contrary to those here evinced. Says Alanus: "If one should propose that freedom be further extended in a State, show that the virtue resides rather in not so extending it. The freedom of a people is, and should be, to serve freely. If a people restrained by the reigning authorities wishes to have freedom, then its freedom perishes through the greater freedom it desires." Alanus does not enlarge on this theme. One recalls, in the

---

[5] *Renaissance in Italy: Revival of Learning* (London, 1904), chap. 9, p. 386.

[253]

philosophical and religious realms, Seneca's words:[6] *Deo parere libertas est,* and the affirmation in *The Union Prayerbook for Jewish Worship,* as also in the "Collect for Peace" in the *Book of Common Prayer:* "To serve Whom is perfect freedom"; in the field of political theory, Plato: "Excess of freedom, in the State and in the individual, seems to pass into excess of slavery"[7] (Socrates is speaking), and Aristotle: "In extreme democracies freedom is supposed to mean doing what one likes; and this is wrong, for to live by the constitution ought not to be considered slavery but salvation."[8] I have yet to trace the history of this concept.

As for specific criticism, Alanus shrewdly sees how the ancient author himself in a number of places employs the method of capturing good will, and how the Introduction to Book IV is artistically developed according to the principles of an epicheireme—a complete argument with several parts; recognizes some of the figures used by the *auctor* in his examples of Style; in the section on mnemonics calls attention to the relevance of auditory images in addition to visual, and to the value of association through the rhythms of verse; and interprets—in an orderly method, and with results that a modern teacher of public speaking might do well to adopt—the doctrine of Introductions by means of the Subtle Approach (which is to be used when our cause is discreditable, or when the hearers have been won over by the speakers of the opposition, or have become wearied by listening to the previous speakers). With good reasoning he corrects Priscian and others who divide the ancient treatise into six books, instead of four.

I have mentioned the kinship between the *Rhetorica ad Herennium* and Cicero's *De Inventione.* Alanus of course thinks

---

[6] *De Vita Beata* 15. 7.
[7] *Republic* VIII (564 A).
[8] *Politics* 5. 10 (1310 a).

that both are the products of Cicero's pen. References to *De Inventione* are naturally very numerous in the commentary; it is there variously called *Rhetorica Inventionum, Alia Rhetorica, Prior Rhetorica,* and of special significance to us, *Prima Rhetorica* (next to *Prior,* most often). This last title it usually held in the twelfth century, the *Rhetorica ad Herennium* being called *Rhetorica Secunda.* Only once in the commentary (the first reference to the work, appearing in the Preface) is the treatise on invention called *Vetus Rhetorica,* the name for it which came into common use in the thirteenth century, the companion treatise then receiving the title *Rhetorica Nova.* Alanus is hard put to it to explain the differences between the two works. His notion is that in *De Inventione* Cicero is following Greek doctrine, and in the other treatise, Latin. He is forced to say that the treatment of the same topic is better or briefer or clearer or more suitable in one work than in the other, now favoring the one, now the other, now reconciling them; and his comments are often sound and keen. He perceives the difficulties in certain textual problems that still bother us, and he is aware that the treatment of the epicheireme in *De Inventione* is on dialectical lines, in the other treatise on rhetorical. He observes that the treatment of Natural Law is fuller in *De Inventione;* and where he supports a statement in the *Rhetorica ad Herennium,* he can point out that Cicero in *De Oratore* (1. 2. 5) repudiated the books of *De Inventione* as the crude and unfinished essays of his youth, or that Cicero is here correcting his earlier work.

Alanus can be adversely critical of the ancient author. For example, when the *auctor,* dealing with Delivery, gives the following definition: "*Figura Vocis* (Voice-Quality) has a character of its own, acquired by method and application," Alanus says: "This definition is quite obscure and troublesome," and substitutes his own: "*Figura Vocis* is the quality or composition of the voice, created by nature, perfected by cultivation, and augmented by exercises." Again, the *auctor* expresses more than once a preference for philosophy over rhetoric. Says Alanus: "The inference that rhetoric is not a part of philosophy is false. There are three divisions of philosophy—ethics, natural philosophy (*physica*), and logic. And logic, in its turn, has three divisions—dialectic, grammar, and rhetoric." Alanus is here heir to the Platonic ordering of these disciplines. To be sure, rhetoric cannot in the Aristotelian tradition belong to philosophy, he goes on to say, for its function is not to inquire after truth. "Perhaps," says Alanus, "the *auctor* meant to limit philosophy to ethics; or he may have considered logic to be inferior to the other two disciplines, whose instrument it is."

The differing classifications of the *artes* in the Middle Ages present a fascinating subject for study, and especially the relations among the arts which comprised the trivium. In the twelfth century the three are interdependent—they borrowed conceptions and terms from one another; the same commentators sometimes glossed both grammatical and rhetorical works; and some, like Alanus, would discuss the connections of rhetoric with other arts. For example, he points out that *pronuntiatio*, delivery, belongs also, in the form of "pronunciation," to grammar. In a Munich manuscript of the twelfth century[9] we learn that Logic, after her marriage with Plato, and the birth of their three daughters, contracted another marriage, with Cicero, to whom she bore the *Topica*.

Through the influence of Aristotle's *Organon*, and especially of Victorinus and Boethius, the method of rhetoric received the stamp of the more influential partner, dialectic, and became a predominantly logical science. Recall Plato's *Phaedrus*, and the first line of Aristotle's *Rhetoric:* "Rhetoric is the

[9] *Bayer. Staatsbibl., Cod. Lat.* 18961, fol. 47. Cf. Alain de Lille, p. 82 above.

counterpart of dialectic." Alanus points out that all the parts of rhetoric except style belong also to dialectic.

The arguments in the text are throughout analyzed by logical categories—*ab habitu, fortuna, officio, natura,* and the like; the seven περιστάσεις—*circumstantiae*—are applied in the interpretation of the ancient author's statement that a narrative must have probability, as topics for finding the truth—*quis, quid, cur, ubi, quantum,* and the rest; and Alanus introduces the *auctor*'s text in an elaborate, schematic fashion borrowed from the philosophers—he asks and answers: *quid sit rhetorica,* what is its *genus,* what its *materia,* its *officium, finis,* and so forth—ten questions on the art, then five on the book—what is its intention, its usefulness, occasion, title, and to what part of philosophy it appertains. To be sure, the ancient *De Inventione* uses five items of the schema; in the Middle Ages these questions became common after Ammonius, at the beginning of the sixth century, had written his commentary on the *Isagoge* of Porphyry. Of the *accessus* I have examined, it appears that Alanus is closest to Gundissalinus, in the *De Divisione Philosophiae,* and to Thierry of Chartres in the commentary on *De Inventione.*

In a commentary of this kind, and of this period, in which the analysis of language was bound up with all the arts, we expect an abundance of etymologizing; Alanus does not disappoint us. Some of his etymologies are drawn from Isidore of Seville, with or without specific attribution, but he has recourse to other sources and perhaps also to his own ingenuity:

ignavus means *igne animae vacuus* (devoid of spiritual fire);
fabula may perhaps come from *for-fari* and Greek ὅλος;
flagitiosus means a guilty man, and so deserving of the *flagellum;*
historia and *histrio* are related;
triceni means *ter centum;*
plebiscitum: plebes and *cita,* i.e. *vocata ad contionem* (summoned to
    obtain its approval).

But to me the most ingenious etymon appears in a Stockholm manuscript of a fifteenth-century commentary[10]; *spurcus* is there derived from *spuens porcus*.

I next present several of the words used by Alanus which, in these forms, I do not find in the lexica: *impreconsiderate, lepiditas, preposteratio, salsinarius, regularitas—regularité* appears in French in the fourteenth century

Nor must I neglect to mention Alanus' fondness for proverbs —edifying rules of life were popular in the Middle Ages, and I list a few:

Magnos magna decent (Great exploits befit great men).
Similia similibus gaudent. In this form the maxim comes from Macrobius (*Sat.* 7. 7. 12).
Quanto plus senescit, tanto plus enitescit (The older he grows, the more brilliant he becomes).
Docenda est ars ut pateat, utendum est arte ut lateat (An art should so be taught as to become manifest, but art should so be employed as to stay concealed).

And echoed later in Shakespeare's famous line, "One touch of Nature makes the whole world kin": *Natura omnes parificat.*

Does the commentary contain mediaeval notions of what we may call "science"? Alanus has this to say on memory: "Memory and wit vary according to the nature of one's brain. If you take in quickly what you hear, and quickly forget it, that follows from the fact that the dense part of the brain is moist; if you acquire slowly and forget with difficulty, that means that your brain is dry; and if you acquire quickly and do not easily forget, the anterior part of the brain is neither too dry nor too moist"—an echo of the Aristotelian principle[11] that too much fluidity as with the quick-witted prevents retention of the image, and too much density as with the very

---

[10] See p. 267 below.
[11] *De Mem. et Recollect.* 45 ab.

slow prevents the image from getting fixed. But Alanus sees that there is more to memory than the ancient author allows in his definition of that faculty as the grasp of the matter, words, and arrangement of your discourse. Three processes are involved, says Alanus: the taking in (*percipere*), the discriminating (*discernere*), and then finally the learning (*memoriae mandare*).

Memory without imagination is impossible. Philosophers say that birds have images, for they know the way back to their nests. So, too, certain brute animals who return to their stalls must have a natural memory.

I read with special eagerness the section on humor—we may with profit look to the rhetoricians for theories on this subject —but I fear that our commentator's illustrations do not stamp him as either a major theorist or an exceptional wit. The ancient author advises that if our hearers have been fatigued by listening to the other speakers, we should open our speech with something that can provoke laughter, and he offers eighteen means of doing so. Alanus provides his own examples, and I give a few of these.

To illustrate distortion (*imitatio depravata*): A speaker quickly regretted the slip he had committed; he had intended to say "*Leo* Episcopus," not "*Leno* Episcopus."[12]

To illustrate ambiguity: A thief, climbing up to break the leg of an image containing golden ornaments, fell and broke his own leg, and when asked what he was up to, replied: "I have broken a leg."[13]

A pun: Instead of *legislator* (mover of the law) say *legislatro* (brigand of the law).

---

[12] The ancient author (to illustrate the figure paronomasia) played on the words *leones* and *lenones* (4. XXI. 29). Cf. also Tertullian, *Apol.* 50. 12.

[13] Cf. Vespa Terentius' like equivoque in Cicero, *De Oratore* II. lxi, 253: he excuses the absence of the ball-player Titius from the Campus on the ground that Titius "has broken an arm."

A retort courteous (to illustrate a faulty kind of Introduction, which
your opponent can turn to his own use against you): Sallust's jibe
to Cicero:[14] "*Your* family *begins* with you." Cicero to Sallust:[15]
"and *yours ends* with you."

The Stockholm manuscript[16] offers additional examples—of
a pun: from Suetonius' life of Tiberius (sec. 42), the name
coined when the emperor-to-be was a young soldier fond of
wine—Biberius Caldius Mero; of exaggeration: "My opponent's eloquence is well-known; it habitually draws to him
rocks and trees"—meaning stones and cudgels; of ridicule:
"No wonder your attention has been caught by my opponent,
that follower of Cicero, Fabius, and Boethius"—meaning that
he likes chickpeas, beans, and beef.

This manuscript supplies us also with a detective story. The
text concerns clues as evidence in a criminal case: a wife-killer
lost his shoe in crossing a stream; a soldier found it; the cord-
wainer who sold the shoes to the murderer verified the sale.

Occasionally Alanus passes literary critical judgment of a
general nature. On imitation: "Do not restrict yourself to one
model of style alone, for no model is altogether perfect, but
imitate now one in the respect in which he is perfect, and now
another in the respect in which he is perfect. I will not imitate
Cicero in every respect, since he speaks with too great abundance"—obviously Cicero is not the exemplar he was to
become in the early Renaissance—"nor will I imitate Seneca,
since he speaks with too great conciseness, nor Sidonius since
it was his habit to speak with too great *lascivia*." This estimate
of the fifth-century author would have been commended by
W. B. Anderson, who discussed the "absurdly stilted and

---

[14] Cf. Ps.-Sallust, "In Ciceronem Oratio," 1. 1. and 3. 4.
[15] Cf. Ps.-Cicero, "In Sallustium Responsio," 2. 5.
[16] See p. 267 below.

obscure" language of Sidonius, with its "rhetorical tricks exaggerated *ad nauseam.*"[17]

Alanus' definition of comedy and tragedy reflects the prevalent mediaeval concept of dramatic form, as we see it, for example, in Vincent of Beauvais,[18] Dante,[19] and Chaucer.[20] Says Alanus: "Comedy always begins with sadness and ends with joy, tragedy the reverse." But he realizes from Virgil and from Horace's *Ars Poetica* that tragic and comic elements can blend.

The ancient author gives us our oldest extant treatment of the three styles. Alanus assigns the use of the grand style to tragedy, the simple to comedy, and the middle—interestingly enough—to satire.

If you wish a model for the employment of the figure of speech *effictio* (Portrayal), read Dares Phrygius—the prose rendering of the Fall of Troy, written perhaps in the fifth century; for *notatio* (Character Delineation) Terence is the master in setting forth the ways of courtesans.

Indeed Alanus maintains the tradition of ancient rhetoric in drawing many of his own illustrations from the poets. Virgil is most often cited; Terence and Horace come next; then Ovid, the *Metamorphoses* and *Ars Amatoria,* Lucan, and Statius; Plautus' *Amphitruo* is quoted once, Juvenal once. One passage from Ennius, without mention of his name, came to Alanus, indirectly of course, through either Quintilian or Boethius. The prose authors, too, are those we would expect a twelfth-century author to cite: Caesar's *Bellum Gallicum;* several of Cicero's works, the *Tusculanae Disputationes, De Amicitia,* the

[17] Article on Sidonius Apollinaris in the *Oxford Class. Dict.*
[18] *Speculum Doctrinale,* chap. 109.
[19] Letter to Can Grande, sec. 10.
[20] "The Monk's Tale," Prologue, and beginning of text.

Paradoxa, of the speeches the Verrines being most favored; Sallust; Seneca; Vitruvius; Suetonius; and Quintilian, often. Alanus must have had access only to mutilated French manuscripts of Quintilian's *Institutio;* as expected, he quotes mostly from Books II and III—and loosely, as from memory; a reference to Quintilian's *Orationes* may be to the *Declamationes*, and it is possible that a couple of citations are from lost *Declamationes*. A citation of Varro (in the *Disciplinae*) he doubtless drew from Victorinus.[21] As for later authors: of the third century, Ulpian; of the fourth, Marius Victorinus—to his commentary on *De Inventione* Alanus is, as I have said, heavily indebted; of the fifth, the fabulist Avianus, a single general reference to Martianus Capella, whose influence was slight also in the earlier commentaries on *De Inventione* and the *Rhetorica ad Herennium* that I have mentioned, Macrobius, without name, Grillius' commentary on *De Inventione*, Vegetius, and Dares; of the sixth, Boethius of course—his influence is manifest throughout the work, especially by way of the *De Differentiis Topicis*—Priscian, and Justinian; of the seventh, Isidore of Seville; and of the ninth, Remigius' edition of Donatus. Examples from the Bible intermingle with those from secular literature.

And here I must report an arresting statement. Alanus knows about Cicero's *De Oratore* from notices in Quintilian, but at one point says about this book: *quo caremus*—"a work which we lack." Only a mutilated text of *De Oratore* was known until Landriani's discovery of the Lodi manuscript in 1421. When, upon his death in 1180, John of Salisbury left his library to the cathedral church of Chartres, the sole representative of the Ciceronian works on rhetoric was a manuscript copy of the *Orator*.[22]

21 See Carolus Halm, *Rhetores Latini Minores* (Leipzig, 1863), p. 170.
22 J. A. Clerval, *Les Ecoles de Chartres au Moyen Age* (Chartres, 1895), p. 278.

Several other statements show Alanus in his time, a mediaeval scholar reacting to a pagan work. For example:

(*a*) In ancient doctrine courage is a primary virtue, important to consider in a speech of praise or censure. The *auctor* defines courage as the reaching for great things and contempt for what is mean—for *res humiles*. This provides Alanus with the chance to say that *res humiles* here signifies *res viles*, and that the books of the Gentiles do not know the *humilitas* which the New Testament preaches.

(*b*) In deliberative speaking Honor is a chief consideration. The ancient author divides the Honorable into the Right (*rectum*) and the Praiseworthy (*laudabile*). The *laudabile*, says Alanus, is in ecclesiastical causes suspect, for it seems to appertain to vainglory. In the Introduction of an epideictic speech, says the ancient author, we ought from our praise of others to show what our own character is. Good advice for Cicero's time, says Alanus; no people was so avid for praise as the Roman. He adds that Priscian, too, in his letter to Julian[23] evinces a craving for glory such as the present, and better, time rejects— Priscian hopes that glory will accrue to him for the labor he has undertaken. In the present, better, time we say with the Book of Proverbs (27:2): "Let another man praise thee, and not thine own mouth."

(*c*) The ancient author tells us that the Statement of Facts will achieve plausibility if it answers the requirements of the usual, the expected (*opinio*), and the natural. Thus, says Alanus, if you should say that a *religiosus* has committed adultery, your *narratio* would not be consonant with what is expected, and so would not achieve plausibility.

(*d*) The ancient author: In epideictic physical qualities— like good health—are subject to praise. Alanus: So in choosing

<hr />

[23] Keil, *Gram. Lat.*, II, 1–3.

a bishop, the possession of this attribute is an important consideration.

(*e*) To illustrate his definition of equity, the ancient author takes an example from the field of substitution in legal procedure: "A man who is more than sixty years old and pleads illness shall substitute an attorney for himself." So with us, says Alanus, a priest who is more than sixty years old and can no longer administer the sacraments, may substitute another for himself.

(*f*) Finally, among the departments of Law the ancient author lists *judicata*, Previous Judgments. When different past judgments are offered for a like case, compare the judges, the number of decisions, and the *circumstances*. Thus circumstances have changed, says Alanus, since Pope Gregory decreed for the English that they might take wives in the fourth degree of kindred—a position which the Church does not now (that is, at the time when Alanus wrote his commentary) hold.

This passage may serve as internal evidence for dating the composition of the commentary. Innocent III in the Fourth Lateran Council in 1215 had liberalized the legislation, yet restricted the impediment to the fourth degree of consanguinity. I must betimes examine further the history of the enactments, to learn whether Alanus' statement reflects conditions that obtained before 1215.

Other reflections of an ecclesiastical character: The Florentine and Cremona manuscripts remind us that we find the figure Hyperbole even in the gospels; in the Harley manuscript we are advised that when defending a pauper—an honorable thing to do—we may begin our speech with the Scriptural verse: "Blessed are the poor in spirit, for theirs is the kingdom of heaven" (Matt. 5:3, Luke 6:20). No mention is made of preaching as an oratorical art, although I observe that in the Stockholm manuscript of a commentary on our ancient author[24] the use of the figure Apostrophe is declared to be favored by preachers. Nor is any mention made of the art of *dictamen,* another kin of rhetoric.

Still another kindred art is alluded to in a couple of the manuscripts—the *ars notaria;* when the *auctor* disapproves of the mechanical memorization of a great number of images, we are told that he did not have the notarial art in mind. This art, which was connected with the study of law, was to rise to full stature in the thirteenth century, with regular instruction being provided by the universities, Bologna especially.

A word about Alanus' knowledge of Greek. He is sometimes aware that a locution in the ancient treatise is Greek; he will say: "This is a Greek idiom." He will use accurately Greek terms like *hypallage, parabole, paradigma, schemata, phrasis, characteres, tropi,* and *hybris,* but confuse *epodos* and *ephodos.* Proper names and technical terms are often grossly distorted in the text: Croas for Corax, Istarenus for Aristoxenus, Polydecius for Polycleitus, epicarope for *epitrope,* caratismus for *characterismos,* aperiodos for *aporia;* and these corruptions cannot all be accounted merely scribal errors. He admits that he does not know the Greek equivalent for the trope *abusio,* yet applies the Greek term for it, *catachresis,* to *pronominatio*(= *antonomasia*), while yet discerning the difference between the two tropes. The Greek names are provided for all but seventeen of the sixty-four figures of speech; of these the majority are correctly identified, several others are commendable approximations, and a few are egregious errors. Synonymy he calls *polyptoton,* and *antimetabole* (Reciprocal Change—Socrates' "You must eat to live, not live to eat") he calls *homoeoteleuton.* This acquaintance with some Greek terms doubtless stems from the grammarians, lexicographers, and glossographers;

[24] See p. 267 below.

we know that in his Priscian-commentary Peter Helias at Paris had introduced many new Greek etymologies.

The Greek authors cited by Alanus are not many: the *Timaeus* of Plato, obviously in the fourth-century Latin rendering by Calcidius; several works of the *Organon* of Aristotle; Themistius (fourth Christian century), known to him from the *De Differentiis Topicis* of Boethius. There are a few general references to Homeric personages, and one to Socrates. I have yet to learn whose translations Alanus used of the *Topica* of Aristotle, and of the *Sophistici Elenchi;* these two works belong to the *Logica Nova,* and did not exert much influence until the thirteenth century, but Martin Grabmann tells us[25] that there were Latin renderings of the *Elenchi* in the twelfth. A manuscript of one translation belonged then to the library of St. Victor in Paris; and the work is cited in the *Heptateuchon* of Thierry of Chartres. Authorities now seem to agree that Jacob of Venice translated both these Aristotelian works in the first half of the twelfth century.

Alanus cites by name only four recent authors. Constantine the African (eleventh century) is quoted for a statement in his *Pantegni* (*The Complete Art,* a Latin rendering of the tenth-century medical work of Ali Ibn Abbas) to the effect that he wished his students of medicine to be learned in all the liberal arts. Peter Helias, interpreter of Priscian, who taught grammar by the method of logic at Paris and was active there certainly from 1140 to 1150, is cited for one interpretation of a passage in the *Rhetorica ad Herennium,* and his contemporary Thierry of Chartres for a different interpretation of the same passage—a striking juxtaposition in light of the fact that in the *Metalogicon* (2. 10. 868b) John of Salisbury says he learned more about rhetoric from Peter Helias than he had earlier learned from the meager treatment of the art by Thierry. The

---

[25] *Geschichte der scholastischen Methode* (Basel and Stuttgart, 1961), II, 64–81.

fourth reference is a tantalizing one: in the interpretation of a passage in the ancient author Alanus says that the inexact use of the word "all" to include less than strictly everything is a *figura dictionis* according to Magister Ber—and the full name remains to be filled out! Is Berengar of Tours here indicated? Or is it likely that "Ber" stands for Bernard of Chartres? Bernard Silvestris? A sure answer I have yet to find; I hope it may come when I have explored the possibilities further. The passage does not appear in the other manuscripts. My guess: Bernard of Chartres. We do not have Bernard's works, and know of him mostly through John of Salisbury.[26]

As long as this one passage is uncertain, a conclusion about the date of composition of the commentary must of course be very tentative. But to limit myself for the present to these three possibilities, Berengar of Tours died in 1088, Bernard of Chartres before 1130, and Bernard Silvestris was active, we know, between 1145 and 1153. The latest of these in time, therefore, belongs roughly to the middle of the twelfth century, the time also of Peter Helias and Thierry of Chartres. I find no reference in the work to conditions or events which would help us to fix a specific date of composition. But we may, for the present, assign the work to the latter half of the twelfth century, the middle of that century representing a *terminus non ante quem*.

I should at this juncture mention that in 1905 Magne Wisén published excerpts from a commentary on the *Rhetorica ad Herennium* contained in a manuscript—now at Stockholm[27]— written at Laon in the year 1468. Fortunately, I now have a photostat of the complete manuscript. Some of Alanus' material appears here, but the contents mostly show the results of reworking, and of subsequent scholarship. I have examined

[26] See J. De Ghellink, *L'Essor de la litt. Lat. au XIIe siècle*, Brussels, 1954, pp. 62 ff.

[27] *Kungl. Bibl.*, MS. Va 10.

manuscripts containing related commentaries or marginal glosses, of the thirteenth, fourteenth and fifteenth centuries, in libraries of Oxford, Cambridge, Florence, Assisi, Rome, and Perugia, but I have not yet studied them thoroughly. They appear to use like methods to those of Alanus, and some contain material in common with him. A fifteenth-century manuscript in the Vatican (Rossianus 975), containing a full interlinear and marginal commentary, mentions Al(l)anus on the first folio (verso). A manuscript in the Balliol College library contains an interesting commentary which refers frequently to Alanus. And I expect in time to make certain a surmise that several Renaissance commentaries—including those by Gasparino Barzizza (died in 1435), Guarino of Verona (died in 1460), and Lorenzo Guglielmo Traversagni of Savona (died in 1503)—drew upon the work of Alanus. I can report also that Alanus is cited twice in an extremely interesting Hebrew rhetoric, *The Book of the Honeycomb's Flow* (Sēpher Nōpheth Ṣūphīm), printed in the eighth decade of the fifteenth century by a Jewish humanist of Mantua, Judah Messer Leon, whose treatise applies the principles of rhetoric in a critique of the Old Testament.

The question has occurred to you: Is Alanus to be identified with Alain de Lille, Doctor Universalis, allegorical poet, the author of *Anticlaudianus* and *De Planctu Naturae?* First, the commentary was probably written during Alain de Lille's lifetime—he died in 1203. Secondly, on the last page of the Harley manuscript are inscribed two of the three hexameters constituting the epitaph on the tomb that was erected to Alain at Cîteaux in 1492 and which is found also in manuscripts of Alain's works:

> Alanum brevis hora brevi tumulo sepelivit
> Qui duo, qui septem, qui totum scibile scivit.

"A brief hour has confined in a small tomb Alanus, who knew

the two, the seven, and all that can be known"—the "two" doubtless referring to the Testaments, the "seven" to the liberal arts. Another couplet reads:

Qui Ciceronis avet compendia pandere sanus
Hec sibi dicta putet rhetor que scripsit Alanus.

"Whoever is eager to make a sound interpretation of the Ciceronian manuals should regard as addressed to him what the rhetor Alanus has written here." Thirdly, two or three scholars have, without—I am certain of this—examining any of the manuscripts, assumed that Alain de Lille was the author. But a recent student of Alain, Reynaud de Lage, wisely, I think, lists the commentary among the spurious or doubtful works.[28] Until I have examined all the manuscripts carefully and made a more thorough study of the authentic works of Alain de Lille, I shall hesitate to assign the work to him. The manuscripts which carry Alanus' name are not more explicit; there is no reference in the commentary to any of Alain's works, and even Claudian is not mentioned; and one finds no sign here of Alain's manner or usual preoccupations, although the *Anticlaudianus* does treat the three styles. The question requires further study, and especially of other Alani of the period.

But I am sure that we must look for a Frenchman. Alanus several times uses the *phrasis Gallica*, as Du Cange terms it: *per excellentiam (par excellence)*. Two (fourteenth century) manuscripts of another, kindred, commentary in one connection refer to the two chief Parisian monasteries of the day—those of St. Victor and St. Germain—expressing the judgment that the former is of a higher order. But so far as I can see, Alanus in the Harley manuscript clearly betrays his nationality in one passage. The ancient author, defining *Latinitas* (which renders Ἑλληνισμός of the Greek), equates it properly with purity—

---

[28] *Alain de Lille* (Montreal and Paris, 1951), p. 17.

freedom from faults like solecisms and barbarisms. Says Alanus: "Thus *Gallicum* is said to be pure when Normanisms do not intrude"—an extremely interesting reminder of the time when the dialects, especially the Norman, had been rivals of the French of Paris and the Ile de France in the race to become the national language. Now Norman and the other dialects, including the Picard, Walloon, Champenois, and Lorrain have come to be regarded as peripheral, and the dialect of Paris, having won its victory by its geographical position and through political and religious developments, has become the κοινή.

Bibliography of the Writings of
Harry Caplan

BOOKS AND ARTICLES

"The History of the Jews in the Roman Province of Africa: A Collection of the Sources." Unpublished Ph.D. dissertation, Cornell University, Ithaca, N.Y., 1921.

"The Latin Panegyrics of the Empire." *Quarterly Journal of Speech Education*, X (1924), 41–52.

"Communication, the Basic Principle." In *A Course of Study in Speech Training and Public Speaking for Secondary Schools*, edited by A. M. Drummond. New York, 1925. Pp. 29–34.

"A Late Mediaeval Tractate on Preaching." In *Studies in Rhetoric and Public Speaking in Honor of James Albert Winans*, edited by A. M. Drummond. New York, 1925. Pp. 61–90.

"Rhetorical Invention in Some Mediaeval Tractates on Preaching." *Speculum*, II (1927), 284–295.

"The Four Senses of Scriptural Interpretation and the Mediaeval Theory of Preaching." *Speculum*, IV (1929), 282–290.

"The Influence of Classical Rhetoric on Mediaeval *Artes Praedicandi*." Summary of an address read at Cardiff, Wales, on April 9, 1929. *Proceedings of the Classical Association*, XXVI (1929), 8–9.

Editor and translator, *Gianfrancesco Pico della Mirandola: On the Imagination*. New Haven, 1930.

"Classical Rhetoric and the Mediaeval Theory of Preaching." *Classical Philology*, XXVIII (1933), 73–96. Reprinted with revisions in *Historical Studies of Rhetoric and Rhetoricians*, edited by Raymond F. Howes. Ithaca, N.Y., 1961. Pp. 71–89, 387–391.

"'Henry of Hesse' on the Art of Preaching." *PMLA*, XLVIII (1933), 340–361.

Bibliography

Mediaeval Artes Praedicandi: A Hand-List. Cornell Studies in Classical Philology, XXIV. Ithaca, N.Y., 1934.

Mediaeval Artes Praedicandi: A Supplementary Hand-List. Cornell Studies in Classical Philology, XXV. Ithaca, N.Y., 1936.

"The Decay of Eloquence at Rome in the First Century." In *Studies in Speech and Drama in Honor of Alexander M. Drummond,* edited by Herbert A. Wichelns. Ithaca, N.Y., 1944. Pp. 295–325.

With H. H. King. "Latin Tractates on Preaching: A Book-List." *Harvard Theological Review,* XLII (1949), 185–206.

"Rhetorica ad Herennium." In *Oxford Classical Dictionary.* Oxford, 1949. P. 768.

With H. H. King. "Italian Treatises on Preaching: A Book-List." *Speech Monographs,* XVI (1949), 243–252.

With H. H. King. "French Tractates on Preaching: A Book-List." *Quarterly Journal of Speech,* XXXVI (1950), 296–325.

With H. H. King. "Spanish Treatises on Preaching: A Book-List." *Speech Monographs,* XVII (1950), 161–170.

With H. H. King. "Scandinavian Treatises on Preaching: A Book-List." *Speech Monographs,* XXI (1954), 1–9.

With H. H. King. "Dutch Treatises on Preaching: A List of Books and Articles." *Speech Monographs,* XXI (1954), 235–247.

Editor and translator, [*Cicero*] *Ad C. Herennium de Ratione Dicendi (Rhetorica ad Herennium).* Loeb Classical Library. Cambridge, Mass., and London, 1954.

With H. H. King. *Pulpit Eloquence: A List of Doctrinal and Historical Studies in English. Speech Monographs,* XXII (special issue, 1955).

With H. H. King. *Pulpit Eloquence: A List of Doctrinal and Historical Studies in German. Speech Monographs,* XXIII (special issue, 1956).

"Hortensius." *Encyclopedia Britannica* (14th ed., 1964).

"Quintilian." *Encyclopedia Britannica* (14th ed., 1964).

"Ars Praedicandi." *New Catholic Encyclopedia* (1967).

"Memoria: Treasure-House of Eloquence." Pp. 196–246 above.

"A Mediaeval Commentary on the *Rhetorica ad Herennium.*" Pp. 247–270 above.

BOOK REVIEWS

Lane Cooper, *The Poetics of Aristotle: Its Meaning and Influence* (Boston, 1923). *Cornell Era,* LVI (1924), p. 85.

Bibliography

The Works of Aristotle, translated into English [vol. 11, W. D. Ross, editor]: W. Rhys Roberts, *Rhetorica;* E. S. Forster, *De Rhetorica ad Alexandrum;* Ingram Bywater, *De Poetica* (Oxford, 1924). *Quarterly Journal of Speech Education*, XI (1925), 299–301.

M. A. Grant, *The Ancient Rhetorical Theories of the Laughable* (Madison, Wis., 1924). *Quarterly Journal of Speech Education*, XII (1926), 210–211.

G. R. Owst, *Preaching in Medieval England* (Cambridge, 1926). *Quarterly Journal of Speech Education*, XIII (1927), 323–324.

C. S. Northrup, editor, *Representative Phi Beta Kappa Orations*, Second Series (New York, 1927). *Cornell Alumni News*, XXX (1927–1928), 498.

G. W. Robinson, editor, *Autobiography of Joseph Scaliger* (Cambridge, Mass., 1927). *Philosophical Review*, XXXIX (1930), 87–89.

Lane Cooper, *The Rhetoric of Aristotle: An Expanded Translation* (New York and London, 1932). *Cornell Alumni News*, XXXIV (1931–1932), 193.

G. R. Owst, *Literature and Pulpit in Medieval England* (Cambridge, 1933). *Philosophical Review*, XLII (1933), 639–640.

M. Levy, *Der Sabbath in England* (Leipzig, 1933). *Modern Language Notes*, L (1935), 544–545.

F. A. R. Carnegy, *The Relations between the Social and Divine Order in William Langland's "Vision of William concerning Piers the Plowman"* (Breslau, 1934). *Modern Language Notes*, LI (1936), 561–562.

J. Marouzeau, *Traité de stylistique appliquée au Latin* (Paris, 1935). *Classical Weekly*, XXX (1936–1937), 169–170.

P. F. Saintonge, L. G. Burgevin, and H. Griffith, *Horace: Three Phases of His Influence* (Chicago, 1936). *Philosophical Review*, XLVI (1937), 677.

G. Kowalski, *De Arte Rhetorica*, I (Lwow, 1937). *Classical Weekly*, XXXI (1937–1938), 136–137.

Th.-M. Charland, *Artes Praedicandi* (Paris and Ottawa, 1936). *Speculum*, XIII (1938), 352–354.

E. Anagnine, *G. Pico della Mirandola* (Bari, 1937). *Philosophical Review*, XLVII (1938), 438–439.

B. V. Wall, editor, *A Medieval Latin Version of Demetrius: De Elo-*

cutione (Washington, 1937). *American Journal of Philology*, LIX (1938), 113–115.

H. M. Smyser, editor, *The Pseudo-Turpin* (Cambridge, Mass., 1937). *Classical Philology*, XXXIV (1939), 82–83.

G. van der Veldt, O.F.M., *Prolegomena in Psychologiam* (Rome, 1938). *American Journal of Psychology*, LII (1939), 667.

W. H. Hay II, translator, *Petrus Pomponatius: Tractatus de Immortalitate Animae* (Haverford, 1938). *Philosophical Review*, XLIX (1940), 273.

E. E. Burriss and L. Casson, *Latin and Greek in Current Use* (New York, 1939). *Quarterly Journal of Speech*, XXVI (1940), 128.

S. F. Bonner, *The Literary Treatises of Dionysius of Halicarnassus* (Cambridge, 1939). *Classical Weekly*, XXXIII (1939–1940), 247–248.

C. E. Lutz, *Johannis Scotti Annotationes in Marcianum* (Cambridge, Mass., 1939). *Philosophical Review*, XLIX (1940), 587–588.

S. Belkin, *Philo and the Oral Law* (Cambridge, Mass., 1940). *Philosophical Review*, LII (1943), 214.

L. F. Smith, *The Genuineness of the Ninth and Third Letters of Isocrates* (Lancaster, Pa., 1940). *Classical Weekly*, XXXVI (1942-1943), 224.

R. C. Goldschmidt, *Paulinus' Churches at Nola* (Amsterdam, 1940). *American Journal of Philology*, LXIV (1943), 479–480.

A. D. Menut, editor, *Maistre Nicole Oresme: Le Livre de Ethiques d'Aristote* (New York, 1940). *Philosophical Review*, LIII (1944), 78–79.

M. Grabmann, *Methoden und Hilfsmittel des Aristotelesstudiums im Mittelalter* (Munich, 1939). *Philosophical Review*, LIII (1944), 79–80.

Sister Mary Catherine O'Connor, *The Art of Dying Well: The Development of the Ars Moriendi* (New York, 1942). *Modern Language Notes*, LIX (1944), 191–193.

J. W. Cohoon, editor and translator, *Dio Chrysostom*, Vol. II, Loeb Classical Library (Cambridge, Mass., and London, 1939); J. W. Cohoon and H. L. Crosby, editors and translators, *Dio Chrysostom*, Vol. III, Loeb Classical Library (1940). *Classical Philology*, XXXIX (1944), 262–263.

V. M. Hamm, editor and translator, *Pico della Mirandola: Of Being and Unity* (Milwaukee, 1943). *Philosophical Review*, LIII (1944), 587–588.

Bibliography

A. Dulles, *Princeps Concordiae: Pico della Mirandola and the Scholastic Tradition* (Cambridge, Mass., 1941). *Philosophical Review*, LIII (1944), 588–589.

G. L. Hendrickson, editor and translator, *Cicero: Brutus*, and H. M. Hubbell, editor and translator, *Cicero: Orator*, Loeb Classical Library (Cambridge, Mass., and London, 1939). *American Journal of Philology*, LXVI (1945), 85–86.

A. Erikson, *Sancti Epiphanii Episcopi Interpretatio Evangeliorum* and *Sprachliche Bemerkungen zu Epiphanius' Interpretatio Evangeliorum* (Lund, 1939). *American Journal of Philology*, LXVI (1945), 86–87.

H. S. Wilson, editor, and C. A. Forbes, translator, *Gabriel Harvey: Ciceronianus* (Lincoln, Neb., 1945). *Classical Philology*, XLII (1947), 130–132.

E. B. Atwood and V. K. Whitaker, editors, *Excidium Troiae* (Cambridge, Mass., 1944). *American Journal of Philology*, LXIX (1948), 231–232.

E. W. Robbins, *Characterization in Printed Commentaries on Terence, 1473–1600* (Urbana, Ill., 1951). *Journal of English and Germanic Philology*, LII (1953), 110–112.

H. M. Hubbell, editor and translator, *Cicero: De Inventione, De Optimo Genere Oratorum, Topica*, Loeb Classical Library (Cambridge, Mass., and London, 1949). *Classical Philology*, XLVIII (1953), 134–135.

M. Boaz and H. J. Botschuyver, editors, *Disticha Catonis* (Amsterdam, 1952). *Classical Weekly*, XLVIII (1954–1955), 18–19.

J. Warrington, translator, *Demosthenes' Orations* (London and New York, 1954). *Quarterly Journal of Speech*, XLI (1955), 69.

J. O. Burtt, editor and translator, *Minor Attic Orators*, Vol. II, Loeb Classical Library (Cambridge, Mass., and London, 1954). *Quarterly Journal of Speech*, XLII (1956), 190–191.

D. Hurst and J. Fraipont, editors, *Bedae Venerabilis Opera:* Part III, *Opera Homiletica* and Part IV, *Opera Rhythmica* (Turnhout, 1955). *Speculum*, XXXIII (1958), 376–378.

A. Quacquarelli, editor, *Q. S. F. Tertulliani ad Scapulam: Prolegomeni, testo critico e commento* (Rome, Paris, Tournai, and New York, 1957). *Classical Journal*, LIV (1958–1959), 273–275.

D. L. Clark, *Rhetoric in Greco-Roman Education* (New York, 1957). *American Journal of Philology*, LXXX (1959), 213–215.

Bibliography

J. Humbert and L. Gernet, editors and translators, *Demosthène, Plaidoyers politiques II: Contre Midias, Contre Aristocrate* (Paris, 1959). *Classical World*, LIII (1959–1960), 261–262.

P. O. Kristeller, editor, *Catalogus Translationum et Commentariorum: Mediaeval and Renaissance Translations and Commentaries*, Vol. I (Washington, 1960). *Renaissance News*, XIII (1960), 306–307.

Curriculum Vitae

Born January 7, 1896, Hoag's Corners, New York. Attended the
public schools of Albany, New York; won the valedictorian's
medal and the prize in Greek at Albany High School, 1912.
Higher education:
B.A., 1916; M.A., 1917; Ph.D., 1921, Cornell University.
Undergraduate prizes and distinctions: Phi Beta Kappa, 1915; Sec-
ond Prize, Prohibition Speaking Contest, 1915; Barnes Shakes-
peare Prize, Frances Sampson Fine Arts Prize, 1916.
Graduate scholar in Archaeology and Comparative Philology,
1916–1917; Graduate Fellow in Latin and Greek, 1917–1918.
United States Army, 1918–1919.
Academic career, Cornell University:
Department of Public Speaking: Instructor, 1919–1923.
Department of Classics: Instructor, 1924–1925; Assistant Pro-
fessor, 1925–1930; Professor, 1930–1967.
Chairman, 1929–1946.
Goldwin Smith Professor of the Classical Languages and Litera-
ture, 1941–1967; Emeritus, 1967.
Visiting Professor:
Andrew Mellon Professor, University of Pittsburgh, 1967–1968;
Walker-Ames Professor, University of Washington, 1968;
Ziskind Professor, Brandeis University, 1968–1969; University
of Minnesota, 1969; Stanford University, 1969.
Summer sessions: University of Wisconsin, 1925; University of
Michigan, 1932; Northwestern University, 1938; Stanford Uni-
versity, 1942 and 1948; University of Chicago, 1945; Columbia
University, 1946.
Lectures delivered at:
University of California at Berkeley, Columbia University,
Elmira College, Hebrew Union College–Jewish Institute of
Religion, Hobart and William Smith Colleges, University of

[277]

Illinois, University of Iowa, University of Michigan, Northwestern University, University of Notre Dame, Ohio State University, Stanford University, State University of New York at Albany, State University of New York at Buffalo, Syracuse University, Wells College, Wesleyan University, University of Wisconsin, Yale University; and, since retirement: Brandeis University, University of California at Davis, California State College at Hayward, Gonzaga University, Haverford College, Macalester College, University of Massachusetts at Amherst, St. Michael's College at Winooski, Vt., University of Minnesota, Mt. Angel College, State University of New York at Binghamton, University of Oregon, Pennsylvania State University, University of Pittsburgh, Queen's University at Kingston, Ontario, Swarthmore College, University of Vermont, University of Washington.

Fellow, Center for Advanced Studies, Wesleyan University, first semester 1962–1963, and January 1964.

Membership in learned and professional organizations:

American Philological Association, Mediaeval Academy of America, Classical Association of England and Wales, Speech Association of America, Modern Language Association, Linguistic Society of America, Renaissance Society of America, American Association of University Professors; Delta Sigma Rho, Phi Delta Kappa, Phi Kappa Phi, Phi Eta Sigma.

Editor:

Cornell Studies in Classical Philology, joint editor; *Quarterly Journal of Speech*, assistant editor, 1923.

Honors and distinctions:

President, American Philological Association, 1955; Fellow of the Mediaeval Academy of America, since 1957; Fellow, John Simon Guggenheim Foundation, 1928–1929 and 1956. Grants: American Council of Learned Societies, 1934 and 1949; Wesleyan University, 1963. Honorary degree, *D.Litt.*, Wesleyan University, 1967.

Subject Index

(Specific references to texts of ancient, mediaeval, and Renaissance authors are to be found in the Index Locorum)

[279]

Index Locorum

Aelian, *De Nat. Animal.*, 216, 226
Aeschylus, *Choeph.*, *Eumen.*, *Prom.*, 213
Alain de Lille: *Anticlaudianus*, 82, 120, 269, *Summa de Arte Praedicatoria*, 81–82, 85, 88–89, 91, 110, 119, 120
Albarus, Paulus, *Epist.*, 114–115
"Albertus"-tract, 111–131 (*passim*); *see also* William of Auvergne
Alcmaeon of Croton, 196
Aldhelm, *De Virginitate*, 98
Ambrose, Preface: *Explanatio Psalmi* xxxix. 22 (=xl. 18), 215–216; *In Psalmum* xxxvi *Enarratio*, 65
Ammianus Marcellinus, 215, 227
Angelom of Luxeuil, *Enarrationes in Libros Regum*, 100
Anon. on Hermogenes, 212, 214, 226
Anon., *Twofold Debates*, 225
Anthony, St., 87
Antiphon, 207
Appian, Preface, *Roman History*, 179
Aquinas, Thomas, *Summa Theologica*, 97–98, 100, 199–200, 242; *Epist.*, 215
Aristotle: *De Anima*, 202–203, 213, 228; *Categ.*, 121; *Eth. Nic.*, 55, 59, 148; *De Generat. Animal.*, 203; *De Iuventute*, 203; *De Mem. et Recollect.*, 202–203, 212–213, 228, 258; *Metaph.*, 202; *De Partit. Animal.*, 203; *Physics*, 149; *Pol.*, 254; *Post. Anal.*, 202; *Rhet.*, 83, 130, 211–212, 256; *De Sensu*, 203; *De Somniis*, 224; *Soph. El.*, 207, 266; *Topica*, 121, 206, 228, 266
Athenaeus, 199
Augustine: *De Anima et Eius Orig.*, 219; *De Civ. Dei*, 224; *Conf.*, 115, 214–216; *De Doctr. Christ.*, 41, 53, 80–81, 115–116, 237; *Sermones*, 59, 148; *De Trinit.*, 199–200; *De Utilit. Cred.*, 97
Ausonius, 33, 219, 236, 237

Bacon, Francis, *Advancement of Learning*, 201, 214, 215, 241
Bacon, Roger, *Opus Tert.*, 108, 109, 132
Bernard of Clairvaux: *In Psalmum* xc; *Sermo* x, 74
Berthold von Regensburg, "On the Angels," 46–47
Bonaventure: *Opusc.* xiii, 129, 130; *Opusc.* xvi, 130
Bromyard, John, *Summa Praedicantium*, 83, 117, 127

Caesar, *Bellum Gallicum*, 198, 261
Cassian: *Collationes*, xiv, 8; *De Spiritali Scientia*, 98–99
Cassiodorus: *De Anima*, 199, 213–215; *Inst.*, 215, 238
Chytraeus, *Praecepta Rhet.*, 133
Cicero: *Acad.*, 213, 216–217, 223, 232; *De Amic.*, 261; *Brutus*, 10, 163, 177, 188, 190, 192, 206, 208, 217, 227; *Pro Cluent.*, 232; *Div. in Caec.*, 232; *Epist.*, 208; *De Fin.*, 83, 199, 223; *De Inv.*, 1, 2, 8, 13, 16, 18–20, 25, 83, 188, 211, 247, 248, 252, 254–255, 257; *De Lege Manil.*, 192; *De Legibus*, 205; *Orator*, 188, 262; *De Orat.*, 2, 16, 23, 25, 83, 188–189, 201, 212, 214, 216–217, 223, 231–233, 255, 262; *Paradoxa*, 262; *Partit. Orat.*, 212–213, 214; *Pro Reg. Deiot.*, 232; *De Senec.*, 198, 217, 227; *Topica*, 83, 256; *Tusc. Disp.*, 177, 213, 216, 217, 261; *Verrinae*, 262

Dante: *Convivio*, Tract. II, 98; *Letter to Can Grande*, 98; *Paradiso* and *Vita Nuova*, 126; *Purg.*, 197
Dio Cassius, *Roman History*, 170
Diodorus Siculus, 201

[286]

Index Locorum

Diogenes of Apollonia, 196
Diogenes Laertius, *Pythagoras*, 198

Epictetus, Arrian's *Discourses* of, 179
Erasmus: *Ecclesiastes*, 50, 241; *Moriae Encom.*, 227; *De Rat. Stud.*, 241
Eucherius of Lyons, *Formulae Spiritalis Intelligentiae*, 98
Eumenius, *Paneg. Lat.*, 32
Eunapius, *Lives of the Philosophers and Sophists*, 218
Euripides, *Electra*, 177

Fortunatianus, *Ars Rhet.*, 239
Fridericus de Nürx, *Ars Praed.*, 138

Gellius, Aulus, 2–3, 200, 217
Geoffrey of Vinsauf, *Poetria Nova*, 239
Gerson, *Opera*, 101, 108, 131–132
Gesta Romanorum, 65, 146
Gregory the Great: *Epist.*, 95; *Pastoral Rule*, 45, 53–55, 131
Guibert de Nogent, *Liber Quo Ordine Sermo Fieri Debeat*, 85, 90–91, 93

"Henry of Hesse," *Tractatulus de Arte Praedicandi:* authorship, 135–136; comparison with "Aquinas"-tract, 140–142; editions, 137–138; manuscripts, 138–139; style, 140; text and translation, 143–157
Herodotus, 201
Hesiod, Theogony, 200–201
Homer, *Iliad*, 201, 203, 210
Homer-Relief of Archelaüs of Priene, 200
Homeric *Hymn to Hermes*, 200
Honorius Augustodunensis, *De Animae Exilio et Patria*, 117
Horace: *Ars Poet.*, 121, 261; *Epist.*, 205
Hrabanus Maurus: *In Epist. ad Gal.*, 98; *De Rhet.*, 116
Hugh of St. Victor, *De Sacramentis*, 96
Humbert de Romans, *De Eruditione Praedicatorum*, 49, 81, 85–87, 119, 131

Iamblichus, *Vita Pythag.*, 198
Isocrates: *Antidosis*, 206, 208; *Epist.*, 208; *Philippus*, 208

Jean de Châlons, *De Modo Praedicandi et Syllogizandi*, 124
John of Salisbury: *Metalogicon*, 116–117, 214–215, 238, 266; *Policraticus*, 98
John the Scot (Erigena), *De Div. Nat.*, 101, 107
John of Wales, *Ars Praedicandi*, 112, 123
Julius Victor, C., *Ars Rhet.*, 232, 239
Juvenal, *Sat.*, 169, 183–184

Katherine, St., 87

Livy, 175, 177–178, 194, 195, 201
Longinus, Cassius, *Ars Rhet.*, 214, 227–228
"Longinus," *De Sublim.*, 12, 176–177, 185–186, 189
Lucan, *Civil War*, 184–185
Lucian: *Pseudologistes*, 208; *Rhet. Didask.*, 170–173, 236; *Zeus Trag.*, 209–210
Lysias, *Characters*, 207

Macrobius, *Sat.*, 258, 262
Mamertinus, Claudius, *Paneg. Lat.*, 32
"Mamertinus," panegyric addressed to Maximian, 33–37, 192–193
Manuscripts, Latin: Basel, *Universitätsbibl.*, A.vi.4:139; Berlin, *Preuss.-Staatsbibl.*, *Theol. Fol.* 287[=527(2)]: 129; Bruges, *Bibl. Pub.*, 546:117; Einsiedeln, *Benediktiner Stiftsbibl.*, 332:138; Erfurt, *Stadtbücherei* (Amplon.), Qu.151:138; Erlangen Univ. 729, 775:138; Munich, *Bayer. Staatsbibl.*, *Codd. lat.* 2689: 119; 3590, 5683, 15548, 16226:138; 18635:133; 18961: 256; 19670, 21708, 23836, 24516, 24539, 24571: 138; Paris, *Bibl. Nat.*, *Nouv. Acq. Lat.* 280:125; Skt. Florian, *Stiftsbibl.*, xi. 113:139; Vienna, *Nationalbibl.*, 4121, 13707:138
Marmor Parium, 223
Martianus Capella, *De Nupt.*, 106, 214, 232
Melanchthon: *De Off. Concionatoris*, 133; *Elementa Rhet.*, 102, 241

[287]

Index Locorum

Nazarius, *Paneg, Lat.*, 32

New Testament: Acts, 86, 148; Col., 59; I Cor., 152; II Cor., 213; Ephes., 69, 155; Gal., 69, 156; John, 57, 65, 66, 68, 70, 90, 95; Luke, 61, 63, 68, 69, 71, 146, 152–154, 264; Mark, 54, 64; Matt., 56–57, 64, 66, 75, 95, 101, 151, 156, 264; I Pet., 156; II Pet., 62; Romans, 55, 64, 70; I Tim., 72

Odo of Cluny, *Moralium Epitome S. Greg. in Job*, 100–101, 103

Old Testament: Dan., 71; Deut., 116; Eccles., 65, 90, 94; Ecclus., 58–59, 77, 148; Exod., 75, 148; Gen., 56; Is., 58, 148; Jer., 59; Job, 56, 63, 75, 90; Josh., 57; Vulg. II Kings, 69, 144; Vulg. III Kings, 144, 152; I Macc. 69; Num., 57; Prov., 115–116, 213, 263; Vulg. Ps., 58, 61–64, 68–69, 70–71, 89, 125, 148–149; Rev., 59, 66, 90, 94, 148; II Sam., 56, 59, 64, 69; Song of Sol., 64; Wisdom of Sol., 59, 69

Origen, *De Principiis*, 97–98

Pacatus Drepanius, Latinus, *Paneg. Lat.*, 32

Parmenides, *Fragm.*, 196

Pausanias, *Descript. Greece*, 197, 200

Persius, *Sat.*, 195

Petilia Tablet (Orphic), 196

Petronius, *Satyricon*, 30–31, 166–167, 178

Petrus Cantor, *Verbum Abbreviatum*, 124, 130

Philolaüs, *Fragm.*, 199

Philostratus, Flavius: *Life of Apollonius*, 218; *Lives of the Sophists*, 200, 216, 218, 219, 226, 236

Pindar: *Nem.*, 214; *Olymp.*, 213

Plato: *Gorgias*, 207; *Hipp. Major*, 216; *Hipp. Minor*, 224; *Menex.*, 206–207; *Meno*, 226; *Phaedo*, 196–197 ,202; *Phaedrus*, 197–225, 256; *Philebus*, 213; *Protag.*, 246; *Rep.*, 197, 254; *Theaet.*, 202, 203, 212; *Timaeus*, 266

Plautus: *Amphitruo*, 261; *Pseud.*, 213

Pliny the Elder, *Nat. Hist.*, 178–179, 216–217, 227

Pliny the Younger, *Epist.*, 161, 168–169, 182–183, 218–219

Plotinus, *Enneads*, 198

Plutarch, *Lives: (Cicero)*, 178, 232; *(Demosthenes)*, 221–222; *(Marius)*, 199, 214

Pollux, Julius, *Onomast*, 216

Porphyry, *Vita Pythag.*, 199

Ps.-Cicero, *In Sallustium Responsio*, 260

Ps.-Plutarch: *De Lib. Educ.*, 205–206, 214; *Lives of the Ten Orators*, 205

Ps.-Sallust, *In Ciceronem Oratio*, 260

Publilius Syrus, 224

Quintilian: *De Corrupt. Eloq.*, 29, 179; *Inst. Orat.*, 2–7, 13, 16, 29, 31, 161, 164, 179–181, 189, 190, 205, 207–208, 211–212, 214, 216–217, 219, 221–223, 226, 229, 232–235, 245

Rabelais, *Gargantua et Pantagruel*, 227

Rhetorica ad Alexandrum, 221

Rhetorica ad Herennium, 1–25 *(passim)*, 83–84, 108, 121, 208, 210–212, 214–215, 225–226, 228–231, 255, 259, 266

Richard of Thetford, *Summa de Modo Praedicandi*, 125

Robert of Melun, *Sententiae*, 116

Sallust, *Cat.*, 253

Seneca the Elder *(Rhetor)*: *Contr.*, 29, 163, 164–165, 181–182, 190, 213, 217–218; *Suas.*, 162–163, 165

Seneca the Younger: *De Benef.*, 215; *Epist.*, 164, 167–168, 195, 226; *De Ira*, 132; *Nat. Quaest.*, 178; *De Vita Beata*, 254

Sextus Empiricus, 213, 214

Sophocles: *Philoct.*, 213; *Trach.*, 213

Stephen, St., 87

Suetonius: *Lives of the Caesars*, 220, 237, 260; *De Rhet.*, 165

Surgant, Ulrich, *Manuale Curatorum*, 120, 126, 130, 134, 141, 142, 159, 216, 238